PURPLE
PROSE

PURPLE PROSE

Bisexuality in Britain

Kate Harrad

Thorntree  Press

THORNTREE PRESS, LLC
PO BOX 301231
PORTLAND, OR 97294
PRESS@THORNTREEPRESS.COM

COVER AND INTERIOR DESIGN BY JEFF WERNER
COPY-EDITING BY ROMA ILNYCKYJ
PROOFREADING BY AMY HAAGSMA

LIBRARY OF CONGRESS CATALOGING-IN-PUBLICATION DATA
Names: Harrad, Kate, editor.
Title: Purple prose : bisexuality in Britain / edited by Kate Harrad.
Description: Portland, OR : Thorntree Press, 2016. | Includes bibliographical
    references.
Identifiers: LCCN 2016011558 (print) | LCCN 2016018344 (ebook) |
    ISBN 9780996460163 (paperback) | ISBN 9780996460170 (Epub) |
    ISBN 9781944934033 (Kindle)
Subjects: LCSH: Bisexuality--Great Britain. | Bisexuals--Great Britain. |
    BISAC: SOCIAL SCIENCE / Gay Studies. | SOCIAL SCIENCE / Lesbian Studies.
Classification: LCC HQ74.2.G7 P87 2016 (print) | LCC HQ74.2.G7 (ebook) |
    DDC 306.76/50941--dc23
LC record available at https://lccn.loc.gov/2016011558

10 9 8 7 6 5 4 3 2 1
Printed in the United States of America

EDITOR: KATE HARRAD

Individual chapter editors:
Jacq Applebee
Meg-John Barker
Elizabeth Baxter-Williams
Jamie Q Collins
Grant Denkinson
Kate Harrad
Symon Hill
Juliet Kemp
Fred Langridge
Marcus Morgan
Kaye McLelland
Milena Popova

Contents

INTRODUCTION

Hi.

This book is here to tell you something we hope you already know—that bisexuality is real and valid. And to talk about what that means: how it's defined, who's included, how to deal with people who don't understand, and where to find support and a community if you want it.

Maybe you already identify as bisexual. Maybe you're wondering about it. Maybe you're bi-curious, or just generally curious. Maybe you have a friend or partner or family member who's bisexual. Whatever your reason, we hope this book will be useful. It's designed so that you can dip in and out of it, picking which topics are relevant to you.

Purple Prose is edited by multiple people. I'm the overall editor, and I've written some of the chapters, but others were produced by individual chapter editors, whose bios you can find at the back. Some of them are bi activists, some are academics, some are writers, some are all three. They wrote their chapter and interviewed people for quotes; you'll see a lot of quotes used throughout, and mostly these are from people who were interviewed specifically for this book, via social media or email or face-to-face discussions.

We've also used (with permission) excerpts from websites, books, newspapers and conversations on social media. The aim is to get a reasonable variety of voices represented—although it's still true that many of the voices are from a specific UK bi community and mostly represent those views. However, we have tried to keep the different voices and styles of writing, which is why different chapters may read differently. In a way, it's an anthology of bi writing, although it's also a coherent book you can read from beginning to end.

Why is it called *Purple Prose*? Because purple has become the colour associated with bisexuality, as pink is associated with the gay community. The bi flag is pink, purple and blue.

Why have we written a book about British bisexuality in particular? Because although there are several excellent books out there about bisexuality, they are US-based, or over twenty years old, or aimed at a mostly academic audience. We felt there was room for a contemporary, accessible book from a British perspective, and we hope this is it. However, this book should also be useful for anyone from any country who wants to know about bisexuality and the many issues associated with it.

We hope you enjoy it.

One final note about our use of language. Sexual politics, and identity politics in general, is a fraught area in terms of language, and we have tried to be as careful as possible when choosing which terms and acronyms to use; for example, we use 'LGB' in some contexts, 'LGBT' in others and 'LGBTQIA+' as our default term for the community we're describing. The glossary at the end should help if you come across any unfamiliar terms.

1

THE BASICS

Editor: Kate Harrad

Part One: Definitions and Numbers

'For me, it is that I am missing a little bit of wiring that allows other people to discriminate between the genders when it comes to attraction. Not that I consider it a deficit—it is a little like the unusual brain symmetry that allows someone to be ambidextrous.'
  DH Kelly

Are labels really necessary?

People often say things like 'labels are for jars' and 'we're all just human, so why divide people up by race/gender/sexuality?'

It's a reasonable question. The answer is that language matters, and it matters just as much here as it does anywhere else. Apples, strawberries and grapes are all fruit, but nobody says 'all fruit is fruit, so why distinguish?' Gender and sexuality labels give us potentially useful information about someone, just as it's often useful to know whether someone is tall or short, or vegetarian, or terrified of snakes. The important thing is that the label is accurate and descriptive, and not imposed by someone else.

So that's why we think it matters that some people are bisexual and are able to call themselves bisexual.

'I could finally describe what I felt. And what's more, I could describe it using existing words, which made it easier for others to understand what I meant.'
Mharie

Definitions

If you asked random people in the street for a one-sentence definition of bisexuality, you'd probably get two things: a weird look, and a sentence such as 'someone who's attracted to both men and women' or 'someone who has sex with both genders'. This is also what you get if you search online for a definition, and from most dictionaries.

If you ask someone in the UK bisexual community how they define bisexuality, there's a good chance you'll get something slightly different from the above. This is because the current dictionary definitions aren't the ones used by a lot of bisexual people.

Why not?

Well, several reasons:

⇨ They focus on sex and sexual attraction—but bisexuality isn't just about who you're sleeping with.

⇨ They make people assume that to be bisexual, you have to be equally attracted to men and women. Not true!

⇨ They're based on the idea that bisexuality is a half-and-half sexuality: you're half gay half straight. Lots of problems with this one. For one thing, bisexuality is a sexuality in itself, not something you can divide up. For another, much of the LGBTQIA+ (lesbian, gay, bisexual, transgender, queer, intersexual, asexual, plus) community doesn't view gender as binary.

All of these issues will come up later in the book. Let's quickly address one thing, though: sex. Or rather, the potential absence of sex.

How do you know you're bi if you've only slept with one gender?

We can't emphasise this enough: *you do not need to have slept with anyone to know what your sexuality is.* After all, heterosexual people are allowed to call themselves heterosexual before they've had any sexual partners. So, equally, lesbian, gay and bisexual people should be allowed to know who they fancy before they've done anything about it.

That doesn't mean you have to decide on a label early on; it means that you can choose one at any age if you find one that fits. And you can change it later if it stops fitting. Sexuality labels can be applied and then removed and then applied again, just like...well, actual labels.

And if you have had sexual experiences, *it's still okay to define yourself based on attraction and not who you've slept with.* You can be a bisexual person who's only ever slept with women. Or you mostly sleep with men but feel romantic only about women. Or you don't want to have sex with anyone, but you fall for all kinds of people. Or you'd like to experience sex with men, but you haven't found the right man yet. If a label feels right, go for it.

> 'I've had relationships with men, women and people who those categories don't fit—but it's the attraction that makes me bi, not the actions. I was every bit as bi when I was fifteen and had only ever dated and kissed boys.'
>
> Fred Langridge

Some useful definitions
So, do we, the bi community, have our own official definition of bisexuality?

Not exactly. For one thing, we're lots of overlapping communities, plus loads of people who never go near a community, so it's not as though we have monthly meetings where we sign off new bisexuality laws. But these are two of the most useful and frequently quoted definitions out there:

'I call myself bisexual because I acknowledge that I have in myself the potential to be attracted—romantically and/or sexually—to people of more than one sex and/or gender, not necessarily at the same time, not necessarily in the same way, and not necessarily to the same degree.'
Activist Robyn Ochs, *robynochs.com*

'You're bisexual as soon as you stop being exclusively attracted to only one sex.'
The Bisexual Index, *bisexualindex.org.uk*

People also often find they have personal definitions of 'what my bisexuality means to me'. For example:

'I'm attracted (romantically and sexually) to people whose gender is like mine and to people whose gender is different from mine.'
Fred Langridge

'I tend to define my sexuality as "attracted to people regardless of gender".'
Milena Popova

'It means gender isn't a limiting factor when considering who I might want to be in a sexual relationship with.'
Karen

'If one day I feel attraction to a woman, I don't have to think "Does this mean I'm gay?" or "If this carried on, would it mean I was a lesbian?" If one day I feel attraction to a man, I don't have to think "Does this mean I'm not gay after all?" or "If this carries on, at what point do I lose the right to call myself lesbian?" If one day I feel attraction to someone who identifies as neither binary gender, I don't have to think "What does this mean about me?"

None of that noise exists in my life. As far as gender-linked sexuality is concerned, there isn't some territory over here where I'm officially supposed to walk, and some territory over there where I'm not supposed to walk. It's all one whole, and I already live there.'

Jennifer

Numbers

It's quite hard to work out how many people are bisexual. In 2010, a UK study asked people to pick one out of 'heterosexual', 'gay/lesbian', 'bisexual' or 'other'. The study found that 0.5% of the population said they were bisexual, 1% said they were gay or lesbian, 0.5% said 'other' and 3% declined to answer. The rest, 95%, said they were heterosexual. A 2011 survey in the US got a slightly higher number: 1.8% of adults defined as bisexual, and roughly the same amount as lesbian or gay.

So, are we looking at something like one in a hundred people? Well, maybe not. A more recent poll by YouGov in the summer of 2015 phrased its questions differently: as well as asking for people's labels, the survey asked respondents to place themselves on the Kinsey scale. This is a scale which goes from '0 = exclusively heterosexual' to '6 = exclusively homosexual', so anything between the two is arguably bisexual. (Very arguably!)

This got quite a different response. In fact, 19% of the UK population chose a number between 1 and 5. And when just eighteen- to twenty-four-year-olds were considered, that figure went up to a hefty 43%.

Does this mean that nearly half the young adult population of the UK is bisexual? For the sake of selling this book, we'd like to think so, but in fact, in the same poll, 89% of people (and 83% of eighteen- to twenty-four-year-olds) described themselves as heterosexual.

So the truth is probably complicated, as it usually is: a lot of people aren't completely gay or straight but wouldn't call themselves bi, perhaps because they prefer to identify as pansexual (for example) or perhaps because they would 'round up' their identity to gay or straight. The label of bisexuality isn't always a popular one.

Nevertheless, it's clear that many people regard their sexuality as capable of change: 60% of heterosexuals and 73% of homosexuals in the YouGov survey agreed that sexuality was a sliding scale. And when YouGov asked the people who defined themselves as heterosexual if they could ever be attracted to someone of a different gender, 44% said that would consider it. Again, the younger they were, the more likely they were to entertain the possibility: the percentage was 58% for ages eighteen to twenty-four.

It's a cheering survey for those of us who stand to benefit from a less black-and-white view of human sexuality.

Part Two: How Will I Know?

'When people find the Bisexual Index website through search engines, the most common question they've asked isn't "Where are the bisexuals meeting these days?" or "What are some films with bisexual characters?" It's the same question over and over again.

"Am I bisexual?"'

Marcus Morgan, founder of the Bisexual Index

How can you tell if you're bisexual?

We quoted above the Bisexual Index's definition of bisexuality. This is a fuller extract, from their tongue-in-cheek 'Am I Bisexual?' page:

'If you're asking yourself "Am I bisexual?", then here's a handy check-list:

Thinking about the people you've been attracted to, so far in your life, were they all of the same gender?

If you answered "No" to any or all of the questions in our list above then we feel it's okay for you to call yourself bisexual. We don't care how attracted you are to the genders around you—you're bisexual as soon as you stop being exclusively attracted to only one sex.

That's it. It really is as easy as that.'

But don't you need to...?

As we've said, people often ask, 'Do you need to have slept with women and men in order to be sure you're bisexual?' No—or at least, not necessarily. Some people do need to have experience with a specific gender before they know for certain if they're attracted to them. Some know what they are well before they've ever done anything with anybody.

> 'I don't remember realising I was bi. I remember being little (five or six) and only registering my crushes on boys as crushes, thinking of (what I now identify as) crushes on girls as a separate thing—and then I remember having distinct crushes on girls that I recognised as crushes when I was fourteen/fifteen. I don't remember the first time I recognised a crush on a girl as the same sort of thing as a crush on a boy.'
>
> Fred Langridge

Of course, you might be told, or tell yourself, that only one kind of crush counts. That one kind is 'normal' and the other is a phase, or something to be ignored.

> 'I'd had "crushes" on girls as well as boys for as long as I remembered but I was always told (even by people who didn't know that about me) that I shouldn't worry if I developed feelings for other girls and that it wasn't really real and was just something that happened as you were growing up and you'd grow out of it. So I was twenty-three and on my first divorce before I realised I wasn't going to grow out of it and should "do something about it".'
>
> Kaye

And maybe you can ignore it, for a while, or even forever. But why should you have to?

Being bi-curious

Being bi-curious gets even more bad press than being bisexual does.

> 'One of the labels used to harm bisexual people is "bi-curious" when it's used to sneer at people who are experiencing similar-gender attraction for the first time. It's common for some people to sneer at bisexual women for "not being able to commit to lesbianism", and say that "bi-curious" women aren't even "proper bisexuals".
>
> This is toxic bullshit. What's wrong with being attracted to someone? What's so distasteful about being the source of someone's desires? I think the main vilification comes from the fact that no one uses "bi-curious" to label people who felt they were previously exclusively homosexual but who have started to have feelings that aren't 'gay enough'. Because these people are seen as "straight but confused" it feels likely to their detractors that they'll go back to being straight, or are just "experimenting".
>
> If no one was curious about "gay sex" would there be this many gay people? If I'm curious about something, I might try it. If I try it, I might like it. If I like it I may love it. If I love it I may make it a major part of my life!
>
> We need curiosity. Thinking, feeling, loving outside of the rigid roles society wants to press us into should be rewarded.'
>
> Marcus Morgan

When do people first realise they're bisexual?

'I had my first crush on a woman maybe around age twelve/thirteen? That was the first one that was clearly "I wanna bang her" rather than "She's cool, I wanna be her." ;-) I'd had crushes on boys/men before so bi was the logical conclusion. (Getting past the gender binary took somewhat longer.) For a very long time I wasn't comfortable actually applying the word "bisexual" to myself. In fact, the first time anyone said it out loud with reference to me, it wasn't me, it was a friend.'

Milena Popova

'Like many folks, I guess I had an idea. David Bowie. Yeah. Anyway... Never being in a world, even at university, where such things could be explored meant exactly that; it was a part of myself I never explored. The fact that I could totally get why women thought certain blokes were gorgeous was put down to me being in touch with my feminine side. It was the '80s and all the cool kids were doing it.

Shutting myself away as a writer didn't help. It wasn't until I got a job as an in-house writer in a game studio more than twenty years later that I was finally out in the open long enough to realise I really understood why women dug on certain blokes.'

Iain Lowson

Of course, not everyone comes out as bisexual from being straight— some people first identify as gay or lesbian and then later identify as bi.

'I finally admitted [my bisexuality] to myself at about twenty, having failed to sufficiently bury it for three or more years. I'd been out as gay for five years. I was twenty-two or twenty-three before I admitted it to anyone else.'

Elizabeth Baxter-Williams

It's also unfortunately true that coming out as bi to the gay community can be met with disbelief or even hostility.

'I called the local lesbian and gay switchboard, and asked about bisexual support groups. I guess they didn't get bisexuality awareness training back in those days because the volunteer I spoke to wouldn't give me the details until after he'd tried to counsel me about how I was in denial about my homosexuality. When I explained I'd already come out as gay he laughed and said that most people who said they were bi did so as a stepping stone to being gay—and maybe I was just making the crossing in reverse. That was the last time I called the switchboard.'

Marcus

What can help with the discovery?

For people who are discovering their sexuality, musicians often seem to provide a way in to finding out about bisexuality, or experiencing bisexual attractions for the first time. If you're one of those people who think pop music is corrupting the nation's youth, you might be feeling smug and validated at this point. (Although if you are one of those people, you may also be reading the wrong book.)

'When I was about ten, I had a grand passion for a little boy my age. When I was twelve, I fell in love with a girl. Both my parents and my schoolmates were pretty homophobic and I was the sort of child who turned to books in times of crisis. Only, I didn't look at a nice glossy book about teen issues or anything so sensible—I went straight for Freud and I discovered I might be "amphigenously inverted". But my next big crush was with another girl, a long time had passed since primary school, so I began to think I was probably a lesbian.

I know this is going to sound daft, but Oasis didn't help matters. I was at high school at the height of Britpop and one of the regular discussions among my friends was "Which Gallagher brother would you most like to sleep with?" Now I realise that there were almost certainly straight girls amongst us who were lying about it, but I looked at these two men who were supposed to be objects of universal female lust, considered my attraction to ordinary unglamorous schoolgirls around me and had no doubt.

So I thought I was a lesbian up until I got together with my first husband, then flitted about a bit; I was with a man now, so that had to be a phase and I was straight. Or perhaps he was the exception, or perhaps I had only convinced myself I fancied him at all. My first husband didn't help at all, because [he thought that] if I was bisexual I would enjoy not just porn, but the exact same porn as him, and I would enjoy threesomes with women he happened to fancy, etc....

Conversations with an older gay friend helped a lot, because it was not only obvious to him, but he described me as 'very bisexual'—other bisexual people he'd met, he felt, tended to lean slightly one way or another, whereas I seemed to be—as Michael Stipe once put it—an "equal opportunities lech".'

DH Kelly

'I wouldn't say I knew I was bisexual that far back, but back in the late '80s I had very definite crushes on Kylie and Jason. I wouldn't say I quite succeeded in coming out age nine because I think my friends thought that by 'liking' Kylie that I liked her music (which I did, and still do when I'm in one of my cheesy queer disco phases). I was aware of the idea of bisexuality around this time—if I recall correctly I'd learnt about bisexuality from the *Usborne Book of Growing Up*, but probably didn't think that it applied to me because I was very much preadolescent and this book was aimed at teenagers (my parents didn't really vet what I took out of the library).

For much of the next five years I was pretty much asexual (no other pop star–inspired crushes, but I certainly found Madonna and her pointy bra very, er, interesting...). Then when I was fourteen and my teenage hormones were in full swing I started crushing again. On boys and girls. And, like an enormous lightbulb going off, it dawned on me that I was bisexual. I still thank the *Usborne Book of Growing Up* to this day for letting me know that being bisexual was a thing and saving me much turmoil and angst in my teens.'

Cat

Cat's experience with the *Usborne Book of Growing Up* underlines the point that telling teenagers—or even pre-teens—about homosexuality and bisexuality doesn't turn them into anything. It just gives them a description of something they're already feeling. And it can be an incredible relief to find that you're not the only person with those feelings.

So the question 'How will I know?' can be answered in all kinds of ways. It might be a gradual realisation.

'I was five when I first got a crush on a girl, twelve when I first fell in love with one, seventeen when I came out, eighteen when I first kissed a girl, and nineteen when I first had same-sex sex. Knowing I was bisexual was a product of all of those experiences, as well as all the equivalent experiences I had with boys.'

Joanne

Or it might be a sudden moment of realisation.

'I was playing a truth game with friends and out of nowhere, one of them asked if I had a crush on another friend, a girl. I said yes without even thinking about it, although I'd never admitted it to myself before. The next question was "So are you bisexual?" I said yes. I hadn't known I was till I said it out loud. It changed everything.'

Faith

Being a proper bisexual

It should be obvious by now that we don't think there's any such thing as a 'proper' bisexual. Your identity is for you to decide. You'll probably find, though, that it takes some courage to keep remembering that, because there are a lot of people out there who want to define you on their terms. 'He's not really bisexual, I only ever see him with women.' 'She's not really bisexual, she just wants the attention.' 'They just think it's trendy.' 'She's had sex with twenty-five women and only two men, she's a lesbian really.'

'I've been asked to qualify my claim to be bisexual with stats about who I've had relationships with, by gay people and by straight people, and by someone who felt she had to justify her lesbian identity by pointing out she'd slept with more women than men, and therefore "needed" me to agree that I was "essentially straight" because we had similar stats in opposite directions.'

Anon

'The first time that I remember talking about my bisexuality to somebody gay or lesbian was back in my early twenties. I'd met my then partner at BiCon and he and I were round at his best friend's place having dinner. His friend was lesbian herself and I remember expecting/hoping that we'd have a bit of a connection because of that. I couldn't have been more wrong. First she quizzed me on whether I'd ever had sex with a woman. Then, when I said that I hadn't at that point, she totally dismissed my bisexuality, claiming that I couldn't know that I was bisexual without having had sex with women.

Back then I hadn't heard the retort that we're happy with people saying they're heterosexual before having sex with somebody of a different gender. I just felt really small and excluded.'

MJ

'When I was younger I used to beat myself up about not having an equal amount of crushes on male- and female-shaped people, and not having slept with equal numbers from each group (it's also worth noting that back then my experience of gender was pretty much binary). But then I discovered the Kinsey scale and worked out that as long as I didn't fall at either end of it—i.e. exclusively homosexual or heterosexual—then I had the right to call myself a bisexual. It's also been interesting to watch over time how my preferences have continually shifted. At present I am more attracted to female-shaped people than male-shaped people, but I currently have a male partner and my sexual experience is more skewed towards sleeping with male-shaped people.'

Cat

You may have noticed that some of these stories feature hostility or ignorance from the lesbian and gay communities. This isn't always the case, of course, and it may seem odd that people whose own sexuality may have been excluded or undermined might want to exclude or undermine yours, but unfortunately it does happen. So keep remembering: *it's not about who you've done or what you've done*, and it's not about what other people think.

(And it's definitely not about being trendy. If bisexuality was an automatic passport to being cool, the bi community would be very different. And probably much less fun.)

It's about you, and your desires, and they're real and they're valid.

> 'A tiny minority of people will say they're bi because they think it's cool or because they're afraid to say they're homosexual. But we firmly believe that all people who are attracted to more than one gender should be free to describe themselves as bisexual without anyone telling them off by saying "Just being bisexual isn't enough, being 'a proper bisexual' is more complicated than that."
>
> Bisexuality isn't more complicated than that—"attraction to more than one gender". It's not incompatible with identifying as gay, either. Bisexuality is proof that sexuality isn't "either/or", it's "and".'
>
> The Bisexual Index

Unfortunately, it's not just the outside world that thinks in terms of 'proper bisexuals'—there may well be part of you that's thinking it, too. Even people who have been happily identifying as bisexual for years can find their internal voice grumbling that they're not doing it properly.

> 'I spent a long time thinking that I must not "really" be bisexual because although I was attracted to (some) other women, I was more often attracted to men, and I had never actually done anything sexual with women.
>
> I still have intermittent angst about the fact that my sexual history (and particularly my relationship history) is heavily skewed male, and perhaps that means I'm not "really" bisexual. (This is strong at the moment, as both my partners are male, I have zero energy for any other romantic/sexual encounters, and this has been the case for a couple of years.)
>
> My belief is that being bisexual is only about being attracted to people of more than one gender. I wouldn't hesitate to apply that to someone

else; but emotionally I sometimes find it difficult to apply to myself. (Social programming, I suppose.)'

Juliet

Ultimately, you can only decide for yourself whether the label of bisexual works for you. And we hope you'll also allow other people the freedom to choose their own labels. Girls who snog other girls in bars with their boyfriends watching, men who go to Clapham Common after their wives are asleep, fifty-year-olds who had one same-sex experience at college, teenagers who have never snogged anyone at all: anyone at all gets to call themselves bisexual if it's a word that they feel fits them, and if anyone argues with you about that, please buy them a copy of this book.

It's all about what it means to you.

What does your bisexuality mean to you?

These comments from members of the UK bi community give some idea of how varied people's conceptions of their sexuality can be, even when they all fall under the label 'bisexual'.

'In itself, my bisexuality doesn't mean much to me. It means I have options. It means I'm as likely to be distracted by any person I consider to be interesting-in-that-way. My personal acknowledgement and acceptance of my bisexuality, however, means the world to me. I'm too big, too old, and too ugly to really give much of a monkey's what anyone else thinks.'

Iain Lowson

'In essence it means that not everyone I'm attracted to is the same gender. It also means that gender isn't the primary determining factor in whether I'm likely to be attracted to someone. That's not to say that I'm never attracted to people's gender. I tend to find it attractive when people have given some thought to gender-related things or when they do their gender in interesting or non-standard ways—but other factors are way more important. I also identify as queer.'

Kaye

'Theoretically, my bisexuality means that I am sexually and romantically attracted to people across the gender spectrum. In real life it means no, I'm not a lesbian, as is generally assumed.'

Elizabeth Baxter-Williams

'It means gender isn't a limiting factor when considering who I might want to be in a sexual relationship with. It's that simple, yet it's also highly political/intellectual; it's about making up my own mind about people, taking into account everything that is important to me and not ruling people in or out arbitrarily on the basis of one characteristic.'

Karen

2

COMING OUT (AND STAYING IN)

Editor: Kate Harrad

Once you've decided that you do identify as bisexual, your next move might be deciding whether to come out—whether to tell people about your sexuality. This can be difficult in some situations: for example, if you're living with your parents and think they would react badly, or if you're older and everyone in your life knows you as straight. It's okay to take some time to think about what to tell people, who to tell and how to do it.

Equally, though, it's okay to just spread the news as much as you want to! Some people—mostly people who've never had to do it— don't see why anyone should come out. You might hear people say things like 'What people do in bed is none of my business', or 'Why do you have to make such a fuss about it?' On the surface, this might look like a reasonable argument—after all, the exact details of sex aren't usually discussed in public, and people often feel uncomfortable hearing them.

But coming out isn't about giving people blow-by-blow accounts of your sex life. (Probably. Best not start with that, anyway.) It's being able to bring a girlfriend or boyfriend home to your parents. It's walking down the street hand in hand with the person you love.

It's being able to say at work that you're going to a gay club that night, or a bi community event that weekend. It's being able to tell your doctor that you have lovers of more than one gender at STI check-up time. It's being able to write blog posts about LGBTQIA+ issues. It's about sitting in the pub with your friends and casually saying, 'Tom Hiddleston and Queen Latifah are both really hot.' It's about not having people constantly assume that you're straight or that you're gay.

You should be allowed to do any or all of that without getting arrested, or judged, or thrown out, or ostracised. Ideally, you should be encouraged and supported in doing it. In the UK, thankfully, being arrested is extremely unlikely, but it's still possible to be mocked or criticised or even disowned or divorced for being open about your sexuality. So yes, it does matter. Coming out isn't always a big deal, but sometimes it can be an enormous one. And if people don't see that, lucky them for not having ever had to deal with it.

Coming Out as Bi to Straight People

'The words "I think I'm probably bisexual" were out of my mouth and hanging in the air before I'd had time to think about them.'
Kaye

The chances are that the people you're coming out to are straight. It's also very possible that they haven't really met anyone bi before and that they have some weird ideas about it. They might think bi girls are just trying to be cool, or that bi boys are 'on the way to gay'. They might worry that you suddenly fancy them or that you're going to sleep with everyone you meet. They might not have any specific worries but might feel it's not 'normal'. And, of course, they might have religion-based objections. It's worth bearing all these possibilities in mind. Equally, they might be absolutely fine with the whole thing, or even have already guessed.

'I told my parents and my older sister and they were a bit confused because they thought I knew that they already knew I was bi.'
    Fred Langridge

'When I told my wife, her comment was along the lines of "That's nice dear. Oh, and the rest of us worked that out ages ago."'
    Iain Lowson

Ways to come out can vary widely. You could do a 'Big Bang' version, where you just tell everyone as quickly and forthrightly as possible. Sit-down conversation, group email, Facebook announcement, branded hot-air balloon—the world is your coming-out oyster.

Or you could try dropping hints into conversation for a while to gauge reactions. 'My friend just told me she was bi' is a useful way to get an idea of how your parents, partner, children, workmates and so on might react. Or discuss a news story, preferably one that mentions bisexuality in a positive light (if you can find one!). Lend someone a book with a bi character or two. Start conversations like 'People say you can't fancy more than one gender, but I don't see why not.' In fact, if you spend enough time bringing conversation round to the subject, there's a good chance people will work out for themselves what you're actually trying to say.

Don't feel guilty if you're not the kind of person who can just come out. Even if you have no reason to expect bad reactions, it can still be daunting and difficult to discuss. It's fine to work up to it.

'Certainly at school and university I never really said "I'm bisexual" to anyone—I just dropped enough hints/talked about attractions to people of different genders until people worked it out.'
    Milena Popova

Coming Out as Bi in the Lesbian/Gay Community

'When I first told my lesbian friends that I was definitely bi they pretty much abandoned me. That was pretty unpleasant.'
Elizabeth Baxter-Williams

Depressingly, it's not always easy to announce your bisexuality when you're part of the lesbian or gay community. It should be easier, you might think, than coming out to straight people—after all, this is a group who should already understand about minority sexualities and the importance of acknowledging that you are what you are. And, indeed, many of them do understand, and many of them are fine with bisexuals. Others are definitely not. Bisexuality doesn't always have a good reputation in lesbian or gay groups. There can be a tendency to think that a bi partner will cheat on you or always be looking over your shoulder, or that bi people are just trying to fit in with mainstream society and 'pass' instead of admitting their 'real' sexuality.

'As a teenager, I was gay. I was only attracted to other guys. I worked very hard to keep this information secret, I didn't tell my parents or school friends. Accusations of being gay were a common bullying tactic so I was sometimes called gay at school, but I knew in the back of my mind that this was guesswork and I tried not to let people see they'd hit the mark.

When I went away to college I had a chance to discover the 'gay' community, and this was the main reason I dropped out of college— the bright lights of the big city took up too much time to actually do any studying.

Eventually my parents worried about my silences and asked how the course was going. I took a deep breath and told them everything. That I was gay, overdrawn, failing the course. It took them a long time to get over their shock, especially as my boyfriend wasn't white.

A few years later, I found my attraction had shifted. I was starting to find women attractive too. I didn't know what to do about that at all—there was no obvious place to go, and I knew the gay scene wasn't going to be very friendly about the shift. One of my lesbian friends stopped talking to me, another accused me of "poisoning gay spaces with [my] thoughts". Eventually I called the local lesbian and gay switchboard, and asked about bisexual support groups. I guess they didn't get bisexuality awareness training back in those days because the volunteer I spoke to wouldn't give me the details until after he'd tried to counsel me about how I was in denial about my homosexuality. When I explained I'd already come out as gay, he laughed and said that most people who said they were bi did so as a stepping stone to being gay—and maybe I was just making the crossing in reverse. That was the last time I called the switchboard.

More than twenty years later I'm glad I found the bisexual community, glad I came out as a bisexual man, and haven't gone straight. I know sexualities can be fluid—mine was, but I also know that they can stop changing just as easily as start.'

Marcus

One way to attack this way of thinking could be to introduce gay and lesbian friends to more bi people, or send them online articles on the politics of bisexuality. Or buy them this book!

Should I Come Out?

Obviously, it's up to you. Coming out has two major advantages: it means you're not having to keep part of your life secret, and it means you're increasing the visibility of bisexual people, which could make it easier for other people to come out. On the other hand, if you're likely to face bad reactions—particularly if coming out might put you in danger—then it's absolutely valid not to do it, or to do it slowly, or to come out to some people and not others.

The relief of telling just one person can be huge—if you don't feel able to tell someone you know, you could try calling the Samaritans and telling them, or just saying it out loud to yourself, or writing it down on a piece of paper. Part of coming out is coming out to yourself: it's probably a good idea to do that first.

'I worked my way up to telling my mum by blogging about my teenage confusion—I knew she was unlikely to read it, but there was courage required to write about it openly where anyone, theoretically, could read.'
DH Kelly

Coming Out Again (and Again and Again)

'One thing that's not obvious about coming out until you do it is that it's not a one-off thing. You meet new people and have to decide whether to tell them, too. If you're bi, you also have the potential frustration of people deciding you're "gay now" or "straight now" on the basis of a partner's gender, and then you get to come out to those people all over again.'
Fred Langridge

'I came out to my mother about eighteen months ago, and for the following nine months she completely ignored it.'
Milena Popova

The narrative around coming out makes it sound as if it's a one-time thing. But—perhaps especially with bisexuality—it can be ongoing. Not just in terms of meeting new people that you have to come out to again. You might find people you've come out to somehow forget about it after a while, or hadn't really taken it in—particularly if you're a bisexual in a long-term relationship with someone of a different gender. If you're a married woman with kids and a house in the suburbs and so on, it's not always easy for people to remember that you're also bi. But if it's important to you—and it's okay for it to be important to you—you can keep reminding them.

'I find I have to keep coming out—it's not like making one announcement and suddenly everyone knows. And occasionally I have to keep coming out to the same people because they conveniently forget and continue to conflate the gender of my current partner with my sexuality.'
Milena Popova

The good news is, once you've started coming out, it's usually easier the second time, and the third.

On Passing Privilege

By Emily Wright

I wrote this to try to tease out what I think about 'passing privilege' and why *I* find it difficult.

I find 'passing privilege' really difficult to talk about. On one hand, it does give me access to privileges and acceptance that non-passing people do not get, but on the other hand, those privileges are conditional on me keeping myself closeted.

There is a gulf between 'passing' and being accepted. Passing is explicitly being accepted on false pretences. I have a male partner, I look pretty heteronormative and people read me as straight. My alleged straightness is not a lie I am telling. It is people's stupid assumptions that bisexuals don't exist, that a woman partnered with a man must be straight and that there is a queer 'look' that can be easily identified. Either I am constantly outing myself or I am being constantly pushed back into the closet.

Am I to blame when people make false assumptions about me? Where is the line between accepting that people will mislabel me and taking advantage of that mislabelling? How soon do I need to out myself to avoid being considered 'deceitful' and 'untrustworthy'? (It is no coincidence that these are negative stereotypes of bi people!) How much should I do to make myself look queer in straight people's eyes, even if it doesn't feel comfortable for me? It is really difficult to avoid blaming myself for people's homophobic and biphobic assumptions about me, my appearance, my relationship, my queer identity. It is difficult to avoid internalising the belief that I am not queer enough, not brave enough, not honest enough.

Passing as straight gives some conditional privileges in straight, mainstream society (even if it is not true acceptance), but it can lead to rejection and harassment in LG communities unless I choose to 'pass' as lesbian, closeting myself again. The assumption is that because I pass in straight communities, I do not need queer community and I am greedy for expecting the community to include me. But I am *not* fully, genuinely accepted in either community, and two half-hearted welcomes do not add up to a community where I can feel safe and respected. 'Passing privilege' can be used to blame bisexual people for their own oppression, unless they meet a set of shifting, unstated requirements: looking queer enough, being out enough in straight spaces but not too out in LGBT ones, having an appropriate sexual CV to demonstrate our queerness.

And yet...I took my time coming out to my family, and it didn't get questioned, because I had this convenient male boyfriend to bring home for the holidays. I can talk about my partner at work without playing the pronoun game. My appearance fits a norm, and that gives me some protection against harassment by randoms. Passing has brought me some privileges, and I have been able to avoid internalising some of the negative effects because I have access to a bisexual community. This has helped me identify and fend off bi-erasing microaggressions from straight and LG(bt) communities.

Some people have a worse experience and are marginalised in both straight and LG(bt) spaces. I am pretty convinced that this experience of dual marginalisation is the underlying cause of the horrifying statistics about bisexual people's mental health problems, experience of violence and reluctance to be out. Being constantly isolated and undermined is destructive, and that experience is emphatically not a privilege.

I approach the issue of passing privilege from a quite defensive posture in two different ways. I think that people mistake passing for acceptance and therefore dismiss the way passing harms us. On the other hand, I have not experienced much direct oppression myself, and I am wary of 'playing the victim' by claiming to be more oppressed than I am. I suspect being relatively privileged on other axes plays into that defensiveness, and I don't want to ignore those factors.

However, it strikes me that I have viewed passing privilege as a specifically bisexual issue because I have seen it used to undermine and exclude bi people. However, the same criticism (of 'taking advantage' of passing) would apply to any queer person who is ever misidentified and does not immediately correct that identification. Holding bisexuals *more* accountable for that than monosexuals is another way of saying we are only conditionally welcome.

I do think that there are actual benefits to passing, and I think they make life easier for people who can pass. For example, I work with a homophobe, and I am not out, so it does not affect our working relationship. My friend is a non-binary trans woman who does not pass as cis—she could not work with my homophobic co-worker in the same way because she does not pass as straight even for a minute. Feeling erased is *not* as bad as fearing for my job. Not outing myself to a homophobe is a choice I can make. It is not a uniquely bisexual thing, and it does not make me responsible for his homophobia (he is a twat), but it does benefit me.

Coming Out Stories

Coming out as bisexual is a widely varying experience. Here we've collected some examples of people's coming-out stories.

'Coming out at work is all kinds of fun because most of my colleagues know me as "Mili, who has been with Paul for longer than she has been with the company". But at the same time, I was heavily involved with running our work LGBT network for years, and that raised questions. My favourite is still "But why are you doing that, you're not lesbian, gay, or…Oh…"—and I've had that from gay and straight colleagues. I've also had colleagues who know about my involvement with the LGBT network but not about my partner assume that I was a lesbian.

I am not completely out to my family. Both my parents have made homophobic remarks in front of me in the past, so for a long time I thought I'd never come out. After a while the fact that I wasn't out started affecting my relationship with them. So much of what I do in my life (e.g. blogging, charity work, some of my day job) has to do with my sexuality that I ended up not being able to talk to my parents about huge chunks of my life, and they started noticing. I came out to my mother about eighteen months ago, and for the following nine months she completely ignored it. We talked about it a little bit when I took her on holiday last year, but she still doesn't really get why it's important to me, so we really don't talk about it a lot. I think I may have semi-accidentally outed myself to my father when he read my blog at Christmas, but he's never explicitly acknowledged it. We did have a very weird conversation after that which either was the world's most avoidant "Why are you flaunting your sexuality" conversation or I have no idea what it was about. I'm still on good terms with my parents, but we may have reached a stalemate on this one for the moment.'

Milena Popova

'I suppose the first person you always come out to is yourself. I guess that may be more true of those of us who arrive at the realisation of our sexuality outside of our teens and twenties. I don't know—I can only speak about my own experience. The thing I found most odd about it all, and why I didn't talk about it for a while, was one simple fact.

It didn't feel like a big deal.

I'd already snogged one guy before this point (but not figured out the whole bi thing) and been in...situations that looking back post-realisation made me go "Ohhhhhh, right. Got it now." Still, I always figured that such revelations would be a Big Thing. The fact that it wasn't was the source of my confusion, not the revelation in itself.

The first person I came out to was a very dear female friend while we were on a work trip. We got chatting into the wee small hours, and it became part of the conversation. Chatting with my chum allowed me to stream-of-consciousness it all out, sorting out the stuff in my head. When I told my wife when I got home, her comment was along the lines of "That's nice dear. Oh, and the rest of us worked that out ages ago." I love my wife very much.

Since then, I've never really done the whole coming-out-to-people thing. I talk about it now and then on Facebook and stuff, normally as a qualifier when I'm off on some political, social justice rant (I do a lot of those). It comes down to the fact that it's not a big deal for me. I don't keep it a secret, but I don't introduce myself as "Hi! Iain Lowson. Writer. Bisexual," much in the same way that I don't go, "Hi! Iain Lowson. Writer. Hazel eyes." I'm not ashamed, scared or anything else. It's worse than that; I'm content.

The only "fallout" from the whole thing, really, again came from the lack of internal kaboom. The fact that it was all a bit of a non-event event in my head, as well as elsewhere in my life, led to me questioning whether I really was bi. I felt like I was, but... There's not a guidebook for this stuff, and everyone's experience is going to be different—be deeply suspicious of anyone who tells you otherwise. Turns out I needn't have worried.

Yum!

Anyway...

I've never come out to the rest of my family. Again, no hiding it. I've never felt the need to shout about who I am in a Coming Out Day context. I think that is an age thing and a time-of-life thing. I'm (does a quick count) forty-five, settled in my own house, with a wife (with her own stories) and kids, shed, video game habit, etc. Again, though, that's just me. For you it might be different. No, actually, for you it will be different, or it is different, even if it's similar.

My dad used to read my Facebook stuff, as do my sisters. With my mum, it's just not come up in conversation (and the digital age is something she hasn't engaged with). With everyone in my life, the subject has either come up naturally in conversation or it hasn't. I want the day to arrive where it doesn't matter to anyone what your sexuality is, so I act as though that day is here. I will stand up, online or in person, to talk down (or slap down) the uninformed or the scumbags, but I don't engage with trolls. Life's too short, and they really are not worth the time it takes for you to realise they are not going to change their minds.'

Iain Lowson

'The big catalyst to my coming out was becoming an aunt, when I was twenty-five. I had told a few friends, which was only once received with anything other than acceptance—the one friend who informed me that I merely "liked the idea of being bisexual". I told my sister and was met with "How can you know, if you've never had sex with a woman?" I pointed out that we had young straight friends who hadn't slept with anyone at all, but we believed them when they said they were straight. That seemed to fix that.

My parents and I had often had arguments about their homophobia. I had been completely in the closet in my teens, but just internalising that stuff had been hard and contributed to a big, dangerous depression I went through when I was about eighteen. I didn't want my nephew to go through anything close to that if he happened to be queer in any way—and even if he wasn't, I hoped my example would make a difference to his attitudes. I worked my way up to telling my mum by blogging about my teenage confusion—I knew she was unlikely to read it, but there was courage required to write about it openly where anyone, theoretically, could read it.

I remember bits of the conversation we had. I didn't sit her down but took an opportunity when it presented itself, when we were travelling somewhere together. I think the conversation may have started with Elton John; it certainly worked its way through homosexual behaviour in ancient Greece and ended in a rather unexpected place. At some point I threw in that I knew I was bisexual because I had been in love with both men and women. I explained that in ancient Greece and also in single-sex environments like boarding schools and prisons, straight people often had sex with people of the same gender, but it wasn't that act that defined sexuality. It was something deeper, something fundamental and more about love.

Anyway, it was all fine, and I was trying to describe this difference between sexuality and behaviour and said something like, "Pretty much any two people have the capacity to get one another off if they really want to, regardless of actual attraction."

And she said, "Do you mean like John Major and Edwina Currie? That's against nature!"

I was going to come out to my dad but I was informed that he knew, so I guess Mum told him. It made a big difference. My parents still have socially conservative ideas, but subsequent arguments have taken place in the knowledge that I am queer—I'm sure they probably count me as something like a half-lesbian or something, not entirely "one of them". But the homophobia has significantly mellowed over the last seven years—I'm honestly quite proud of the way that, realising this stuff isn't about an abstract group they have nothing to do with but about their family too, my folks have become far more egalitarian.

There are people I'm not out to. There are lots of people who know my husband and me and will thus read me as straight. I'm extremely close with my in-laws, and I've got a ninety-year-old granny I love dearly, but I can't conceive a way in which that conversation would ever arise with them. However, what I never do is attempt to conceal anything about my sexuality. If anyone who doesn't know learns by accident—such as through something I've written—then that's fine.'

DH Kelly

'Around age twenty-three, I was in a pub with a group of people and chatting to an old school friend about his holiday dalliance with a Turkish waiter. Then he mentioned a girl he fancied. "But I thought you were gay," I said. "Oh, I'm bisexual," he replied. The words "I think I'm probably bisexual" were out of my mouth and hanging in the air before I'd had time to think about them. Once I'd said it, it felt absolutely accurate, but until that moment I hadn't articulated it, even in my own head. After that I came out to close friends individually. I was very nervous about it and, especially with women, I felt the need to soften it with "I don't fancy you though" or something similar. It mostly went well. I did lose one friend who just stopped speaking to me and wouldn't return my calls. Everyone else was fine, though, and a couple of them came out to me in return. Since then I've varied a lot in how much "coming out" I've done. I'm pretty open, but sometimes I just decide I don't owe people that information. Being an out bi person in a small-town lesbian scene was particularly difficult. I got told all sorts of hurtful nonsense about myself. I eventually came out to my father by email about five years ago. He said he didn't want to talk about it, so we don't (he belongs to a pretty homophobic religious group). Sometimes I mention something bi-relevant in passing, but he mostly pretends not to hear.'

Julie

'Very boring: I told my parents and my older sister, and they were a bit confused because they thought I knew that they already knew I was bi. I don't remember actually telling people at school, but I must have at some point—everybody knew. It must just have been very undramatic.

I was lucky enough to be in a situation where it never occurred to me that it might be a problem. I knew about societal homophobia, but I was also totally confident that my family and friends wouldn't have a problem with me being bisexual. I was kind of blind to biphobia to begin with: I happily described myself as lesbian and heterosexual and bisexual, and was a bit perplexed when I went to join the local LGB (at least in theory) youth group and was told (by one of the adults) that I'd grow out of the bi thing and become a proper lesbian.'

Fred Langridge

'I came out to my parents kind of by accident, during a (friendly) argument while we were eating at a restaurant with friends. Some years later, it turned out that they hadn't actually registered that I meant it. Since when I discovered this I was in the process of telling them that I was poly and had both another boyfriend and a girlfriend, the bisexuality was not the bit that really caught their attention at that point, either.'

Anon

'Like every non-heterosexual person, I've got a million "coming-out" stories, most of which are hideously dull. But there is one that's rather more notable: how I came out to my friends at college. I'd told maybe a couple of my closest friends, but managed to not just come out of the closet, but burn it down in spectacular fashion at a party when I was interrupted fisting another girl. It makes for an interesting story now, but at the time I was mortified, and it wrenched my coming out firmly out of my control.'

Anon

'An awful lot of my friends are socially connected to others in ways that mean they will know about/will probably have guessed my bisexuality. Others would know if they read what I say on Facebook. At work, even though a number of people I work with can read what I say on Facebook, I seem to have to come out once a year when I say I'm going to BiCon, because my bisexuality seems to get forgotten.'

Karen

'I'm out to my friends and family. I'm not out at work, though—however, if the subject did come up, I probably would come out (there just doesn't seem to be a particularly good way of doing it so far...).

I came out to my friends first. It was hard not to when they saw me kissing girls at clubs and eventually dating them, as well as kissing boys and dating them as well. (But not at the same time—I didn't start doing the poly thing until I was in my twenties.) I guess other people at school knew, but I didn't give a shit what they thought because I was a bit of an outcast anyway (being into alternative music and having a stay in psychiatric hospital under your belt didn't do your reputation much good in the '90s).

Out of my family, I came out to my sister first. Again, it was hard not to, as we were in overlapping social circles, so if she hadn't heard about my sexual and romantic entanglements with various genders she would have seen it herself sooner or later. My sister then outed me to my parents when she was drunk; I was in a fairly serious relationship with a girl, and my sister told my parents. My dad's reaction was to decide that I was a lesbian, my mum's was to think that I was "going through a phase". However, they never treated me any differently, and they did get the right message in the end.'

Cat

'I came out very tentatively to my friends once I'd realised. I was worried that it would make things awkward or they'd think it was a trying-to-be-trendy phase. Fortunately, the reactions of my friends have been pretty good. In fact, an ex that I was still on good terms with then confided with me that he, too, was bi!

Coming out to my mother was something that felt a lot more tricky. She was a lot older than the parents of my peers and is quite active in the church. I decided that I wouldn't say anything unless I really had to. This wasn't such a big deal, as we generally didn't talk about relationships.

Then came the conversation where she asked me if I was seeing anyone, right when I was seeing my first girlfriend. I replied yes, but there was an obvious hesitation in my tone which she caught on. She went through a list of reasons she could think of that I might be hesitant to tell her, including race, religion and class, till, exasperated, she asked, "What is he?", to which I replied that "He is in fact a she." There was a processing pause, after which she got very flustered, said "Well I hear that can be a very satisfying lifestyle", and swiftly and uncomfortably changed the subject.

...In general, though, coming out is a continual process as you meet new people. I've been presumed both lesbian and straight at various times, and setting the record straight is awkward for all involved.

...In regards to coming out in general, I've also found I've had to come out to the same people multiple times, as there seems to be some form of 'mental Teflon' about bisexuality.

I remember a conversation with a friend after a break-up with a guy where he said, "Well I'm not surprised it didn't work out; you're gay!" I reminded him that actually I quite liked both women and men, but it didn't seem to impinge on his mind at all.

...I've been told I shouldn't concern myself with others labelling me incorrectly. What other people think is their own concern, but I liken it to someone consistently getting your name wrong, or presuming you to be a nationality you are not and continually referencing it; maybe not too bad at first but very irksome after continued exposure.'

Linette

'I don't remember having any specific coming-out moment. At school and university I had a friendship with a woman where there was increasingly open recognition between us that there was a sexual element that might be acted upon at some point. That went alongside having a few different relationships with men. I was aware of the word but didn't use it much at that point.

A few years later, I remember wanting to come out to a female friend who I think was straight, because it was part of me that I couldn't talk about. But I didn't do it, because I worried she might think it meant I was attracted to her.

Going to BiCon for the first time was great because being out was a non-issue there, and I met a partner there, so it was always out in the open between us, and with all subsequent partners who I mostly met through bi or LGBT communities in one way or another.

I don't remember particularly mentioning it to my family until my sister came out to them, at which point I think I just made it clear that it applied to me too. That made it a lot easier, actually. I realised that the one thing I've had to come out as which didn't also apply to her was much more difficult than the things I could just say "me too" about!'

Meg-John

3

GREEDY, CONFUSED AND INVISIBLE: BI MYTHS AND LEGENDS

Editor: Kate Harrad

There is a really impressive collection of stereotypes about bisexuals around the place. Some are well meaning, some are naive or ignorant, and some are actively hostile, but they all contribute to biphobia: prejudice towards bisexuality. Here, we'll look at some of the most popular options.

Erased

Image by Jennifer Moore, from 'Three Levels of Bi Erasure'

Obviously, we can't know what goes on in other people's minds, but the evidence suggests that a lot of straight and gay people are instinctively suspicious of bisexuality. Which leads to an exciting variety of methods for pretending we're not there. Let's start with the most basic one: denial.

Bisexuality doesn't exist

> 'I went to a Lesbigay meeting in Freshers' Week and got told by a pair of stereotypical short-haired lesbians that they were fed up of "obviously straight" long-haired women turning up and claiming to be bisexual, because everyone knew bisexuals didn't really exist.'
>
> Hessie

There's just gay and straight and nothing in between, and if you think otherwise, you're deluded or lying. This is a popular one and makes everything very simple for people. Well, it's simple as long as the person who believes it is themselves gay or straight, and as long as they manage to avoid meeting anyone who isn't.

This type of thinking leads to the belief that the slightest drop of gayness makes you gay, like ink in water. One kiss. One thought. And that's it—you've crossed the divide, and there's no going back. After all, gayness is so pervasive that sometimes even hearing that it exists is enough to turn you (which is why young people must never be allowed to find out about it).

The idea that your only choices are heterosexuality or homosexuality is an appealing one because it's simple and because people tend to like to think in binaries: gay/straight, black/white, normal/weird. But although it might look okay at a distance, close up it's clear that sexuality is much more detailed and much more colourful than that.

A variation on this kind of denial is the belief that while bisexuals might exist in general, certain types of bisexual don't: 'There aren't any black bisexual people' or 'Women can be bi, but men aren't.' The truth is, anyone can be bisexual.

But denying the very existence of bisexuality isn't the only way to discredit it. There is a whole collection of assumptions, prejudice and ignorance which have the effect of making bi people feel like their sexuality isn't genuine.

Gay but scared

'Bi now, gay later' is one of the phrases people often use, describing bisexuality as a stepping stone for people who aren't ready to come out as gay. In 2014, actor Christopher Biggins told *Pink News*, 'I think the people who fear homosexuality most are the ones who could be gay. The world is full of bisexuals because that's the way they want to do it. What do they do? They ruin a woman's life. It's so wrong, because you're not owning up to what you are. You lead a double life so how can you be a real person?'

It's true that some people do come out as bisexual and then later come out as gay. Maybe they're actually changing their sexuality, or maybe they really were gay all along. The problem here isn't the change of label but the level of homophobia in society which makes it hard for people to be themselves.

And it doesn't invalidate bisexuality as a sexuality. If one person identifies as vegetarian but craves meat and eventually decides to start eating it, does that mean vegetarians don't exist?

Bisexuality as trendy or appealing

'A faux bisexual is a naive, conforming girl who pretends to be bisexual because being a bisexual girl is currently considered "cool" in pop culture.'
Urban Dictionary

There's a lot of hostility towards people who 'pretend' to be bisexual, for example two girls who snog each other for the enjoyment of men. Many bisexuals get annoyed by this behaviour. But bisexuality is a very broad church. Maybe one of the girls, or both of them, are acting out their actual desires in the only way they safely can. In any case, even if there are people who identify as bisexual just because they like the sound of the word, it doesn't mean everyone is doing that.

It's also often true that bisexuality is not at all a cool label to have. Especially if you're (for example) fat or disabled or not conventionally attractive.

Implicit erasure

The phrase 'gay marriage' has been in the news a lot over the last few years. But it's not gay marriage. It's same-sex marriage, because it also means that bi men can marry bi men and bi women can marry bi women. Does that seem like nitpicking? It's actually part of a whole culture of ignoring the bisexual aspect of issues. If denying bisexuality is explicit erasure, this is implicit erasure.

> '**Implicit** class erasure is people repeatedly **leaving out** the word and idea "bisexual" where it would make sense to include it. "Blah blah gay and straight", "heterosexual and homosexual", "gay and lesbian".
>
> This way of talking and thinking links up with mistaken logic such as: "Is so-and-so gay?" "No, he's straight—I know his girlfriend." Or "Is so-and-so gay?" "Yes—I've met his boyfriend."
>
> Unintentional, unthinking erasure of this **implicit** kind is very common in present-day mainstream culture. It's even done by bi people ourselves by accident sometimes. It can take work to **unlearn the habit**: first, making a conscious decision not to erase/forget/ignore bi people any more, and then practising and failing, failing and practising, till it becomes more usual to remember.'
>
> Jennifer Moore, from 'Three Levels of Bi Erasure'

Maxine Green

Prove it!

'The idea that you have to "**prove**" your bisexuality by having some particular sexual history; e.g. people nosily questioning "So have you ever been with a woman?", and/or talking as though it's **up to them to decide** whether your history "counts".'

Jennifer Moore, from 'Three Levels of Bi Erasure'

Jennifer Moore, from 'Three Levels of Bi Erasure'

How often are heterosexual people asked to prove that they're heterosexual? Bisexuality doesn't need to be proved.

Organised biphobia

In the not-too-distant past, it was perfectly normal for organisations to be lesbian and gay only, and even to specifically refuse entry to bisexuals.

> 'As a public sector worker, one obvious union to join was Unison. Who had a lesbian and gay group that explicitly banned bisexuals—apparently their issues were too different from gay people's. This was a bit ironic, as the rest of the world was saying bisexuals had exactly the same issues of homophobia—if they existed, which they didn't because none were out as such at work. Some bisexuals tried to get Unison to change their policy, but it took over a decade of insulting debates.' [Unison's policy has now changed.]
>
> Hessie

Now, mostly, organisations are LGBTQIA+ at least in name. And yet, it still seems very easy for bisexuals (and indeed trans people) to be forgotten. This can lead to bi issues being ignored and a lack of funding for bi events. In fact, at the time of writing, no bi groups, organisations or events in the UK have any outside funding—it's all entirely self-supporting. This has meant a very grassroots, community feel, which is not a bad thing, but the lack of money has made it difficult to organise certain types of events. For example, finding a suitable venue for a central-London one-day bi event with virtually no budget is verging on impossible.

It's assumed that organisations such as Stonewall look after bisexual rights, but historically Stonewall's focus has been on lesbian and gay issues, although times are slowly changing.

Organisations such the Bisexual Index have increased bi visibility and provided the media with someone to contact, but lack of funding remains a major issue.

It's Real, but It's Wrong and Weird

The next stage of biphobia is people admitting that bisexuality does exist, but making all kinds of assumptions about it.

Making your mind up: The confused, indecisive bisexual

> 'Ever since I told my boss I was going to a bi event she seems to treat me as a flake. She makes little comments all the time about how I can't stick at things, how I'm not a team player. One time she told me not to apply for a promotion because they wanted "someone loyal, who could commit". I think I'd have got that one too. I wish I'd never mentioned it now.'
> *The Bisexuality Report*, p. 24

There's this idea that bisexual people are confused about who they 'really' fancy, haven't decided on their sexuality or are trying to have it both ways. Like the 'Bisexuality doesn't exist' trope, there's a superficial appeal to this. People failing to choose a side, or trying to be on two sides simultaneously, is traditionally a sign that they're untrustworthy: they're trying to play both sides off against each other, they're double agents, they're disloyal.

Part of the problem is that analogies are weirdly powerful things. One popular description of bisexuality is 'batting for both teams'. This immediately sets up a few interesting assumptions. In any game with two teams, playing for both sides at once is clearly unsportsmanlike; you'd only ever play for one team, and even switching between games would be seen as dodgy. Supporting a team is even more polarised; players might move to different football teams, but a football supporter usually sticks with supporting one team over a lifetime. In this context, it's easy to see why the idea of bisexuality looks like a kind of betrayal. Other analogies have a similar feel to them: trying to have your cake and eat it, hunting with the hare and running with the hounds, sitting on the fence.

However, just because you can make a striking visual metaphor about something doesn't mean you've arrived at any kind of truth.

Bisexuality is just a type of sexuality, nothing more; it doesn't imply anything else about you. And it's not a choice, so any comparison involving a decision—like being a double agent—won't work. A better analogy would be someone who has dual nationality. Or quite liking (but not loving or hating) Marmite.

It's a phase!

This is slightly different to the accusation of indecision, because it allows for the idea that you may be genuinely bisexual now, but it won't last. Obviously, this is usually aimed at younger people, so at least you're likely to hear it less as you get older.

'When I came out to them aged nineteen, my mum told me it was just a phase and I'd grow out of it. Now I'm forty-two, she can't exactly say that any more—it's clear that if I was going to grow out of it, I'd have done so by now!'
Joanne

Of course, bisexuality can be a phase. So can heterosexuality and homosexuality—many bi people identify as straight or gay on the way to eventually settling with a bi identity. The fact that sexuality can change, and that the labels people want to use can change, doesn't mean that anyone's current sexuality or label isn't valid. After all, ultimately, everything's a phase.

Everyone's bi, really

This is something often said by bisexuals and non-bisexuals alike: everyone's a little bit bisexual. It feels right to a lot of people, and it's a positive thing to say, surely? Well, not necessarily. For one thing, it's not true. Most people aren't bisexual and don't identify as such. And the rules about not imposing your labels on other people apply here too: don't label your gay, lesbian or straight friend as bisexual if that's not something they'd call themselves. It also doesn't really

45

help bi visibility. If everyone's bi, people could argue, why make a fuss about it?

Everyone isn't bisexual, and that's okay.

Needing both genders/the unfaithful bisexual

'I've lost count of how many people, especially lesbians, have said they aren't bisexual because they've only slept with/had relationships with one/two/not as many people of the other sex.'

Hessie

'I was once told by a lesbian friend that I wasn't a proper bisexual because I had slept with more men than I had women. I then told her that she couldn't be a proper lesbian because I'd slept with more women than she had. Not entirely fair, I know, but saying something that stupid deserves an equally stupid answer.'

Cat

The idea that proper bisexuals are exactly 50-50 in their sexuality has been mentioned elsewhere in this book. It's a silly idea but it's extremely popular, presumably because it helps people keep a sort-of-binary view of things: if you can't be one side or the other, then you must be precisely in the middle, like the world's best trapeze artist permanently balancing on a wire suspended over a net of monosexuality. Wobble slightly in one direction or the other, and you lose your right to be bi.

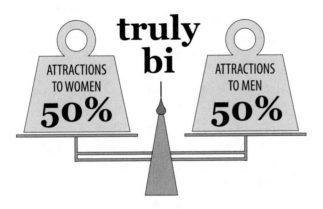

Image by Jennifer Moore at uncharted-worlds.org

Now, the existence of non-binary genders undermines this argument to start with: there isn't a 50-50 you can be, because gender isn't neatly divided up into a half-and-half arrangement. But even if that weren't the case, it would still be true that bisexuals don't have to like men and women equally. How would that work, anyway? As soon as you see a man you fancy, you have to look round for a woman you also find attractive, so the Sexuality Police don't get you? Do you have to keep a scorecard of everyone you sleep with and make sure it adds up at the end of every year, or decade? Or are you allowed to wait till the end of your life before you calculate your final score and then finally claim the True Bisexual crown?

And what counts? Is it sleeping with precisely equal numbers of men and women, or is it who you eye up in the street? What about kissing? What about celebrities? Or do only actual relationships count towards the total? Maybe fancying equals one point, kissing two points, sex five points and dating ten points? At this point, being bisexual is starting to feel both complicated and a bit too much like someone marking a sexuality test.

It's a small step from this belief to the next idea.

Bisexuals have to have sex with both genders

Don't bisexuals, by definition, want to have sex with men and women? Would they be unsatisfied if they didn't? Well, we talked in chapter 1 about that definition not necessarily being the best one—and not just because of the problem with saying 'both' genders—but let's assume that a majority of bisexuals do enjoy sexual activity with men and women, because that's a fairly reasonable assumption. Does that mean that if you have a bisexual partner and you're monogamous with them, they'll always be looking over your shoulder yearning for another gender?

No, it doesn't. The desire to date multiple people isn't the same thing as bisexuality. Some bi people feel unfulfilled without access to multiple partners, some are perfectly fine with one. This is also true of all other sexualities.

'Why do so many bisexuals end up in heterosexual relationships?'

A lot of bi people are in relationships with different genders. We don't have statistics for how many, because many bi people in that situation wouldn't identify themselves as bi on any survey. A lot of bi people are in relationships with the same gender too, and many of those also wouldn't put 'bisexual' on a survey form.

However, it's quite likely that a majority of bisexual women are in relationships with men, and bisexual men with women. This is because if you're a bi woman (for example), your dating options are confined to people who fancy women, and most of those are men. So, statistically, it's just more likely that you'll end up dating a different gender to yours.

It's all about sex

Imagine that your friends Alan and Beth get engaged. When Alan tells his friend Charlie the news, Charlie says, 'It doesn't matter to me what you do in bed.' That would be a weird response. Alan's not telling Charlie what he does in bed, he's telling him an important piece of news about his life and his relationships.

What happens when bi or gay people come out? They often get responses like that: 'I don't care what you do in bed. I don't need to know that! Your private life is your private life.' Essentially, people are reacting as if they're being told something very sexually personal. But they're not. They're being told a basic piece of someone's identity.

'Bisexual' as a search term is often blocked from public Wi-Fi, even when 'gay' and 'lesbian' aren't—as some of this book's editors found when trying to research it. That means blogs about being bisexual, educational resources and so on get blocked. And if you *can* search for 'bisexual', you'll get a lot of porn links unless you turn SafeSearch on. Bisexuality is a very sexualised identity in popular culture.

We're not anti-sex, or anti-porn. This is about people trying to live their lives without the assumption that they'll fancy absolutely everyone and will be up for threesomes within five minutes of meeting.

'Over the weekend, I was helping a friend sell merchandise on her company stall at a large trade show up in Manchester. I had a great time, as I always enjoy meeting new people and chatting with them—even if they don't end up buying anything! I also have a fair bit of experience in this particular field, and really like getting to know people in order to signpost them on to websites and events that I think they would enjoy and find useful.

Around midday on the second day, I chatted to a couple who I would guess were about 20 years older than me, possibly even double my age. They were very nice and lived in the East Midlands too and we were talking for about five minutes before they carried on looking round the event.

By the time I had arrived home that evening they had already messaged me to tell me that they were seeking a "suitable and enthusiastic submissive female", and wondered whether I would consider having a relationship with them. From the way they described it in the message, this relationship would seemingly take the form of meeting up for sex a few times a month.

Needless to say I was a bit stunned. I had only spoken to them for a few minutes to recommend events in their area. I didn't know their names, nor could I even remember what they looked like. I gave them my username for networking purposes as they were potential customers. I certainly didn't think any of my actions during that brief time were flirtatious or suggestive.

I'm a very smiley, sociable person. I would never want to restrict that in order to reduce inappropriate and unwanted attention from others. I shouldn't have to. No one should be making these kind of assumptions based on my sexuality and the fact that I was friendly towards them.

The sad thing is this kind of experience is really common for me. I hate how I never get asked how *I* am in a message, or asked what *I* want or what *I'm* looking for. People only state their wants and needs, as if I will immediately stop what I'm doing so I can fly over to theirs. (Presumably leaving a trail of condoms and sex toys along the way, as I'd be unable to carry much whilst using my unicorn wings.) People never speak of what they could bring to *my* life, they only write about what they want me to do for their sex life. They never offer to go out or do anything together or get to know me.

The myth that bisexuals are all super-horny greedy sexed-up individuals is just that, a big stupid myth. All I really want is someone to share my life with, so it would be nice if I could be considered for someone's primary relationship for a change.'

Hannah Bee, 'Hypersexualised Objectified Bisexual'

Bisexual sexuality is fluid sexuality

Sexuality often is fluid. People can change their sexuality across their lifetime, across a year or even in the space of an evening, and then change it again, and again. But people, especially in the media, often assume that bisexuality is the same as having a fluid sexuality. This isn't true, because just like being gay or straight or anything else, you can be bisexual from a very young age and carry on being it for the rest of your life.

'I don't feel *fluid*. I feel **stable**. I feel settled. **I arrived already**. I'm not going anywhere.'
Jennifer Moore, from 'Bisexuality: Integrated, Stable, Peaceful'

Internalised Biphobia

By Milena Popova

A lot of focus in the bisexual community is on the biphobia we experience from the lesbian and gay people in our lives. This is understandable. Growing up, we learn to automatically expect hostility from many straight people. At the same time, we have an expectation of the so-called LGB community to provide a safe space and support. When we are met with hostility instead, we feel betrayed.

This double marginalisation has dramatic impacts on our lives. According to the *Bisexuality Report*, bisexual people experience more mental health issues than either straight or gay people. We are significantly less likely to be out to friends, family or colleagues than lesbian and gay people. We experience erasure and biphobia from healthcare providers, which affects our physical health. We experience stigma around sexual health, including being blamed for the spread of HIV to both straight and gay communities, and struggle to get appropriate advice and information. Bisexual people are at higher risk of domestic abuse from same-gender partners than lesbian or gay people (and statistics for different-gender partners are not available). Bisexual asylum seekers experience even more intrusive questioning by agencies of the state in order to 'prove' their sexuality than lesbian and gay asylum seekers do, and are often sent back to countries where their lives are in danger with instructions to simply live a 'heterosexual life'.

It is important to remember that the roots of monosexism lie with the heterosexual majority and that we should target our efforts to combat biphobia and monosexism at those roots, while looking to carve out a truly welcoming space for ourselves within the LGBTQIA+ community too.

Living in a monosexist world and constantly experiencing biphobia from both straight and gay communities leads many bisexual people to internalise certain biphobic attitudes and thought patterns. It often takes years to even recognise such thoughts and feelings as internalised biphobia, and shedding them may take even longer. This is a process that many, if not most, bisexual people go through, and it can be accompanied by many negative emotions: distress, anger, self-blame, shame, sadness. It may help to recognise that this is a normal process, and that in many cases internalised biphobia is a survival mechanism: by mimicking oppressive thought patterns and actions, we feel we may better 'fit in' with dominant social groups and experience less overt hostility.

Some common forms of internalised biphobia

We asked people about their experiences of internalising anti-bi prejudices.

Worrying that I am not 'bi enough'

> 'I frequently worry that I'm "not bi enough", that there are particular boxes I should be ticking in order to legitimately "count" as bi. I don't believe that when I think about it, but it's definitely hiding in my back-brain.'
> Juliet

This is a very common concern for many bisexual people. It takes a while to realise that the standards monosexual people set for what counts as 'bi enough' are impossible to meet. No particular gender ratio among our sexual and romantic partners, no polyamorous or monogamous relationship model, no amount of rainbow flags all over our kit will make others recognise us as 'bi enough' or 'gay enough'. But neither do other people's definitions trump our own experiences of our sexuality.

The 'privilege of passing'

'Currently both my relationships are with men, so I'm also uncomfortable about "bi invisibility". But as I'm aware that that can be a privilege as well, it doesn't feel okay to complain about it. I guess that's a form of internalised biphobia.'
Juliet

Those of us in relationships which look heterosexual from the outside are often subjected to accusations of betraying the LGBTQIA+ community, 'passing' as straight and thus becoming oppressors of lesbian and gay people ourselves. It is easy to internalise such feelings of alleged privilege, even though they rarely mesh with our lived experience of the pain every time our identity is erased or assumed away based on the gender of our current partner. We experience a series of such microaggressions but find it difficult to challenge them, as we are told we should be glad that people assume we are straight. Straight privilege exists, but bisexual people don't automatically have it.

Feeling 'too sensitive' or like I am 'making a fuss'

'I feel frustrated and uncomfortable when I encounter monosexism. It feels like a choice between an erasure of an important part of my identity and "making a fuss".'
Juliet

An accusation often levelled at bisexual people when we correct a false assumption about us is that we are 'too sensitive' and 'flaunting our sexuality'. The implication is that somehow bisexual people have less of a right for our sexuality to be recognised than straight people wearing wedding rings or gay people casually slipping the name or pronoun of their partner into conversation.

Feeling that bi issues come last

'I have been an LGBT activist for nearly fifteen years now. For the first decade of that, I wouldn't touch bi issues with a barge pole. It took me years to realise that there even was such a thing as bi-specific issues. I thought for a very long time that, as one of those "privileged bisexuals" in a "straight" relationship, it was my duty to actively work on lesbian and gay issues and simply shut up about things that affected me and my community. At work, I was reluctant to speak to senior management, despite being on the leadership team of our LGBT network, because I felt I would only confuse straight people and be a distraction from the "real" issues of my lesbian and gay colleagues.'
Milena

Feeling that we somehow have to 'atone' for not being 'properly gay' and to earn our credibility within the LGBTQIA+ community by putting our own issues last is quite common. Finding a supportive bi community can be really helpful in working through this and in lending legitimacy to our feelings of oppression.

Feeling that relationships with people of a particular gender are somehow less legitimate

'It took me years to feel confident enough to take my straight male partner to LGBT events. The first time I held his hand at Pride was a deeply surreal experience which in some ways I am still processing a year later.'
Milena

'I've got a boyfriend. The phrase still feels odd in my mouth, like I'm using a forbidden word. I've had one for just over a year now, and those words haven't got much easier to say. Here, in a cosy south-London flat, just me and my netbook on the sofa, it's marginally easier, but out in the world it's almost impossible. Among friends, many of them bisexual activists, in the most accepting community I have ever had the good fortune to be a part of, the words choke me. Boyfriend. Even now I hesitate over the keys. To admit that I have a boyfriend—a cisgender man who I love and whose bottom I have seen—feels like a betrayal.'

Libby

No particular gender of partners will make us feel any more or less bi, or will make other people accept us as such—but sometimes that is difficult to remember. The best we can often hope for is partners who are supportive and understanding of the inner turmoil we go through, and a community around us that will accept us and not cast us out the minute we don't meet impossible standards.

Most of us have many layers of internalised biphobia to work through, and each individual will be at a different place in that process. It is important not to judge others for the coping mechanisms they have developed to deal with both external and internalised biphobia, and to focus on our own personal growth and helping others where that help is appropriate and welcome.

4

THE GENDER AGENDA

Editors: Fred Langridge and Meg-John Barker

Content note: While there are no graphic, specific or detailed descriptions in this chapter, there are mentions of transphobia, biphobia, homophobia, sexism and mental health issues in a broad sense.

This chapter covers bi people's experience of gender: how we identify our gender and sexuality, and how they relate to each other, how our gender and sexuality change—or not—over our lifetimes, how they're linked to the relationships we form, and how they play out in the communities we're part of.

We've included the experiences of bisexual men, women and non-binary people throughout the chapter, including our own experiences. Some of the people we include identify as trans, some as cisgender, and some question this distinction as well, due to having a trans history but no longer regarding themselves as trans, for example, or feeling 'cis-ish', due to having some degree of fluidity or experimentation when it comes to gender.

We were keen particularly to include plenty of non-binary bisexual experience because there are existing collections on the experiences of bi men and bi women, but none that we're aware of on non-binary or genderqueer bis. This is an important absence to address because recent statistics suggest that around 1% of the general population identifies as something other than male or female, and that this rises to 5% among young LGBTQIA+ people and 25% among trans people, and around a third of people in general experience themselves as the 'other' gender, both genders, and/or neither gender.

Before we explore bisexual people's experiences of gender, it is important to say something about how the people we spoke to thought that gender and bisexuality were represented in the wider world they occupy. Of course, this is already covered elsewhere in the book, so we'll just summarise the main points here.

How Gender and Bisexuality Are Related in Representations of Bisexual People

Generally, people agreed that men, women and non-binary people were represented in different ways:

'Men are more likely to be perceived as being "secretly gay" and women as hypersexual or indecisive. Bi women are more visible in the media but only certain versions: white, thin, non-disabled, cisgender, attractive. Other bi women remain invisible. Men tend to be mocked and doubted a bit more.'

Emma

Suzy agreed with Emma that bi women tended to be more visible than bi men.

'Bisexuality as a whole is still associated with negative connotations, but in terms of public acceptance, I'm glad I'm a bi woman. Even though I know that acceptance is to the cost of being heavily fetishised. I think it must be much more difficult to be a bi man.'

Suzy

Matt confirmed these stereotypes and went on to suggest that non-binary people were even more invisible.

> 'I think we all know the classic stereotypes: bi men are gay men in waiting, bi women are putting it on to titillate men. So few people can see outside of the gender binary that I'm not sure there are stereotypes of non-binary bi people: most don't realise they exist! I definitely feel like bi women are more visible than bi men. For what it's worth, I'm trying my best to be as visible as possible!'
> Matt

However, Anon felt that both bi men and bi women had their identities erased more than they did as a non-binary person.

> 'It definitely feels as though bi men and women have their bisexuality erased more than mine is—particularly with the idea that all bi men are "really" gay, and all bi women are "really" straight.'
> Anon

Meg-John concluded that whether we are men, women or non-binary, the ways of being bi that we see around us tend to be pretty limited.

> 'Bi women are probably most visible. For a long time there was a real invisibility of bi men, but now we have Captain Jack and Alan Cumming. There's still a sense that the only way to be an acceptable bi woman or man is to fit a culturally understood version of "hotness" and being quite highly sexual.
>
> With non-binary, depictions of androgyny have often gone hand in hand with bisexuality, so the two are linked together in people's imaginations. David Bowie is the obvious example. But, as with bi men and bi women, the acceptable face of bi-androgyny is very slim, white, sexual, stylishly dressed.'
> Meg-John

Given that these were the versions of bisexuality that people saw most represented in the world around them, we next explored how they saw their own gender and sexuality in relation to this.

How We Identify Our Gender and Sexuality

A number of people labelled their gender and sexuality in relatively straightforward ways; for example:

'Male, man and bisexual.'
   Clive

'"Woman" is as good a word as any to describe me.'
   DH Kelly

Some mentioned further aspects than just their gender and bisexual identity as being equally important labels:

'Cis male. Monogamous, bisexual, kinky.'
   Matt

'A bisexual genderqueer person born in a male body. I also find aspects of asexual identity as being helpful in making sense of my experience.'
   Steve

Several mentioned more than one label feeling appropriate for them.

'Bi or bisexual, sometimes queer, occasionally pansexual. Primarily male, but I don't feel totally anything, so I also use genderfluid where that seems appropriate.'
   Ed

Non-binary or genderqueer people in particular often explained a little further what that aspect of their identity meant for them.

'I'm bisexual and genderqueer. I'm a mixture of masculine and feminine and I'm happy with the umbrella term "non-binary gendered". I am transgender: my gender doesn't match the "girl"/"woman" label that society has assigned to me; I've been through transitions in my understanding and expression of my own gender and am continuing to transition.'

Fred

Ash explained why 'bisexual' was a particularly important label as a genderqueer person.

'I am grateful that I can use the label "bisexual" because if I only liked one gender, then, as a genderqueer person, would that make me homosexual or heterosexual? Gay and straight can be really problematic labels for people who don't have a binary gender.'

Ash

Kaye explained that 'femme' was another term that required rather more explanation, due to having different connotations for different people.

'Often I describe myself as something like "haphazard femme" because I feel a bit "thrown together". In recent years, I have heard a lot about femme as drag. I see the reasons behind this, but I don't see my own femme as drag, any more than any other gender is drag, and I wouldn't want it to become a general assumption that that was the only way to do it.'

Kaye

Many people found they used different labels in different contexts, with different people, or at different times. For example, several felt the term 'queer' fitted better, but that people would understand 'bisexual' more easily.

'I like "queer" but I more often use "bisexual". "Woman" (I struggle a bit with this occasionally but think it is basically applicable).'
    Juliet

'I generally use the words "non-binary" and "bisexual" to capture the fact that I don't identify with binary genders (man or woman) or sexualities (gay or straight). The word "queer" is also quite a good encompassing one for not experiencing either gender or sexuality as binary, but not everyone is familiar with that word.'
    Meg-John

'I use "non-binary", though "genderflux" and "agender/genderqueer" also feel like accurate descriptors. What terms I use to describe my sexuality often depends on the space I'm in: I'm fond of "queer" but am aware that reclaiming slurs means I have to tread with caution; I don't want to risk triggering people. "Bisexual" works for me, though I do find I'm constantly battling misconceptions. I also fall somewhere on the asexual spectrum: "ace-ish" is my placeholder on that.'
    Jamie

'I tend to use "bi" or "bisexual" around people who I think don't know much about the diversity of sexual identities, but I use "queer" around my friends because I think this fits how I feel a bit better. It also has different connotations, not necessarily more positive but less tiresome than the bi stereotypes!'
    Emma

Ash described some further reasons why 'bisexual' didn't always feel like quite the right term.

'I do use "bisexual". Sometimes it feels right and comfortable, but at other times it doesn't. It's hard to decide how long a period of not fancying any people of a certain gender qualifies as a period of being monosexual (indeed, it's hard to decide how long a period of not fancying anyone qualifies as a period of being asexual) as opposed to just not having met anyone I like of a certain gender for a while. Sometimes I have long periods of being so in love and in lust with one particular person that no other people really interest me sexually.'

Ash

Ash and Suzy also spoke about how they related to the labels that other people assigned to them. Ash said that it could feel okay.

'I see myself as having been different things at different times in my life and in different contexts. Sometimes it's about how someone's reading me. I'll be talking to someone, they'll label me, I'll think "Oh, I'm that, am I?" and I'll accept that label at that time even if I wouldn't have chosen it for myself.'

Ash

Suzy expressed more ambivalence, suggesting that she used 'bisexual' more for others' benefit even though she didn't like the word.

'Female, girl, tomboy. Bisexual/bi; though I deeply dislike those words, they are practical to use and a good fit.'

Suzy

There was a sense that some people appreciated times and spaces where identification with labels was less necessary.

'"Trans" and "bisexual" to people who are broadly uninformed about gender and sexual diversity, "trans" *and* "genderqueer/androgynous" and "queer" to those who know more, and to the people who know me best, I don't have to identify myself with words at all.'

Anon

H seemed to sum up the limitations of labels well.

'Labels around sexuality and gender are only useful for me when they are descriptive: when they help me describe myself to others, help me find

community, help me find friends, partners, lovers. When they become prescriptive, they have lost their use, and more than that, they can be hurtful.'
    H

Following on from this, we asked people to say some more about whether their gender and bisexuality felt linked.

How Gender and Sexuality Are — or Aren't — Related

Some people didn't feel there was much of a link between these aspects of themselves.

'For me they are not related identities. They feel very distinct within me.'
    Suzy

'They're not really related, but my understanding of the gender spectrum has shaped my understanding about the fluidity of my sexuality and my ability to be more comfortable about who I find attractive.'
    Ed

Ed also pointed out that his gender was related to his bisexuality in the way that other people saw him: a point that was echoed by Matt and Clive, meaning that their gender and sexuality was linked at least to some extent.

'First of all, as a bi man I want to be clear that I do exist and I am not a figment of anyone's imagination: I am male and I do find people of more than one gender attractive. I think it is often easier for women or people of a non-binary gender to be out about being bi.'
    Ed

'There is an *absurd* amount of pressure on men to not be attracted to other men.'

Matt

'Men are encouraged not to say they're bi: "straight but browsing", "gay but hanging on to straight ideas". I had no bisexual role models and plenty of stereotypes growing up. I don't know if internalising those led me to not discover I was bi until later, or if I genuinely changed.'

Clive

People also spoke about the ways in which bisexuality could be linked to gender for women.

'I think it's difficult to be a feminine-presenting bisexual woman. People tend to assume I'm heterosexual based on the way I look. I'm in a relationship with a woman and people always ask us "Who is the butch one?" Feminine-presenting bi women are considered "sexy" in a way the others aren't.

I think it's probably more socially acceptable to be a bi woman than non-binary or male.'

Emma

'When I was a butch woman, one of my regular fuck buddies told me that she would never sleep with a bisexual. I corrected her by saying I was bisexual. She was absolutely astounded: her idea of a bisexual woman included being heteronormatively feminine. She did not mind continuing to sleep with me because I was "not like most bisexual women", who would pretend to be heterosexual to avoid homophobia and thus not admit they knew her in public, and would try to make her have a threesome. I tried to get her to understand that loads of bi women wouldn't do those things.

I had mixed feelings about this. It reinforced the realness and importance of my masculinity, which I liked, but I did not like the biphobia.'

Ash

Some of the non-binary people spoke about how being bisexual linked to their gender identity or expression.

'I've probably found it easier to express my non-binary gender clearly with clothes, hair and so on because I was out as bi. Someone society viewed as straight might find that more difficult, but I've mostly been perceived as a woman who fancies women, and butch appearance is seen as related to that. At work I didn't announce my gender identity for a long time, but everyone knew I was bi and probably saw that as explaining my clothing and hairstyle choices.'

Fred

'There's a resonance between bisexuality and non-binary gender which makes a lot of sense for me: that feeling of both being attracted to more than one gender and experiencing myself as more than one gender. I thought of myself as bisexual before I thought of myself as non-binary. I suspect that was mostly about bisexuality being much more available culturally, with a community and events and things.'

Meg-John

There was definitely a sense here of sexuality and gender influencing each other and impacting on how somebody was treated.

'My own sense of gender fluidity has definitely shaped my bisexuality. My partner has a fabulously unique female masculinity. While many who meet us would probably perceive us as a heterosexual couple, the realities of our life together are far more complex (and interesting!).'

Steve

'I probably have it a little easier because I'm seen as being "weird" about gender anyway. It makes sense for a lot of people that that "weirdness" (and do they ever love that word!) extends to my consideration of romantic partners.'

Anon

Having experienced multiple genders, Ash was in a good position to comment on how gender impacts on the way in which bisexual people are treated by others.

'My gender(s) have often influenced the way people relate to me as a queer person. As a queer man and a bi-gendered person I was sometimes met with hostility from homophobic men, and I was sometimes afraid that I would be the victim of violent homophobia. As a queer woman, I have occasionally met with disapproval, but I have never felt that I was being threatened with homophobic violence.'
Ash

Finally, some people felt that their sexuality and gender were completely inseparable and interwoven.

'[My gender and sexuality are] absolutely related. My not relating to a gender binary, and not liking its imposed divisions on the world, is intimately linked with trying to relate to every person I meet as a unique individual. Just as I can't know someone's gender without asking them, I feel I can't know if I'm attracted to someone without getting to know who they are.'
Anon

From what we've heard so far, there is always a sense that some people experience their gender and sexuality as relatively fixed, whilst for others, one or both aspects of them change over time.

How Gender and Sexuality Change — or Not — over Our Lives

When we asked people to comment on this, some said that these things hadn't changed much. However, most reflected that they had learnt different words over time, or discovered other new ways of making sense of their gender and sexuality.

'Broadly the same, but my ways of understanding myself and the words I use have grown over time.'

Anon

'As I grew up, I was aware of both my own gender fluidity and my attraction to a broad range of people. While I identify as bisexual as a general descriptor of my orientation, I also find "queerness" really helpful both in terms of my own punk-rock attitude and my attractions. Generally, female masculinity, male femininity and other non-binary people turn my head and heart. I think that this has always been the case for me, but over time I have found words and community that have helped me make more sense of who I am.'

Steve

Like Steve, Ed found that learning and community influenced how he thought about his gender. Ed and Emma also both spoke about how they made sense of early attractions in different ways over time.

'I am sure I have always been bi, but my initial sexual experiences were with other boys at my all-male school, and I allowed myself to become quickly pigeonholed as gay when I got to university. I did have sexual experiences with women, but it wasn't until I actually had a full-time female partner (aged thirty) that I came out again as bi. As I have grown older, learned more and been in more accepting spaces, I have become more fluid in the way I think about my gender.'

Ed

'I was born female and have always identified and felt comfortable this way. The way I have interpreted my sexuality has changed. Until the age of around eleven, I thought that I "admired" certain women and wanted to be like them. When I went to high school, I began to realise that this admiration was in fact attraction, and I became aware that I was attracted to men and women. I was always comfortable and accepting of this.'

Emma

For Jamie, learning about gender meant some shifts in what bisexuality meant as well.

> 'I was in my twenties before I learned about non-binary identities, and whilst I've privately identified as bisexual since I was thirteen, learning more about my gender and gender politics has changed what bisexual actually means for me. Without LGBTQIA communities, I'd be significantly less comfortable with who I am.'
>
> Jamie

Fred similarly encountered the idea of genderqueer/non-binary gender later than bisexuality.

> 'I first met the word "genderqueer" when I was about twenty-nine—it describes my experience over a long period of time, not just the period when I knew the word. I used to describe myself as a butch woman; I still use "butch". It took a while for me to settle into using "genderqueer": when the whole world had been telling me I was a girl or a woman forever, it took a while to untangle the thought that I'm not.'
>
> Fred

Meg-John also spoke about this process of disentangling earlier understandings and expressions of gender.

> 'As a kid, my gender and sexuality were heading in non-binary directions. Then I got a whole load of messages about what a person with a body like mine should be like and the kinds of relationships they should have. I tried to conform to a kind of femininity which was about being desirable to others, and focusing on romantic relationships. It's taken a decade or more to gradually unpack and disentangle some of that stuff in order to get to something that feels like a better fit for me.'
>
> Meg-John

Clive and Matt both talked about going through periods of experimentation to determine where they were at in terms of their gender and sexuality.

> 'As a teenager, I discovered I was attracted to men and assumed I was trans first, then gay. In my twenties I became attracted to other genders, including female, and started identifying as bisexual. I use the term "cisgender". I don't always feel it entirely applies, but I don't have another term.'
>
> Clive

> 'I've experimented with gender identity from a young age, cross-dressing in secret and sometimes questioning whether I more identified as female or male. I came to the conclusion that I identified as male and simply enjoyed femininity alongside masculinity, both sexually and non-sexually. I've only very recently come to the realisation that I was bisexual. Despite being pretty clued up on homophobia, I was lying to myself about my own sexuality, clouding it in terms like "man crush" and "heteroflexible". Society links femininity in men with homosexuality, which ends up getting flipped into "I can't be effeminate if I'm not gay." Since coming out as bisexual, I've felt a lot more comfortable in being fluid in my gender expression.'
>
> Matt

Suzy and Juliet described shifts in terms of how they felt in their gender.

> 'I didn't want to be a girl when I was a kid. I didn't feel like I was a boy, I just really wished I was. I often dressed like a boy and people sometimes thought I was, which was fine by me. In my twenties I slowly started to change. To enjoy being feminine. I don't know why. When I became a mother, it was like the final piece slotted in. Now I feel happy to be me and for that me to be female.'
>
> Suzy

'I didn't realise I was bisexual until my early twenties. In retrospect, I did have crushes on other women, even if I didn't identify them as that.

I wanted to be a boy when I was younger, and then accepted that I was a girl, and have been fairly comfortable with that (though not with commonly accepted notions of femininity) since. I am a bit less comfortable with it currently... I think that's about gendered societal norms rather than my bodily gender (to the extent that those are separate things!).'

Juliet

For Ash and Kaye, there was even more sense of gender and sexuality being something that had been constantly shifting and fluid.

'For me, it makes sense to talk about [gender and sexuality labels] as if they were fairly changeable and transient things. I'd love to be able to say "I'm bisexual" in the same way I might say "I'm tired", i.e. if you ask me a bit later I might not be feeling like that any more. They've both been very fluid, very changeable. I'd say my gender has varied the most. Some gender labels I have embodied at different times in my life are:

→ **Trans man**: Helpful when I'm talking about the fact that I was born female but then took testosterone, had a bilateral mastectomy and later had a phalloplasty.

→ **Trans woman**: Helpful to describe that I live/present as a woman but I have a penis. As I am a sex worker, the fact that I have a penis is something people need to know.

→ **Woman or cisgender woman**: When the subject is anything to do with my womb, vagina or ovaries [or being] read as a woman.

→ **Man**: To talk about [being] read as a man.

→ **Bi-gendered person**: To talk about periods in my life when passing as male was my default but I also spent a lot of time in drag, attempting to pass as a woman.

→ **Butch woman/butch lesbian**: To talk about the period when I was taking testosterone, shaving my head and wearing masculine clothes but not passing as male and mainly referring to myself as a butch woman rather than a trans man. I was also having a lot of sex with lesbian women and having little or no sex with men.

I identify more strongly with "genderqueer" and "transgender person"
than with any of the other gender labels.'

Ash

'When I was a child, the best description I had for my gender was "tomboy". I didn't (often) want to actually be a boy, but it made my day when
people got it wrong and thought I was one. Being this particular type of
girl who was also a sort of boy was very important to me.

Things didn't really get complicated until puberty, which I hit pretty
young. My gender identity kind of got lost in a whole load of unpleasant
and sexualised assumptions about what busty girls do, especially busty
girls who hang out with groups of boys. I went through my teens fancying camp boys and tomboyish or androgynous girls. Before I went to
uni I shaved my head. When I started work and needed a bit more of a
conventional appearance, I got an undercut for stealth (in my defence, it
was the '90s).

Now I'm in my early forties, I would say that "femme" is my most
commonly professed gender identity. I like it because it has queer asso-
ciations (straight people still tend to talk about "feminine" rather than
"femme"), and I feel like I've reclaimed it from the people who thought
it was so much less. My gender is woman, my gender presentation is
femme, my past is gender variant.'

Kaye

We've heard in some of these stories about the impact of other people on our ways of identifying, and experiencing, our genders and
sexualities. Next we focus on the links that people saw between these
aspects of themselves and the relationships they formed.

Links Between Our Identities and Those of the People We Have Relationships With

Again, diversity was the rule here. Some saw their relationships as highly linked to their identities, some saw them as unrelated, and others described them as everything in between.

The gender or sexuality of their partner didn't feel very important to Emma or Clive.

'I'm just attracted to the individual person; I'm attracted to heterosexual, bi and lesbian people as well as cis and trans people. It's about the person, their integrity and the way they live their lives. My long-term partner is a cis bi woman.'

Emma

'I've always enjoyed sex which played with gender roles, subverting or parodying them. I've had relationships with people from a range of genders and sexualities.'

Clive

Matt and Anon, in contrast, spoke about the way their partners' gender and sexuality had influenced them.

'My partner has been out as bisexual for over a decade and I feel like the way I handled discovering my bisexuality was positively affected by that. She's a big advocate for bi visibility.'

Matt

'Having a relationship with someone whose gender identity is fluid has definitely led to me thinking more about my own gender identity—and experimenting a bit more with gender roles in some situations.'

Anon

Suzy and H reflected on the different kinds of people they were attracted to and what that meant to them in terms of their bisexuality.

'There are certain feminine and masculine traits that I prefer. I simply don't care what gender the person is that has them. So I guess my bisexuality means I am often attracted to androgynous or non-binary gendered people because the mix of traits is pleasing. I much prefer to have relationships with other bisexual or sexuality-fluid people, but that's not about attraction, it's about being understood.'

Suzy

'I have one partner with a similar gender identity and expression, the same genitals, and mostly the same wardrobe. The other partner has a cisnormative gender identity, different genitals to me, and we are radically different in appearance. Both of these partners have been in my life for many, many years, have seen me change pronouns and wardrobes, have seen me both stuff my bra and pack my pants. Has their orientation changed because my gender expression has? When I stopped using female pronouns, did my cisgendered male partner have to suddenly occupy a bisexual identity? Or my other partner, who has had a masculine identity for all time, and always revelled in my high-femme glamour—what happened to their orientation when I became more like them? If, hypothetically, both me and my non-binary partner "transition" in the eyes of society to become binary gendered men, are the three of us now gay? Of course not!'

H

Perhaps most striking here was the fact that many people spoke of negative experiences with monosexual partners in the past, and this had left them seeking bi partners only, or at least partners who were also in bi or queer communities. This seemed particularly to be the case for non-binary people who had struggled to have their gender affirmed by monosexual partners.

'Before I was involved in the bi community, most of the men I dated were straight: some of them explicitly stated a preference for me to look more feminine, and with some others I made the assumption that they'd be more attracted to femininity, so I pushed my presentation further in that direction. In the last few years, I've been almost exclusively dating people I've met within the bi community and have felt more freedom to express my gender; however, I'm feeling it, rather than moulding it to whoever I'm dating. I'm also more likely to be dating people who like my gender presentation in the first place!

I seem to be read by strangers more as queer than as a particular gender, so if I'm on a dinner date with a man the waiting staff tend to call me "sir", and if I'm with a woman they're more likely to call me "madam".'
Fred

'I've had some bad experiences with past partners who considered themselves "mostly gay" or "mostly straight", but who had fallen in love with me—a genderqueer transmasculine person. These partners obviously experienced a great deal of inner turmoil, trying to reconcile how they felt about me with their own ideas of how their sexuality *and* gender should be expressed—but they expressed this by trying to pressure me into being more feminine or more masculine, and saw my being trans as problematic.

My current partner was already out and comfortable in being bisexual, and in being someone who, while benefitting from cis privilege, didn't agree with a binary model. The difference is unbelievable—in the best possible way.'
Anon

'As a non-binary person, I'm really only comfortable dating bi/pansexual folk, regardless of their gender. I no longer feel comfortable dating lesbians or straight men: Lesbians who exclusively sleep with women, but who are willing to make an exception for me, feel an awful lot like lesbians who are refusing to accept my gender identity. As do straight guys who would never sleep with a guy, but are willing to make an exception for me. I just can't shake the nagging doubt that they are not truly seeing me in the way I ask to be seen.'
H

'I don't see myself being in a relationship with someone who isn't bi (/queer/pan). I feel that I need to be with people who understand me and my sexuality, and that is most likely to come from others who have a similar fluidity in those they find attractive.'

    Ed

'I have had more bisexual partners than monosexual partners. I assume that with a bisexual partner/lover I am free to express my gender in whatever way I feel like, whereas with a monosexual partner I generally feel that I have to be aware of my gender and make sure it doesn't go too much in a direction they wouldn't like.

That said, the majority of my clients [as a sex worker] are actually heterosexual. There seem to be quite large numbers of heterosexual men who are attracted to trans women and specifically seek out women with penises to have sex with. I do find that in order to appeal to such men and have them pay me for sex, I need to maintain a more feminine appearance than I would maintain if I did not care about attracting such men. The biggest example of this is that I wear my hair longer than I prefer.'

    Ash

Some degree of non-normative gender on the part of a partner also felt helpful to Kaye.

'I've been in situations and relationships with women and with men who have had quite prescriptive assumptions about what women should be, what femmes should be, what bi women are like, and a load of other constraints. Now I am in relationships with people whose genders are non-binary, otherwise complex, or presented in a non-standard or self-aware way. My gender and my sexuality are no longer being used to tell me what I'm capable of or what's expected of me.'

    Kaye

While most people focused on their relationships with partners, Meg-John spoke of how relationships with other people in their life had been important for their gender and sexuality.

'The relationships between my gender and sexuality and the gender and sexuality of the other people in my life are interwoven. Family relationships were important: my parents didn't conform to all the expected gender roles, and that was a good model for me, and having a bi sister has always been helpful for a sense of not being alone in this. The enthusiasm of some friends in embracing my non-binary name definitely fed into my own confidence in using it and being more open. And, of course, the bi community has been huge in shaping my experience of bisexuality. Partners have often experienced me in ways which have drawn out aspects of gender and/or sexuality which wouldn't otherwise have emerged—like experiencing myself as the more butch/masculine person in a relationship with a woman, or being with a guy in something that felt more like a same-sex relationship than an "opposite-sex" one (for want of a better term)!'
   Meg-John

We've seen that communities can be important for helping people to find ways of making sense of their gender and sexuality, and for finding affirming partners. To conclude the chapter, we explored the importance of community in a little more depth.

Experiences of Our Gender and Sexuality in Communities

Interviewees' experiences of LG(BT) community were mixed. While some preferred LG(BT) spaces to heteronormative spaces, many had experienced problems as bisexual people in LG(BT) communities, related to their gender.

'I liked [gay bars] when I was younger. If I went out drinking I would probably still prefer to do so in a gay or queer venue than a mainstream one.'
    Ash

'My initial experience of the NUS LG(B) campaign was one of deep institutionalised biphobia, and that seemed to be widespread amongst other organisations. I had some (lesbian) friends disown me when I came out as bi later in life, having previously identified as gay.'
    Ed

'In LGBT spaces, people are surprised I'm married to a woman. When I came out as bi to lesbians who'd known me as gay, I lost friends, was accused of being the enemy, of polluting the "energy". Gay men were just confused and offensive, making jokes about female anatomy.'
    Clive

'My first proper girlfriend was a fair bit older than me. I had a very short cropped hair cut and I mostly wore jeans, trainers and shirts marketed at "men". But all of a sudden my girlfriend and her friends in the local lesbian community were telling me I was a "femme", that my bisexuality was a phase, that bisexuals were responsible for introducing AIDS to the lesbian community, and that I'd grow out of it and become a proper dyke. Femmes in that small-town circle in the mid-'90s were treated as bits of fluff, and the butches were taken seriously. I'm pretty sure that the reason they were so adamant I was "femme" was because I was bi. They saw my sexuality as being less authentic, so they positioned my gender presentation the same way.'
    Kaye

Meg-John explored some of the linked reasons why both bisexuality and non-binary gender were not completely welcomed in LG(BT) communities.

'LGBT communities are often problematic about bisexuality and about non-binary gender. Both are sidelined or invisible. I think it is because so much of sexuality and gender rights has been based on a binary as-sumption (that gay people need the same rights as straight people, that women need the same rights as men). It seems very difficult for people to let go of that and not to keep trying to put you in a box. If you're one of us, you should be happy to be under our umbrella (gay or woman), and if you're one of them, then we're not interested in you.'

    Meg-John

H spoke about queer communities as potentially more affirming. However, they recognised that there could still be issues here regard-ing gender.

'There's a lot of discussion around masculine-of-centre non-binary folk having more social kudos, privilege, space, time, etc. in queer space than femme-of-centre folk. Sadly, I have experienced this. Put simply, I feel more welcomed, liked and paid attention to when I turn up in a suit. I have also experienced some misogyny and sexist behaviour when I'm in my femme attire.'

    H

Pagan and BDSM communities had been particularly important to Steve.

'My primary contact and involvement [with the bi community] has been through being a practising Pagan and in being active in the BDSM/leath-er community. As a Pagan with a deep interest in non-binary forms of divinity, I have co-run a group that has gay, bi, trans and leather folks practising together. I have been deeply privileged to explore how such diversity impacts on our spiritual practice.'

    Steve

Turning to bisexual communities specifically, again experiences were mixed. Many found bisexual spaces and events to be welcoming of their sexuality and gender, but this certainly wasn't everybody's experience.

'I've only recently started interacting with the bisexual community, but it has been positive so far. I had a wonderful time marching alongside them at Bristol Pride and surprised myself by feeling truly proud of who and what I am.'

Matt

'I often attend BiCon and have made a lot of bisexual friends through it. I like BiCon, it's a welcoming space with a lot of nice people. I don't feel that one has to actually be bisexual in order to attend and enjoy BiCon, although one has to be comfortable spending time with bisexual people of all genders.'

Ash

'I tend to shy away from "communities", as I just don't feel like I belong there. The people that I have encountered at bi groups don't really reflect "me". Nobody looked similar to me, there were hardly any feminine bi women—most were butch presenting… I only have experience of one particular bi community group, so can't speak for all groups.

I have limited experience of communities, but I would like to think that in general, bi people are more accepting of difference because of the difficulties we have faced.'

Emma

Clive and Ed agreed that bi communities were not equally welcoming to everybody when it came to gender identity and expression.

'It feels sometimes like the bisexual community is where bi women go to meet bi women and where bi men go to meet bi women.'

Clive

'BiCon certainly seems to attract/welcome the more non-normative bi people. That can make it uncomfortable for me, who presents in a more normative way.'

Ed

While gender and body diversity are often more accepted in bi spaces, Meg-John agreed that some wider cultural norms of gender and attractiveness find their way in.

'Part of what I really appreciate about bi spaces is the body diversity and gender diversity there. I think that you can't step outside of culture entirely, so the bi community can include some elements of wider culture around gender. I have noticed attractive women being very welcomed into some communities, whereas men—particularly those who weren't "conventionally attractive"—often really struggled to get accepted. That could be quite isolating for those guys, but also quite overwhelming for those women, as you could feel a pressure to conform and get quite attached to being "that girl". I think that people are becoming more aware of this over time, and useful conversations are starting to happen.'
Meg-John

However, several people agreed that bisexual communities were generally safer, or more affirming, places to be trans and/or non-binary, for various reasons.

'Bisexual space can be more appealing to trans folk than straight/gay space: if I'm cruising in cisnormative spaces (either straight or gay), there's a point at which a potential partner might reveal genital discrimination. If I'm cruising in a bisexual space, and I fancy a guy, and I know that he is bisexual, then regardless of how he is reading me, I feel less terror about both a) the fact that I have a vulva, and b) that I want to be seen as male/masculine, particularly in the bedroom. It's like, bisexuals potentially have experience/interest of both the genitals I own, and the gender I inhabit, even if they've never dated this particular combination before! Sure, they might not fancy me, but it's probably not going to come with the shame/horror of transphobia.'
H

'BiCon does seem to be very relaxed about gender compared to a lot of more mainstream events. For example, people who make a big effort to dress up seem to be given roughly the same amount of "Oh wow, you look great!" regardless of whether the dressing up is drag or not. Drag is accepted and treated as normal at BiCon, whereas in some places it might be treated as a really big deal or even a problem.'

Ash

Fred and Suzy agreed that the welcoming stance towards gender diversity often became self-perpetuating in the bi community.

'In my experience, the UK bi community is a notably safe place to be out as any sort of trans. Well over half the trans people I know are or have been involved in the bi community. I think it's a self-perpetuating safe space: the more trans people are involved, the safer bi space is for trans people and for those exploring the possibilities of trans identity.'

Fred

'The bi community is used to non-binary thinking. Being bi allows you to see other issues as gradients. Even if you don't see gender as a gradient at first, you can be shown it, and then you can see it. That makes for a more accepting community. The more non-binary genders are present, the better the understanding becomes, and the more accepting the community becomes, so it becomes more common, and round and round it goes.'

Suzy

From what we've learnt here, it seems that people's experiences of all aspects of gender and sexuality were diverse, so a community with an explicit stance of welcoming and upholding diversity can have a very positive effect.

5

BISEXUALITY AND NON-MONOGAMY

Editors: Grant Denkinson and Juliet Kemp

So, first up: non-monogamy is not required to be bisexual. You don't have to be actively getting it on with multiple people of various genders in order to get your Bisexual Card. (There is no Bisexual Card, so it can't get you 10% off your coffee or your T-shirt, sadly.) You can be in a happily monogamous relationship with anyone of any gender for your entire life and still be bisexual. For that matter, you don't have to be in a relationship at all to be aware of your attractions and sure of your self-expression as bisexual.

But quite a few bisexual folk (and, indeed, non-bisexual folk) do choose non-monogamy, so we thought it was worth a chapter. If you read this and really want to know more, there are resources at the end of the chapter for further information.

Secondly: when most people think of non-monogamy, they think of cheating. Cheating is non-monogamous, yes, but what we'll talk about in this chapter is ethical non-monogamy: relationships where everyone concerned has agreed to what's happening. Having more than one partner isn't automatically cheating if everyone is consenting, and you can cheat even if you're notionally in a non-monogamous relationship already if you break your agreements. Cheating is about breaking agreements, not necessarily about how many people you're involved with. We don't recommend cheating. It's just not good behaviour, and it will probably backfire. Read on for more about managing this stuff ethically.

Non-monogamy has different attractions for different people. Some people may well be thinking about sex with a lot of people, possibly at the same time. Others may have less or no interest in sex. Some may love the variety and newness of intimacy with strangers. Others still may find only their strongest life connections hold sexual attraction.

Non-monogamy can be difficult, too. Being open to, or actively looking for, multiple partners doesn't guarantee finding compatible people to go out with. (But then monogamy doesn't guarantee you a successful date, either.) Being non-monogamous can open all sorts of opportunities, but it does also close down other paths such as monogamy or singleness.

We'll look at several different types of non-monogamy: open relationships, ethical sluttery, polyamory, polyfidelity, friends with benefits, swinging or lifestyling, multiple love, group marriage, relationship anarchy... Sometimes we find ourselves naming different ways of doing relationships in order to focus on the important aspects for us; for example, we might talk about polyamory if we want to emphasise we mean 'many loves' rather than 'sleeping around'. Or we might find certain boundaries important, such as whether and how new people might join the household, relationship web or party.

Some don't use any of these words, either because they have never heard of them, or because they just consider themselves open to love, in whatever form it may arrive, without needing words for it. The rise in media interest in non-monogamy does mean that it's now less common for people to be non-monogamous without knowing there are others out there.

Why Non-Monogamy?

So, why would anyone get into non-monogamous relationships? The short answer is 'Because it works for them.' Some people really struggle with monogamy: they don't see why they shouldn't have romantic relationships with more than one person just as they have friendships with more than one person. What's so special about sex and/or romantic love? (Not all romantic relationships include sex, after all.) Some people have specific needs or desires that their existing partner (whom they love and want to be with) can't or doesn't want to meet. Kinky folk may be more likely to be non-monogamous, for example (but again, it needn't be about sex). Some people just find themselves, one day, in love with more than one person and have to work it out from there. Some couples like to have sex with other people. Some bisexual folk really do find it too restricting to stick to one single gender even whilst wanting to stay in an existing relationship. Some people like sexual variety. Some people... Well, people vary a lot, so there are lots of different reasons why people choose non-monogamy.

Some folks feel their polyamory is pretty hardwired—even as a child back at school they might never have understood the idea of having just one best friend—and might describe it as an orientation in a similar way to their bisexuality. For others, it is more of an option, contingent perhaps on what partner they might meet or on other life circumstances, perhaps closing a relationship when children are due. Some may try out non-monogamy because someone they fancy is doing it: this might open up a new world, they might be okay to experience it for a bit or they might secretly hope their lover will become exclusive.

A few people come to re-examining what relationship shapes they might be open to when they examine other parts of their life after coming out to themselves as bi, changing gender understanding or getting into kink. Perhaps they come to it via anarchism, utopian living, science fiction or fantasy; because friends or people in the media are doing it; or through other introspective or self-development activities like meditation, courses, retreats or LSD.

There is some research on how we use relationships to build a bulwark against life changes such as ageing, or feeling a lack of something, or how relationships mirror earlier family dynamics. Other research talks about adding poly rules as a way to deal with anxiety about an existing relationship. Some of this thinking can sound critical of some relationships, styles or reasons for choices.

While we can unbundle relationships into many components, this can sometimes lead to unrealistic redrawing of boundaries or the creation of boundaries that don't fit everyone involved, or do but only temporarily. For example, one could imagine as an extreme one relationship with a mature, supportive base person who is also a carer, and another relationship with a fun sexy partner for occasional holidays. These assumptions can fit with sexist divisions of emotional and domestic labour.

> 'I'd personally like more people to know about options other than traditional monogamy, including examining what they mean by monogamy, and then choosing—rather than saying that more people should be poly.'
> Grant

Advantages

More support. More love. If one partner hates, say, films which consist only of three-hour shots of the Siberian tundra, and another partner loves them, you have a happy companion to go to the cinema with rather than dragging someone who will fall asleep halfway through. If you choose to pool financial resources or live together, you can get some extra financial stability (perhaps especially valuable if kids are involved).

More space. Some people prefer to be pretty much independent or concentrate on other parts of life, and being in a full-time one-to-one relationship isn't welcome. Being mostly single but with significant others who share your life for specific times or in specific ways only might be the best fit.

Non-monogamy means you can connect romantically or sexually with more people without having to break up with your current partner to do so.

Some people simply aren't cut out for monogamy, and as such, ethical non-monogamy is a better option than unethical non-monogamy.

But the biggest advantage is really just—if it's true—'It works for us.'

'I was rubbish at being monogamous, right from my first teenage relationships onwards. I never really got why it was important to anyone—it wasn't particularly important to me—so I was very bad at "resisting temptation". (Not that that makes my behaviour excusable.) When I found out that there was a way to do relationships without breaking my word, upsetting people or trying to do something that felt so impossible to me, everything got a lot better.'

    J

Disadvantages

Maxine Green, chaosbunny.com

Having more than one romantic/sexual relationship does have its disadvantages. It's more work: you're likely to have to put in more emotional effort to keep things healthy. It keeps you busy: as many polyamorous folk say, love may be unlimited, but time is not. There's a slightly higher chance of getting your heart broken, simply because there are more people who are in a position to do that.

Non-monogamy may allow someone to move away from intimacy with a partner without admitting that things have changed, where in a monogamous relationship they would have to face up to the situation. On the other hand, non-monogamy may also offer more ways for relationships to change, rather than being limited to 'together' or 'not together'.

The freedom afforded by non-monogamy to explore other options and other relationships might lead to someone realising that they would rather be living a different life, where perhaps being in a monogamous relationship might have hidden that from them, as they might never have encountered it. Whether that is an advantage or a disadvantage probably depends on your point of view and how you approach life in general.

People can and do still get jealous in non-monogamous relationships, although jealousy doesn't have to be a deal-breaker. It can just be a signal that there's something you need to work out between you (for example, that one person feels they're not getting enough time).

Depending on your set-up and agreements, you might need to worry more about STIs. (Not to mention the common cold and other germs.)

Depending on where you live and how out you are, you may find people disapproving of you, openly or less openly. Even if you're not out, you may find it hard to hear others disapproving of you without knowing that it's you. Families of origin can be disapproving, or worse. But, just as with bisexuality, you don't have to be out if you don't want to. (In general, people who are 'just' sexually non-monogamous are more likely to keep the matter private than people who are in multiple committed relationships, although as we'll discuss, that boundary doesn't always stay where it is put.)

Why *Not* Non-Monogamy (or, Bad Reasons to Try It)

Non-monogamy can work out wonderfully. But it's not a good fit for everyone, and that's fine. You might not be sure if it's going to work out for you, and want to give it a go, and that's fine too. (Check out the rest of this chapter and some of the resources at the end to prepare yourself a bit and to avoid the most common pitfalls.) But here are a few reasons that probably aren't a good reason to change the way you do relationships:

⇨ 'Because I should.' 'Should' is a word that is best treated with caution. Why 'should' you? Who's telling you this? Non-monogamy isn't better or worse than monogamy. There's no reason why you 'should' try it other than because you think you want to. Having said that, if you regularly find yourself cheating in monogamous relationships, then you might want to rethink the assumptions you're bringing to your relationships, and maybe see if non-monogamy is a better fit for you. But anyone telling you that it is 'better' or 'more evolved' or anything like that is talking nonsense. Ignore them, and avoid them.

⇨ 'Because my partner wants to.' Maybe your partner really wants to open up your relationship, and after a bit of thought, you decide you're okay with that even if it wouldn't have occurred to you on your own. Maybe you're happy with them having multiple partners, but you yourself just want one. That's great. Check out the resources section, and look for advice on opening up your relationship or on mono/poly relationships. But if your partner wants to and you really hate the idea, even when you've thought it over, they don't have the right to push you into it against your will. They don't have to stay with you, either, if they feel that they really can't stay in a monogamous relationship; neither of you owes the relationship anything. If you really don't want to, and you can't find a way of being comfortable with it, opening your relationship just for your partner's sake is likely to end in misery for both of you. You don't *have* to do anything you don't want to, and if that means the relationship isn't a good fit any more, well, that happens, and it's better to acknowledge it than to make one another miserable.

⇨ 'Because real bisexuals aren't monogamous' (or some variation on that). As already discussed above, bisexuality and monogamous relationships are 100% compatible. Anyone telling you otherwise is straightforwardly wrong.

Some people may try a form of non-monogamy and find it hurts too much, takes too much emotional work to be worth the reward or just doesn't feel right when they try it. Perhaps another shape of non-monogamy would work better, perhaps they would be happier with different lovers, or perhaps monogamy or single life might be happier options.

Bisexuality, Non-Monogamy and Monogamy

Some have felt alienated from the bi community because they perceive, if not exactly pressure to be non-monogamous, at least too much emphasis on it; they can feel that 'boring' monogamy might be seen as less cool or queer or evolved or fun. (In reality, there are plenty of monogamous folk in the bi community, and whilst, as in any diverse group of people, some might have judgemental opinions, the vast majority feel that relationship structures are the business of the people involved in them and no one else.) Some people would prefer not to fuel the stereotypes of the promiscuous, unfaithful, undecided, hedonistic and hypersexual bisexual.

Others find the openness to imagine and discuss all manner of human sexuality and relationships in the bi community the most liberating and at-home experience they have encountered.

On the other hand, some people find excessive relationship processing and de-emphasis of sex boring, prudish or simply not what they are looking for. They would rather just enjoy sex without strings or attachment to expectations.

While we know many gay men who do forms of open relationships, and some lesbians and straight people, the bi community is where we've found most discussion of non-monogamy. The *Breaking the Barriers to Desire* book came pretty strongly out of the UK bi community. While bi Polyday organisers have tried outreach to gay and lesbian non-monogamies, those links don't seem to have persisted.

As a bi person in a poly relationship, you can have metamour connections with a community you would not otherwise be part of; for example, a man with a bi partner who has a lesbian girlfriend or acquiring a metamour with links to the rarefied world of elite sport. (A metamour is your partner's partner.) Some people might find this educational and an excellent bridge for ideas. Others might prefer not to be associated with their lovers' other communities or would not be welcome.

With a lot of dating and sex, a small community can feel quite incestuous, and break-ups or abuse can be difficult to contain or recover from without pushing someone out of the community. It can also be difficult to find more objective support from people who still 'get it' but aren't the partner of a partner. This may mirror social connections in more rural societies.

Some people might find open relationships a chance to express aspects of their personality on a temporary or ongoing basis with some significant people and not others: perhaps having a change of gender expression validated or being seen as dominant in a scene. Some things we are into might fit more easily with some people than others. Trying something new can be less scary in a more casual context where there is less to lose if rejected. A partner might be happy with a lover being very different with others than at home and actively support it, or alternatively feel they are being excluded from an important part of their lover's life. Some people love flexibly moving from one part of life to another with different people; others might feel they want to integrate more parts of their life to feel more authentic.

'For me, bisexuality has pretty much gone hand in hand with open non-monogamy from the start. I noticed that I pretty much always had close relationships with, and/or attractions to, men and women simultaneously. I also knew that I always had close relationships in my life that weren't sexual (like the ones with my siblings), so I wanted a way of doing relationships where the romantic relationship wasn't the most important one always to be prioritised over all the others.

I met my second main partner in a polyamory workshop at BiCon. Although we didn't really act on it much for a while, we were always open to that. When I went to my second BiCon a few years later, I started being poly. I have mostly had more than one partner at the same time since then. I've tried lots of variations (primary/secondary, Vs, triads, etc.).

Where I've ended up at this point is something more like where I came in, which is about wanting a way of doing relationships that doesn't make big distinctions between sexual and non-sexual relationships, just as it doesn't make big distinctions based on the gender of a partner. So I'm open to close loving relationships of all different kinds, and sex is a kind of icing on a cake (just like having other compatibilities or shared interests) rather than cake itself.'

Meg-John

'There is a long-running myth I've heard so many times that bisexuals are all greedy. That all bisexuals are non-monogamous because we "need" to be in relationships with "both" genders. Leaving aside the binary genderism of that last sentence (which no bisexual I've ever met subscribes to), this is a stance that annoys both my monogamous bisexual friends and my non-monogamous bisexual friends alike. For monogamous bisexuals, well that's fairly obvious. Monosexual folk (whether straight or gay) often just don't seem to believe they exist. I hear them say "Oh, I'd never date a bisexual person, they'd never be satisfied. I would always be waiting for them to cheat." Like the monogamous part of them is always, inevitably, secondary to their sexuality. Like "relationship" means something different for someone who doesn't see gender as a deal-breaker. Like it doesn't hurt my friends to be distrusted or dismissed over and over for something that's just a ridiculous falsehood.

For a non-monogamous person like me, the issue is different. The expectation is that as a polyamorous bisexual person, the polyamory is a result of my bisexuality. A way to deal with the fact that I "need" to have sex or relationships with more than one gender to be happy. It's a *functional* choice, rather than a romantic urge, from their point of view.

Maybe I confuse the issue because all of my romantic relationships (and the majority of my sexual encounters) are currently with cisgender men (even though I'm more sexually attracted to women). Each of them are different people, with personalities and desires and preferences of their own. However, they are all, unmistakably, cis men. When I am with them, I am often perceived to be straight, because I am equally noticeably a cis woman. There appears to be nothing I can do, short of snogging a woman whilst holding my male partner's hand, to disabuse people of this assumption.

I don't know whether this gender unevenness in my relationships is mostly due to circumstance of timing, statistically probabilities, or the so-called lesbian sheep syndrome or what. Possibly, it's due to my tendency to be very oblivious to flirtation and desire (both from someone else towards me, and my attraction towards others). I need someone to come right out and tell me if they're interested, or ask me if I am, before I start thinking of this as an option, and that has always come from men so far.

Theoretically, I'm supposed to be "on the lookout" for a person of another gender to date, in order to "fulfil those desires", like the final toys to complete a collection. So why aren't I? Could it be that I don't think of gender as a criterion in my dating choices (like, oh, the vast majority of bisexuals I know)? I am one more example that this myth of bisexuals being unable to stop themselves and "needing" partners of multiple genders is, to put it bluntly, bollocks.

My polyamory is not related to my bisexuality. How else can I say it and be believed? It is possible to be both polyamorous and bisexual, and for these to be entirely separate. Even if I hadn't been bisexual, I would still be poly. Even if I hadn't been poly, I would be bi. They are two distinct facets of my sexual and romantic orientations.

Conversely, I almost feel guilty when I tell people that all of my current partners are male, and that I've never dated anyone who isn't a cis man. Almost as if I wasn't being a "good" bisexual—as if I were perpetuating the mainstream myth that bisexual women are only bisexual in order to appeal to men. As if I can't possibly be a "real" bisexual if my partners aren't evenly split between genders. But that's genuinely not why I'm dating my partners, and I wouldn't know how to convince the sceptics otherwise. Bisexual people just tend not to pay as much attention to the gender of the people they date as (surprise surprise) monosexuals. Why is that so hard to understand?

I feel simultaneously guilty for perpetuating a bisexual myth, and also happy not to be perpetuating another bisexual myth—with the same set of choices. I don't feel like I can win this argument. It's a catch-22 that I don't see a resolution for. My relationships were never intended to be political statements, but sometimes I feel like they became so just by dint of them existing. Like many people in gender, relationship or sexuality minorities, sometimes our personal does become "political". Or maybe "symbolic" feels like a better word? Like each one of us are examples, case studies, object lessons for people who don't understand us, but don't care enough to see us as individuals.'

Eunice

Types of Non-Monogamy

There are many ways to be non-monogamous.

Polyamory

Polyamory means 'many loves' (although some people are saddened by the word's mix of Greek and Latin), and polyamorous folk are typically open to multiple emotional relationships, not merely physical ones. That doesn't mean that poly folk don't have relationships or hook-ups that are purely physical, or that that's a bad thing. It just means that getting emotionally involved with other people is fine (in contrast to most swingers, for example).

There are lots of different set-ups: one person with many different partners; three or more people who are all involved with one another (usually three or four people; the relationships get significantly more complicated the more people are involved), one person who is involved with two others who aren't involved with one another (a 'V'), a household where various members are involved with one another, a couple who consider each other their 'primary' relationship but who each have other 'secondary' relationships... Some poly folk really care about hierarchy in their relationships (usually reflecting things like whether they live together or share finances). Some strenuously dislike that sort of structure. Living arrangements are many and varied. Some poly relationships are strictly faithful within the boundaries of the group of relationships ('polyfidelitous'); some people have lots of casual sex. Some people share finances or a house or bring up children together; some prefer to live alone however important their partners are to them (sometimes known as 'solo poly'). As long as everyone involved is happy, you can make it work however seems best to you.

For more detailed information, see Further Reading.

Swinging

'So I'm a swinger. I'd been poly for years, but like the Facebook status, it gets complicated. After the last relationship break-up I decided it might be less hassle to scrap the dating part and just hook up for sexy fun times, and so far that's working quite well. However, I have discovered that I am not too good at staying unattached, so rather than just playing with random people I now have a select bunch of friends with benefits, plus occasional spontaneous fun with others.

It does feel like I'm a bit of a stereotype. Often when I mention being bi, people assume it means I'm a bit of a slut and having regular threesomes and moresomes. Well, while it may not be true for every bi person out there, for me it is, and I feel very lucky that I am able to do so.

Swinging folks seem to see bi people as extra desirable, although I've lost count of the number of guys who have assumed that me being bi means I have a girlfriend who wants to play with them too.

There are a lot fewer female swingers than male, so you find quite a few nominally straight guys willing to hook up with other guys because they like having their cock sucked more than they worry about being

strictly straight. Obviously it's up to them what they define as, but it does suggest that being out as bi still isn't as acceptable as I'd like it to be.'
Carol

Some connect to non-monogamies via swinging and the various established subcultures within it. Others connect their form of non-monogamy with the imagined or lived 1960s, communal living, or experiments in utopian lifestyles, perhaps spiritually or political-ly based.

There are criticisms about the structure and practice of some non-monogamous groups in the past. For example, the free-love movement in the '60s incorporated some unpleasantly misogynist attitudes around the idea that women's bodies should always be available to men.

Cruising, saunas, etc.

Some people have this sort of casual sex alongside more committed relationships (one or more); some people prefer just to have this sort of interaction without any longer-term arrangements. (And, of course, often people may move between these over time and in different life circumstances.)

Some couples or groups like heading out for recreational sex together or to watch a partner enjoy and be enjoyed, either as a turn-on or as a warm fuzzy feeling. Other couples love being togeth-er and also have other relationships, but not together at the same time because they want to keep exclusive focus when together, or because they find their history of coupledom can overwhelm newer intimate friendships.

Don't ask, don't tell

Some people choose to open a previous monogamous relationship with a 'don't ask, don't tell' (DADT) policy. One or both partners are free to do whatever they like with whomever they like (or perhaps with other limits), as long as they don't tell the other person about it, implicitly or explicitly.

This could work for some people. However, it has some big disadvantages, probably the biggest being what happens if someone falls in love? Implicitly or explicitly, a DADT arrangement tends to include a 'no emotional relationship' clause. Even if it doesn't, managing an important romantic relationship without ever letting your other partner know anything about it is immensely hard work and can be very emotionally tough on the 'hidden' partner. It's more likely to work with casual sex, but you can't really guarantee that casual sex will never become anything more emotionally connected.

You also need to carefully consider how you manage safer sex. If you agree that you'll use barrier methods, what happens if the barrier breaks? Ethically, your partner ought to know this, but that is going to mean telling them at least something about what you've been up to. If pregnancy is a concern, how would that be handled if it happened (because even people who are very responsible about contraception have accidents happen)? Is it okay for your partner to take another person to your favourite restaurant? To perform particular sex acts? To do other specific things with them? Bluntly, the more rules you have, the more likely something is to go wrong, but if you can't discuss things as you go, there's way more scope for screwing up.

Cheating

Cheating is technically a form of non-monogamy (sometimes described as 'secret non-monogamy'), but not ethical, and we recommend against it. How big a deal this is will depend on the person: for some it might be a minor infraction, for others it is a deal-breaker and the mistrust, rather than the physical act, can be the most significant factor.

Negotiating Non-Monogamy

Sometimes the freedom of non-monogamy can be confusing; it can be like a restaurant without a menu where you order what you like but with a group of people trying to agree shared dishes.

If you decide to try non-monogamy, you will probably find yourself asking a lot of questions, such as: What do I really want? What do these other people want? What would work best for us all? How do we find other people doing similar stuff? What tends to work for others? What doesn't? For similar reasons, explaining non-monogamous relationships to friends or professionals for the first time can lead to a flurry of questions or assumptions. A single chapter in a book isn't going to cover all of this (nor in fact is any book; a lot of it is about working things through for yourself), but here are some things that might crop up as you explore the idea of non-monogamy.

How does it work in practice?

While people new to poly and the media might be interested in group sex or relationship jealousy drama, much of non-monogamy is quotidian—just everyday life or deciding how to balance time with lovers and also time alone, sleep, hobbies, activism, career, learning, caring responsibilities, recovery time, or unscheduled and discretionary time.

What will the neighbours (or the paper-pushers) think?
Monogamy for life in a nuclear family is increasingly rare, and we are used to extended families, blended families, portfolio careers and the like. So you may find, if you're worrying about what others will think, that in fact you might not be seen as so strange. Also, there may be a British tendency to mind one's own business. As a rule, it's possible to choose how out you want to be, depending on your personal circumstances and preferences.

'I live with both of my partners, one of whom I have a child with, and we're generally "out". But in my everyday interactions it would be easy not to be if we chose otherwise (by, for example, implying that one of my partners is a friend or lodger), and I am pretty sure that our neighbours might think we're a bit weird but haven't made the jump to "poly"! Getting a mortgage for three people was doable, but we did have to jump through slightly more bureaucratic hoops than normal. We did not mention the word "polyamory" to the building society or our mortgage advisor...'

Anon

Sometimes officialdom does not support non-monogamy or actively interferes with it: immigration controls, welfare support or licensing of houses of multiple occupation, for example.

Likewise, so-called mainstream society may be disapproving, jealous, voyeuristic, worried, or oblivious and erasing to non-monogamous relationships. That doesn't mean it's not worth it. But it's wise to be aware that stepping outside the mainstream can have both positive and negative consequences.

Safer sex

A safer-sex agreement is a very good idea to protect everyone involved. You might wish just to stick to barrier contraception methods with all partners, or you might have some partners with whom you have other agreements (for example, if you and a partner have both been tested for STIs, and you use barrier contraception with all other partners, you might decide that you're happy that you're both safe enough). Make sure everyone involved is clear on what acts are considered safe/risky/etc. and how you want to handle that.

If anyone involved can get pregnant, you also need to think about that: what contraception to use, whether you just avoid the sorts of sex that risk pregnancy, and how to handle it if someone ends up pregnant anyway. If you're deliberately trying to get pregnant, think about the possible implications of that with multiple partners. (Some people in that situation might only have pregnancy-risking sex with one person; others might be very happy to have that sort of sex with more than one of their partners.)

Safer emotions

Do poly relationships last? We know people who have been together for lifetimes; we also know people in quite stormy relationships. Ask yourself if longevity is the only or best measure of relationship quality and also how monogamy compares.

Honesty

Lying will generally get you into trouble sooner or later. (See 'Cheating' on page 97.) What level of honesty you want to share with your partners might vary, though. Some people might love (or indeed get turned on by) a detailed account of what you got up to with so-and-so last night. Some people might be happy just to know that you had fun. It's best to discuss that in advance if you can.

Communication

'Communicate, communicate, communicate' is a bit of a poly cliché. But still good advice.

Ground rules and rules to avoid

It's a good idea to have a discussion about basic ground rules before you start out. It might be best to focus on the things that are important to you about your current relationship; you might want to commit to spending an evening together regularly, for example. You might also want to have dates away from home, at least initially, or to agree that you'll talk to your existing partner before you do certain things with another date or partner. However, the more 'rules' you put in place, the more likely you are to find down the line that they're impractical. Some rules are almost always a bad idea; as discussed elsewhere, anything like 'we won't fall in love with anyone else' is fundamentally making a promise you can't keep. Human emotions are not always predictable. You could back out of any relationship that looks like it's getting too emotionally valuable, but that too may lead to distress (and potentially resentment) down the line.

A famous concept is the 'one-penis policy' which some male/female couples have if the woman is bi. This rule basically states that the woman can date other women but not other men. Besides the very binary-gendered nature of this, it's another rule that's likely to lead to trouble and resentment.

For a humorous take on this and other general polyamory advice, try the online essay 'How to Fuck Up' by Elise Matthesen, or there's a less snarky version of similar advice by Rebecca at the *Only More So* blog.

Dealing with jealousy

A lot of poly folk find that jealousy is something that they treat as a warning signal, a sign that there's something a bit awry in the relationship. It might, for example, suggest that you feel your partner isn't spending enough time with you, and that's manifesting as jealousy of the person they are spending time with.

Sometimes, with experience and as you gain in resilience, you might find that something can feel unpleasant but still be okay enough to put up with (especially if your partner is happy), perhaps with support from others.

'First things first: I suck at poly. I hate dating. I also have no time for dating—sometimes by design! And sex is almost entirely off my radar, even with my long-term partner. As for jealousy? It's a definite thing—but that's why poly is crucial to me.

Until I met my current partner, I'd never been in a non-monogamous relationship; I'd also never been in a relationship where I hadn't been cheated on. In one, I had real problems with sex being painful. I was eventually diagnosed with vaginismus, which didn't please my partner. I felt the burden of having to try to have sex with him for his sake, as well as feeling like I'd failed him when I couldn't tolerate the pain any more. I proposed an open relationship, on his side only, so his needs could be met. He declined. I started getting texts, Facebook messages, emails from other girls, saying they'd slept with him. One even showed up at work. He denied it every time and would shout at me for being jealous before refusing to talk to me for hours, even days at a time. Yet he mistrusted my male friends and would get angry if I made a comment that reminded him I was bisexual.

After we eventually split up, I discovered that not only had he cheated on me, he'd done so without protection. He later admitted to me he was cheating on his new girlfriend, though denied doing so to me—even after I showed him emails that had been forwarded to me by one of the girls he'd slept with.

So sure, I get jealous. And paranoid. And mistrustful. It's taken a long time for me to undo the damage he's done on this and other issues. It'll take longer yet for me to fully process and come to terms with everything.

My partner and I are in a poly relationship. It was a non-negotiable for both of us going in. Since meeting my partner, I've worked out I'm somewhere on the asexual spectrum and that sex has pretty much zero interest for me. My partner is 100% respectful of this: we share affection and intimacy in other ways that have far deeper meaning for me.

My partner has dated a couple of people since we became a couple; I've not. (Honestly—dating. I hate it.) So why is poly so important to me? Well, I can ask if my partner likes someone or "likes" someone—though I don't have to, because they'll tell me up front. (Seeing my partner with a crush is the cutest thing.) If they go on a date, I know I'll be informed. If they have sex, unless I've asked to not be told, I'll know—and I'll know they used protection.

By being in a poly relationship, we get to redefine the narrative of what a couple is. We get to share intimacy without the pressure of providing everything. If I do get insecure, I'm not shamed for it. I'm reassured by what we have: it's solid. It's under no threat, because everything is open.'

Anon

What do my relationships look like? What do I want them to look like?

'Words can be descriptive or prescriptive. If someone new comes along and I'm in a long-term closely meshed relationship with someone already, then I would best describe the new person as really quite peripheral rather than an equal partner, even if we might be open to moving to—and here I struggle for words—a more equal, a more fair, a more balanced and more egalitarian set-up. The struggle is a bit about the words being quite loaded: ideas of equality and sharing and equal personal importance for all are important for many of us, but that doesn't necessarily mean we wish to date everyone in the same way or that everyone wants the same quantity and type of time together to feel valued and satisfied.

I don't always know how I'll feel as I get to know someone, and it has taken time to learn that lovers can value my initial feelings, process and intention, including the uncertainty and space to co-create relationships."

Grant

Grant writes on unbundling groups of concepts that come under 'lover', 'partner', 'family' or 'friend', since we can look at what we want each human connection to contain and talk about how to do that if we can—getting too stuck on finding a widely agreed meaning of 'lover' might lead to finding that such words are both important and carry much meaning and also aren't very agreed a lot of the time.

'Other people also try to influence what they want our relationships to be—for our own good, to promote their own ideas of morality, to get laid or to sell us stuff. Possibly they are just to trying to understand in their own terms or deal with their own discomfort. We need words to communicate and express ourselves, although feelings aren't limited to how we might put them in words.

For some, such unbundling loses some useful guidelines for thinking and organising their lives. For others, querying societal mores (and sometimes these are very specific to some times, places and cultures, though they are claimed to be universal) fits well with their projects towards queering boundaries, questioning categories that divide us and breaking down hierarchies and power relations.

We all change over time, and so do our relationships—sometimes slowly and sometimes suddenly with a child, illness, bereavement or career move. Our family systems and networks might be supportive of some changes. Other changes might lead to a re-examination of roles or cause much friction, instability and upset spread widely through the relationship network.'

Grant

If you're currently in a monogamous relationship...

You'll find yourself asking a lot of questions: How and when do I tell someone I want to be non-monogamous? How do I make the change from monogamy, whether explicitly agreed or assumed? You might also ask 'How do I persuade my partner?' or 'How do I get my needs met?'

A reasonably common transition might be from infidelity to wanting to openly have more than one loving relationship—or trying monogamy and chafing too much within it. Having space to acknowledge mistakes, or what hasn't worked and the feelings around that, can be vital before 'moving on'.

Some people are open to, or expect to, date as a couple, either dating other couples or looking for a single person to be with both of them (often, in personal ads, a bi woman—so often that this has been named 'unicorn hunting'). Another transition can be where two people no longer wish to be sexual or as close, but still want to be involved with others in the group.

Managing relationships: Monogamous and otherwise

Ideas and skills from monogamy can be useful to non-monogamous people: working through harder times, reconnecting after breaches in relationship contact, adjusting to changes in desire and sexual expression, and keeping love and lust alive.

Likewise, thinking of what relationships can include or exclude and how to decide wants and needs and negotiate them can be taken from poly relationships and applied to friendships, community building or monogamy.

Finding people

How do you find lovers? If you're thinking about this, it might be useful before you start to try writing some 'personal ads' (for your own information, not for publication!) describing yourself, the sort of person you think you're looking for and what the relationship might look like. You could also think about it in terms of how you would like to be in a poly couple or a larger group. With luck, the more you know about what you do and don't want before you start, the less likely you are to make certain discoveries the hard way. (Having said which, you may find that what you want, or think you want, can change as time passes and you and your loved ones change and grow.)

Sometimes we project all manner of dreams and nightmares onto the unknown. This might mean a potential new lover could be expected to fix all of a person's problems, or a couple's problems. This is unlikely to work (the 'add another person' relationship fix is basically a bad idea, whether the person to add is an adult lover or a baby). It's also likely that those expectations won't remotely fit with what the new lover is looking for. Similarly, a new metamour can embody all of our personal relationship fears, and getting to know them as a real person can help. Being aware of the projection dynamic can also help us spot and work on our own stuff rather than externalising it onto others.

On a practical level, you can try online dating (OkCupid seems to be popular), but do make sure that you're honest about your current relationship status and what you're looking for. You could look for poly groups or meetups in your area: Facebook or the Meetup.com website are places to look for this sort of thing, and you can also search online for groups or online forums. If you're involved with other sexual subcultures, then those may have places where poly folk hang out.

Conclusion

Non-monogamy isn't for everyone, and that's fine. But it's an option that for some people does work out really well, either as a long-term lifestyle choice or as a short-term period of experimentation. As long as you stay honest and ethical, it's all good.

For more information, here are some resources you could try:

⇨ Books: *The Ethical Slut* and *More Than Two*
⇨ Try searching for mailing lists or Facebook groups
⇨ As above, in-person meetup groups can be good too

Postscript: A personal experience

'I'm polyamorous and currently live with my partner, his other partner and our two children (this household set-up is more through accident than design, but it seems to be working).

Like most people, when I started out I was monogamous, but looking back this was because, as far as I knew, it was the only option. Frankly, I was terrible at monogamy and was very bad at limiting myself to one person; I'd end up cheating on people and/or breaking up with people, and looking back on it, this was because I couldn't be tied down to just one person. I accept that this was bad behaviour on my part, but I didn't have any other useful way at the time to handle my desire to be with more than one person.

Then when I went to uni, I got together with someone who expressed an interest at sleeping with other people. For me this broke my head a bit because that was cheating and cheating was bad. It also didn't help that he'd grown up in a dodgy cult where his parents had sex with other people (and the reasons they were doing this—basically to entice people into the aforementioned cult—seemed deeply wrong). Also, this boyfriend didn't seem very interested in getting any sort of agreement from me that it was okay to sleep with other people, which also seemed a bit dodgy ethically. We split up not long after and went our separate ways, and I fell back into doing monogamy badly again.

A few years later, a friend of mine announced to me that she was polyamorous. I didn't know what this meant so had to ask her to explain it. She explained that it meant she was open to having multiple relationships with people. I have to admit that I was a bit concerned because my previous personal experience around non-monogamy had been a bit dodgy; also, the people she had started seeing were considerably older than her, and I was concerned that they would take advantage. However, after a while I could see that my friend's life as a poly person was not turning into a total train wreck. Through her I also met more people that were poly and making it work, and I began to realise that maybe it could work for me. Also, it would be a way to potentially be sexual with people of more than one gender without having to be exclusive with one person of one gender.

Ironically, this came at a time when I was actually single, so I felt faintly ridiculous labelling myself as poly, as "poly" means "many", and I had diddly-squat in the relationship department. A lot of casual sex followed, and eventually I met a wonderful man through friends who was also poly. After much mutual foot shuffling we got together and started seeing each other on a fairly casual basis; around this time I was also seeing a few other people casually, as well as indulging in a variety of one-night stands.

The problems started when things got more serious with this chap and other people became interested in potentially starting something up with me but wouldn't because they were monogamous and I was not. Despite the heartbreak at the time, I'm glad I didn't try to force any of these potential relationships into working, as they would have been disastrous due to my inability to remain monogamous; also, I'm quite glad I didn't break up with the person I was with, as he's still my partner and the father of my children!

Also, there have been strains within my relationship with this person—most notably when his other partner got pregnant. They'd been trying for a while but nothing was happening, so we'd all resigned ourselves to it never happening. When it did, it was a massive shock—I wanted to be happy for them, but I was torn between this and worrying what would happen with our relationship. Things got further complicated when I became pregnant a few months later (this was not planned, and was as a result of a condom splitting). We made the decision to all live together so the children could both be brought up by their father, and could also have the opportunity to not grow up as only children.

Living in a poly family seems to be working out well for us, though. The children seem to thrive on having three parents, and love having each other as siblings. Having three parents also makes childcare a lot easier!

At present, I only have the one partner (a lot of people seem to have a hard time getting their head around us being a V-shaped set-up rather than a triad!), though there have been people in the past. I'm still up for having more people in my life (as well as in the lives of the other adults in the household), but the children will always come first now, which, added to being resolutely poly, makes new people difficult to find. Still, I wouldn't want to change what we have.'

Cat

6

DATING

Editor: Kate Harrad

Compared to the US, Britain's formal dating culture is frankly a bit ramshackle. That *Sex and the City* thing where you chat to someone on the street, get their number, go for dinner, and then either work out what's wrong with them or propose? It doesn't happen much over here. In Britain, asking for the phone numbers of random strangers is not a popular activity, and even the dinner-and-a-movie dating structure is a minority sport. Many British people are happily married to people they have never actually dated. Instead, they went to school with them and just never broke up. Or they got talking at a house party, fell into bed and never fell out again. Or they can't actually remember how they got together or even how they met; it just crept up on them until they woke up one morning and found they had kids together.

Of course, there is online dating. Online dating has a bad reputation with some people, particularly older people who assume everyone on the Internet is a robot or a serial killer (or, in rare cases, both), but it's essentially just another way to winnow down the dating options until you find someone you can stand to live with.

Whatever your chosen approach, dating while bisexual comes with its own specific issues.

Dating While Bi

So, you know you're bi. And you understand that you can identify as bi regardless of who you've dated, slept with, kissed or stared wistfully at through a cafe window. But nevertheless, you'd quite like to take your sexuality out for a test drive and try it on people. How do you go about it?

We've all heard the joke that bisexuality doubles your chances for a date on a Saturday night. It's not true, unfortunately. Firstly, for the simple mathematical reason that about 90% of people who share your gender won't be attracted to it—so you've only increased your chances by about 10%. Secondly, because some straight people and some gay and lesbian people will refuse to date bisexuals. (More on this elsewhere.) Thirdly, because being bisexual does not mean you fancy absolutely everyone!

So, in fact, being bisexual can make dating *harder* in all sorts of ways. For example, the frequent assumption that being bisexual means you'll be up for anything. It's difficult to make connections when one of you wants to talk about shared tastes in music, books and fine art, and the other wants details of what threesomes you've had. The related stereotype that bisexuals will cheat on their partners also doesn't help. From a 2015 Facebook discussion from a BiCon page on the experience of dating while bi:

> 'Dating-while-bi-and-non-monogamous: ALL the cishet dudes assuming I'm up for threesomes. Also trying to impose their One Penis Policies on me ("you can date women but not other men"). Also the endless "I can't date you, you'll leave me for a man" from gay women.'
> Jess-Amy

'People asking about the sex/number of threesomes/kink I have, as soon as I mention I'm bi.'

Eunice

'For me, it was the amount of gay dudes on dating sites who would assume I was just looking for one-night stands and that had the attitude that declaring myself bisexual was an implicit "has no standards and will shag absolutely anything that moves".'

Simon Manley

'"I don't date bisexuals because they always cheat" (screw you)

"Can I watch you and your partners have sex?" (A world of no)

"So are you bisexual all the time?" (on further questioning they thought you could only be bi if you were sleeping with a man and a woman at the same time)'

Anon

And sometimes the responses are really not what you expected.

'My most recent favourite was "I can't date you because my dad is bi."'

Peter

Having said that, it's not all doom and gloom; there are, of course, plenty of ways to have fun dating experiences and fulfilling relationships as a bisexual.

So, let's look at your dating options. First, the important questions: who do you want to date, what do you want out of it and what's your situation?

Who do you want to date?

Some bi people have a definite preference for which gender they want to be romantically involved with; for example, a homoromantic woman might sleep with men but be interested in settling down only with women. But some bi people don't care—or sometimes even notice at first—what gender people are, and happily date across the gender spectrum. Don't assume that being bi means you have to fancy certain genders or combinations of gender all the time, or that your sexual and romantic preferences have to be aligned all the time. Like most things, it's a spectrum, and it's worth viewing it, if you can, as similar to other dating preferences (e.g. tending to fancy people with dark hair, or being more attracted to people who play chess than people who play rugby).

'I fall in love with women and with men. I don't fall in love and/or become attracted to men as easily as I do with women, perhaps, but I find serious relationships with women really difficult and basically stick to men for that. When it comes to relationships, I get on with men a lot better and find them much easier to live with. But when it comes to physical attraction, that fluctuates. I am generally (slightly) more physically attracted to women, but I go through phases when I'm really into men.'
Ronete

'There are at least two ways in which I don't have a 50-50 split in my attractions. The first way is that I am more likely to find a woman attractive than a man. The second is that when I find myself attracted to a woman, the attraction is often both romantic and sexual, but when I find myself attracted to a man, it is usually only a sexual attraction.'
Ciaran McHale

'Gender isn't the main thing about attraction for me. I can sometimes feel attraction even before I'm entirely sure or have even noticed what gender the person is.'
Ronete

'Gender's certainly something I notice and is part of my attraction to people, but I don't find myself more attracted to people of a particular gender than of other genders. It's more like "Oh, this person has freckles

and their freckles are really cute; this other person has gorgeous hair"
than "Freckles are more attractive than nice hair."'
 Fred Langridge

For many people, gender is just another piece of information about
someone, to be put together with all the other pieces of information.

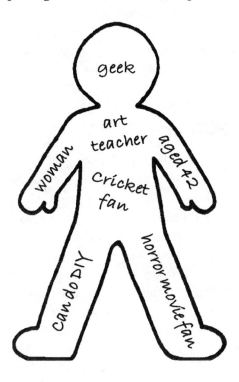

Or maybe it's very important to you. Either is fine.

What do you want out of dating?

When people think about what they want from dating, they often
think in very binary terms: having a one-night stand versus looking
for a potential wife/husband. But there are many more options than
that. You might want a friend with benefits—or a group of them.

You might want a partner, but one that you don't live with. You might want a romantic partner who you don't have sex with at all, or a platonic friend you can have children with, or a couple you can form a triad with, or a partner to have adventures with. Or several of the above. There's really only one rule, and that—to quote Granny Weatherwax—is not to treat people as things.

These questions aren't necessarily related to your sexuality, but being bisexual can lead you to think about them in a way that many heterosexual people might not. For example, while it's not true that all bisexuals need to sleep with more than one gender to be happy, it is true for some bisexual people, some of the time. If you think you fall into that category, it's possible—though certainly not inevitable—that in a monogamous relationship you could find yourself cheating on your partner. Having an honest conversation about that when you first get together could help a lot.

Non-monogamy is covered elsewhere in this book, but one aspect to mention here is that the categories of monogamy versus non-monogamy aren't always as clear-cut as they may look. Some monogamous people are happy with drunken flirting, for example, and some aren't. Some non-monogamous people don't want their partner to date a specific gender, or don't want them to fall in love with anyone else (though this is really impossible to enforce). These are conversations you want to have with a partner early on, but they're also conversations you want to have with yourself before you even start dating. The answers will probably change over time, but the main thing is that you're being aware of your own needs and desires. Bisexual people absolutely can be happily monogamous, whatever stereotypes may say. But like anyone else, they can also be unfaithful, and exploring non-monogamy can be a way to avoid that.

What's your situation?

One way to put this is 'What do you have to offer?', but that makes it sound as though dating is a two-sided job interview. And while it may feel like one sometimes, it's helpful to think in less market-oriented terms. Beyond your bisexuality, who are you? Are you single, or are you someone who already has a partner? If you have a partner, how do they feel (assuming that they know) about you dating? Do you have lots of free time to hang out, or do you have a job and three kids and two existing live-in partners and maybe can fit in an extra date once every six weeks? Do you find yourself arguing with people a lot, and do you enjoy that? OkCupid has a potentially useful set of questions that will give you an idea of what you're like and may help you find other people who are similar (or different in interesting and compatible ways).

Who to Date

Very broadly speaking, these are your choices: you can date straight people, you can date gay/lesbian people, and you can date bisexuals. (Note that other sexualities also exist: see chapter 9.) You're allowed to choose more than one (see chapter 5). Here are some of the pros and cons.

Straight people

Pros:
- ⇨ Easy to find. They're all over the place. On your TV, in your school, in the pub, in charge of stuff. So that's handy.
- ⇨ Many straight people are totally unfazed by bisexuality; it will be just another thing about you.
- ⇨ Your parents/family/co-workers/friends might find it easier to deal with.
- ⇨ You might get some straight privilege by association.

Cons:
Many straight people have never thought very hard about sexuality (in the same way that you probably haven't thought that much about an issue that doesn't really affect you). This may mean that they ask

you naive or annoying questions, such as 'But which gender do you really prefer?' and 'Will you dump me for [other gender]?' If you like them, you may be happy to unpick some of their ideas with them, and this is a very public-spirited gesture on your part, because the more sexuality-aware straight people in the world, the better. Equally, you may find that you just don't want to have to deal with these kind of assumptions, and that's fine too.

Some straight people are actively prejudiced against bisexuality, even the ones who are fine with homosexuality. Maybe they 'just don't understand how it works'. Maybe they 'feel sorry for you being so confused'. Maybe they 'don't see why you have to bring it up all the time' (i.e. any of the time). These may not be the best people for you to date, although again, if you do actually like them and want to educate them, the bi community applauds your sacrifice and would like to buy you a drink sometime. Otherwise, just move on.

If you have a straight partner, it may be even harder to socialise in the gay or lesbian communities (if that's something you want to do).

Gay and lesbian people

Pros:
- Relatively easy to find, depending where you are. Many places have gay bars, clubs, cafes and meetup groups. Dating sites have plenty of gay and lesbian people on them.
- You both fall under the LGBTQIA+ umbrella, which can be very useful; for example, you're less likely to get thrown out of gay bars.
- Hopefully, they will understand what you've been through in terms of coming out, dealing with prejudice and so on.

Cons:
As mentioned elsewhere, some gay and lesbian people are depressingly anti-bisexual. And it can be a harder bias to shift than when it comes from a straight person. Which isn't to say it's not worth trying if you're so inclined, but it's possible it might not work.

Specifically, there is an idea within the gay and lesbian communities that bisexuals are 'slumming' or 'pretending' or 'going through a phase'—that they will leave their gay/lesbian partner eventually and 'go back' to the heterosexual world. If your date has this idea entrenched, there may not be much you can do to get rid of it, since the only way you can absolutely prove you won't do this is to stay with them until one of you dies. Which is a bit of a commitment to make if you're just trying to prove a point.

Other bisexuals

Pros:
⇨ The obvious benefit here is that you—hopefully—won't have to constantly explain or defend your sexuality.
⇨ You should also be relatively free of biphobic stereotypes like your lover worrying you'll cheat on them with someone of a different gender.
⇨ They may already be familiar with issues like non-monogamy, if that's something you want to do, and gender non-binaryness.

Cons:
We're harder to find. There are probably more bisexual people than there are gay and lesbian people—stats suggest so—but there aren't really bi bars, clubs, cafes and so on. There are meetup groups in various places, particularly big cities, and there are dating sites. But dating sites also contain a lot of straight men who want to talk to bi-identified women, so that could get annoying. Still, they are a good place to find other bisexuals.

If you encounter biphobia from your bisexual date—and you might; see 'Internalised Biphobia' in chapter 3—that's going to be *really* depressing.

Where to find bisexuals

Local bi groups. If you're in the UK, a subscription to *Bi Community News* will be immensely useful in keeping you up to date with events and groups. Please note that local bi groups are almost always *not* intended as dating or hook-up events; they are social events, and if you turn up looking for sex or even scouting for a relationship, it might not go down very well. Aim to make friends with people and work from there.

BiFests, BiCons, etc. The UK has a variety of bi events around the country which are designed to be welcoming to new people. If you have children, try Big Bi Fun Day, an annual event in the Midlands. There are bi-activist weekends too, for those who want to get involved in organising. BiFests are one-day events often held in pubs or community centres, usually featuring workshops, social space and crafts. BiCon is an annual three- to four-day event usually held in August which moves around the country and is organised by a different team every year. It can have around four hundred attendees and includes loads of workshops, craft space, quiet space, dancing and much more. Many people find it a life-changing event.

Goths and alternative communities in general are usually good places to be out as bi and to find other people who identify that way.

If you're inclined that way, BDSM/kinky communities are normally extremely bi-friendly. FetLife might be a good place to start.

It is, of course, worth trying gay bars, lesbian groups and so on, as long as you're aware that a few gay and lesbian people can be very odd about bisexuality.

Geeky/science fiction communities are also a good bet a lot of the time (although misogyny can be a problem).

Geek - sexual

Chaosbunny.com

Maxine Green

Dating non-monogamously

In dating terms, it can be awkward to bring up the subject of being non-monogamous, because there's a lot of prejudice about it. Even if your potential date is okay with it, you may still be looking at a lot of explanations. Online dating can be easier for this, since you can specify in advance on your profile that you're non-monogamous and avoid at least some of the initial conversations.

There's a lot of overlap between the bi community and the poly/non-monogamous community, for fairly obvious reasons: it's a relationship style that (typically) allows dating of multiple genders. There are also many bi people who prefer monogamy, though—it's a common trap to assume that everyone you meet in the bi community is theoretically available to date, but it's certainly not true. (It should also go without saying that even if someone is non-monogamous, it does not necessarily mean they will want to date you. Or even that they'll be free to date you: they might want to but not have any free time because they already have half a dozen partners, for example. Not that unusual.)

Finally, if you are non-monogamous, it can be easy to fall into the assumption that monogamous people are less 'evolved', or are too insecure to be open in their relationships, or are too conventional to cope with it. Please do not assume this. In fact, it's best not to assume anything about other people's relationships, if possible, because you never really know what's going on.

Dating in secret

There is a trope about the 'secretly gay' husband who is married to a woman but sneaks out at night to the nearest public toilets to have anonymous sex with men. There's also a trope about the 'secretly lesbian' housewife who has a 'best friend' who's really their lover. And there are the often-publicised cases of people who leave marriages after years and years, having realised they are gay/lesbian. The word 'bisexual' is rarely used in these examples, and it's interesting to wonder why that is. One reason is that often the people concerned don't think of themselves that way. In fact, the world is full of people who behave in a way that would fall under a definition of bisexuality but who would never think of using that label.

What identities people choose to claim are entirely up to them. However, this book would like to suggest that adopting the label 'bisexual', if it felt appropriate, could be helpful to some. It can be deeply stressful being 'outwardly straight and secretly gay' or going from 'was completely straight, now completely gay'. Bisexuality can help tie these identities together into a whole, and perhaps could help some people resolve their need to cheat on partners. On the other hand, we recognise that many people in these situations do not feel that a bi identity is appropriate, and for those who do, they could be risking their relationship by coming out as bi. There are no easy answers.

7

BISEXUAL AND DISABLED

Editor: Kaye McLelland

Content note: frank discussion of illness, pain, medical issues, and prejudice, including from medical practitioners; reclaimed insulting words to describe disability; accounts of people's internalised prejudice towards their own disabilities.

This chapter predominantly uses the social model of disability, which proposes that disability is created by barriers in society or by the way that society is organised which does not take into account the various mental and physical differences and impairments that people may have. We use the term 'impairment' to mean one or more medical conditions that negatively affect a person's ability to carry out day-to-day activities.

A large proportion of people who attend bi events describe themselves as having a disability, be that a mental health condition, mobility difficulties, sensory impairments (e.g. hearing or sight impairments), neurodiversity (autism and similar), learning difficulties (e.g. dyslexia), chronic pain or fatigue, or other invisible disabilities (e.g. diabetes).

Some people behave as though disabled people don't have a sexuality at all. Some people are even told that their impairment is the fault of their sexuality or that their sexuality is a symptom of an illness. People might also find it difficult to use the word 'disabled' about themselves, often because of their own or other people's prejudices. Sometimes it can seem like just another thing you have to repeatedly 'come out' about. Luckily, there are plenty of areas in the UK bi community and elsewhere that have a much better view of disability and disabled people. Here we look at some of the challenges faced by disabled bi people, as well as some of the more positive stories.

'One of the advantages of having a mental health impairment over a physical health impairment is that people seem to at least be willing to accept that I have a sexuality.'
Cat

'I find the medical profession seem to think having a sex life is optional and by no means a priority. They didn't see the levels of pain involved in having sex as a good enough reason to prescribe stronger painkillers even just for occasional usage.'
Carol

'Bisexuality is invisible, so one side of my identity is invisible—although often hypersexualised—and on the other side, there is this very visible physical disability, but disabled people are desexualised.'
Charlie[1]

Charlie has also had partners who have blamed his bisexuality on his cerebral palsy: 'The reason he [an ex-partner] said I wasn't straight was that women are less likely to want to sleep with me because they don't see me as a possible reproductive partner.'

1 Charlie's words, reproduced here with his permission, form part of an interview with Patrick Strudwick, published on BuzzFeed, 11 October 2015.

Intersections

Having a disability or disabilities can intersect with a lot of other things besides sexuality. One of our contributors wrote this poem about how they have to work out their energy levels to manage a sometimes invisible disability alongside prejudices about other aspects of themselves:

Calculations

As I wake up I start doing the maths,
Quickly before it gets too late,
Figure out what I can cope with today:
Capacity to actually get stuff done = hours of sleep + levels of self-hate.

On some days to do even the most simple things
I need to use all my smarts:
Amount of pain × being triggered by my own body =
If I can shower completely, at all or just do parts.

Getting dressed I try to work out the next problem,
Which is particularly mean:
Impact of medications ÷ number of people I'm likely to meet
Must be smaller than how bisexual + foreign + vulnerable I seem.

Clothes carefully chosen I slowly negotiate the stairs while
processing the worst one:
Planned activities ÷ current capacity must be greater than
The impact of all the different discriminations that may come.
Despite daily practice I often get these equations wrong.

Waddling to the taxi the sums continue. They never do slack:
Age of driver × their maleness² + whiteness =
'What's wrong with you Hen?' + 'So, where are you from?' +
My personal favourite, 'When are you going back?'

There's no time for this nonsense at work but still I have to calculate:
The volume of productivity decreases at the rate
Of those kinds of questions + comments + looks
That I am called on to answer, ignore or debate.

At home there is no escape from the need to evaluate:
To get the dishes washed or feed the dog.
Do I have to go to bed now so that I can cope with tomorrow or
Can I afford to watch TV with my Love?

I used to go out to see friends or go to the shops,
Occasionally the movies or even the park.
But the geometry required for such activities became so complex,
I forget now how that used to work.

If the sums don't turn out right I can't afford to take that shower
Or sometimes can't leave my home or at worst my bed.
I'm not very good at mathematics and there are so many variables
I really wish I didn't have to do quite so many complex calculations
in my head.

Sam

One of the things that was a concern for lots of the disabled bi people we talked to was that having more than one label will make people think they're trying to be too special. This is hard when society already tells you bisexuals are greedy and attention-seeking.

'I have multiple disabilities. I don't usually list them all because it makes me feel self-conscious.'
Julie

'Occasionally I run into people who seem annoyed that I tick "too many" diversity boxes…like I've somehow been greedy by being born bisexual AND multi-racial AND disabled.'

   S.B. Stewart-Laing

'I worry in the outside world (at work; at events that aren't in the bi community) that I'm fulfilling stereotypes by being queer as well as disabled, or disabled as well as queer, so people have to make extra allowances for me.'

   Fred

'There's a concern for employees that insisting on reasonable adjustments for disability may not in itself be a sign of a troublemaker, but asking for accommodations for flexible working, maternity leave, part-time hours, etc. as well starts to make you look "difficult", at which point you become reluctant to mention sexuality because colleagues will assume you want to be seen as a special snowflake in every way possible. I keep having to "come out" as disabled in various ways and having to fight to be believed that yes, I really do need certain things to be done, so I find I don't mention my sexuality as freely as I used to, because I'm tired of fighting.'

   Karin

Prejudices and Challenges

If you're bi, then people often make assumptions about the ways in which you have sex; they might assume that you're promiscuous, for example. If people know you're disabled, then they might also make assumptions about how, or why or even *if* you have sex. People can also have some pretty judgemental attitudes to the prospect of having sex with a disabled person. They might also be afraid of accidentally hurting a disabled lover or of saying or doing something wrong. It can be hard as a disabled person who also has a misunderstood sexuality to avoid internalising some of these attitudes.

'My disabilities are usually fairly invisible, which can be troublesome in terms of asking for help or adjustments, but it means I don't have a very obvious thing about me that says "disabled" that might make people speculate about how (or if) I have sex.'

Julie

'Some of my earliest memories are of people refusing to talk to or come near me because they might catch disabled. I didn't know any different at five years old. Even nice children were sometimes scared of me, and I was lucky to have a close infanthood friend, so through her some girls got to know me and were willing to be my friend. Boys usually remained unwilling to come near me unless they were socially excluded themselves for some reason. I only had a handful of male friends before college.'

Natalya

Rude and intrusive questions about sexuality can be hard for disabled people to deflect because they're used to being asked rude and intrusive questions about their impairment. A lot of people think it's okay to interrogate people about disabilities and impairments and ask them to justify themselves. They ask questions like 'Why can't you just…?', 'Have you tried…?', 'How do you…?' or, especially in the case of people who are visibly physically impaired, 'What's wrong with you?' or 'What happened to you?' People don't seem to realise that they're asking a stranger for an account of something deeply personal and very possibly extremely traumatic. If you're also going to get questions like 'So, do you have threesomes?', it gets very tiring very quickly.

'I frequently get [queerphobia] from medical professionals (No, I'm not having sex; yes I'm bisexual, still doesn't mean — No, I'm not telling you what genitals my partner has; how is that relevant to my sprained knee? No, this therapy session doesn't need to hinge on my being bi—), and I avoid doctors where possible. Perhaps then it's little wonder that over the years, my back has got worse and impacts other areas. The way I self-correct my posture means my balance is thrown off; I've fallen down stairs more times than I care to admit and am frequently spraining my knees or ankles.'

Anon

'I see a lot of parallels in my experience of bisexuality and disability and a great intersection between the two. Most queer people occasionally have the experience of being interrogated about parts of their lives which straight people would never get asked about. Some of these questions are simply very personal ("So how many boyfriends and girlfriends have you had?") and some are just ridiculous ("So who is the man in your marriage and who is the woman?"). I think this may be a little worse for bisexual folk than gay people because, in those situations where we are out, there's often scepticism. We're more often asked to justify the label.

Disabled people get this about our impairments and medical history, but in our culture, most people can relate to the idea that our sexual histories and experiences are personal—folk are curious, but have to be fairly crass (or perhaps more likely, drunk) to push the matter. Yet our impairments are considered public property. Scepticism about disability is a massive problem, encouraged by politicians defending welfare cuts and newspapers interested in disability-benefit-claimant-seen-bungee-jumping-type headlines (not that all disability rules out bungee jumping). We've come to expect to have to explain ourselves, to justify our identities and our existence.

In one week, I read three articles by disabled people about the frustration of being asked all about their impairments—information no one had a right to know. Yet every single one opened with a paragraph explaining exactly what their impairment was, a medical explanation and how it affected them every day. We're so used to having every aspect of our lives scrutinised that we can't even complain about this scrutiny without explaining ourselves. We're taught that to say "It's none of your business" is unhelpful, uncooperative or even ungrateful.

So when I was younger, I answered all the questions about my physical health, and I answered all the questions about my sexuality in the same way. Not only did I sacrifice some of my privacy, but I had many very boring conversations I didn't want to have.'

DH Kelly

'If you're disabled, people think it's their right to know how you're disabled, why or how it happened: "What's wrong with you?"'
    Charlie

Mental Health

One of the things that keeps coming up in surveys and studies is the prevalence of mental health concerns for bi people. In 2012, BiUK devoted their biennial BiReCon research conference to discussing mental health and bisexuality. When it comes to mental health, there are things that might take a toll on people, things like invisibility, the need to repeatedly 'come out', or difficulties caused by society's myths and prejudices.

'I figure that the depression and anxiety are often normal responses to [...] not being supported adequately, and compounded by sexuality not being taken seriously.'
    Karin

'As nice as it is to know that there other people out there who are some way "like me" (i.e. bi and mad), I do wish that poor mental health wasn't so prevalent in the bi community.'
    Cat

'I definitely see a relationship between my sexuality and experiences of depression. I think my first experiences of depression—which set the scene for later experiences—were all about not fitting with the standard ways of doing sexuality and gender in the place I was in at that time. The school I was at between ages nine and thirteen had a certain way of being a girl, which was very much about wanting to look a certain way and being attracted to boys. I was rubbish at both elements of that but ended up learning them pretty well in an attempt to fit in, because it felt so horrendous to be isolated and bullied for not doing so.

So it's not at all that being bi, or non-binary gender, has caused a mental health problem (an assumption that is still sadly made by a lot of therapists).

Rather, trying to fit into a heterosexual and binary gender model of femininity, and being told that anything else was unacceptable, definitely laid the ground for a lot of my experiences of depression and anxiety, particularly around low self-esteem, fearing being "found out" and that kind of thing.

Later in life I experienced some bullying at work which also related to my "difference" and openness about that. That left me struggling with anxiety and depression again for a long time because it really triggered those early memories.'

Meg-John

The issue of bisexuality being seen as a symptom or a cause of a mental health issue is a problem that a lot of bi people have encountered, and it can stop people from accessing proper support and treatment for their mental health and sometimes for their physical health too.

'Bisexuality has derailed doctors for years, and they went foraging for a mental health problem and/or STI and/or drug-and-alcohol [problem] when none of the above existed (the latter being "you must be unhappy with your orientation and are self-medicating").'

S.B. Stewart-Laing

'My problem is […] that people see my sexuality as somehow resulting from having BPD.[2] One of the diagnostic criteria in the DSM IV is "Impulsivity in at least two areas that are potentially self-damaging, e.g. spending, sex, substance abuse, reckless driving or binge-eating."[3] Although I can easily see how my historical risky sexual encounters can be categorised in this way, my bisexuality has also been lumped under this umbrella (presumably because bisexuality is all about being promiscuous, yet another one of those old chestnuts). Also, sometimes bisexuality finds itself under another one of the DSM IV diagnostic criteria of "Identity

---

2 Borderline personality disorder

3 The *Diagnostic and Statistical Manual of Mental Disorders*, or DSM, is the main document that medical professionals use to define mental health conditions. It is published by the American Psychological Association.

disturbance—markedly and persistently unstable self-image or sense of self." It's also amazing how clueless mental health professionals can be about bisexuality in general—I've lost count of the amount of times over the years when I've had to explain what bisexuality is to someone whose patient I've been. It's also beyond me how difficult it appears to be for them to grasp the concept when I had no issue with getting my head around it when I came across it at the age of nine.'

Cat

'When I was at university, I ended up going to a university-provided counsellor. It was a few years after my father had died, and at the time I was failing my course, something I'd had the privilege of not experiencing before. Various other things also were going wrong at the time, and I found myself in a very fraught position, bursting into tears with little provocation, and generally wanting to hide away from the world.

The counsellor that I spoke to decided that my bisexuality was "just another way I was refusing to commit to future course of action", and proclaimed that, even though I'd been identifying as bi for a few years at that point, it was merely a symptom of a more fundamental "dysfunction" and that when I was healthy I would "settle", and be okay with my "true orientation". Thankfully, even in my distraught state, having experienced the awesome support of a BiCon by that point, I was pretty darn sure it was a legitimate sexuality (and not a "symptom"), and I found myself another person to assist me through that difficult time.

P.S. Still bi, fifteen years later ;)'

Linette

Labels and Identity

Some people find parallels between disability and bisexuality. Sometimes these are positive things, but sometimes they are reminders of not feeling like they belong in either group: gay or straight, disabled or non-disabled. They might also feel that they're not 'entitled' to their labels and self-definition.

'Bi spaces are usually really supportive of negotiations around safer sex and consent, as well as other needs and preferences. Being in that kind of open environment makes it easier to negotiate sex that works around disability as well.'

Julie

'I struggle to define myself as disabled. The social model of disability doesn't really feel like a good fit for me: it's my body that causes the problems more so than societal failings.

For years, I used the phrase "I have a bad back." More recently, I've adopted "I have chronic pain and mobility issues."

I bought a stick. I had to be nagged into using it. I still don't use it at work, or around my family. Conversely, whilst I don't need it all the time, I feel I'm only allowed to use accessible bathrooms, which I need when the less accessible ones are up/downstairs, or ask for seating on the bus when I have it.

I carried a lot of guilt over both aspects: I'm not disabled, but here I am using a stick and accessible spaces—what a fraud! But nor am I able to do the stuff able-bodied people can do—how pathetic of me! I should try harder.

It was only when someone compared models of disability to models of gender and sexuality that things clicked into place: we're told that you are either disabled or able-bodied, either gay or straight, either man or woman. But I'm none of those things. I exist outside of these imposed binaries: I'm genderqueer, I'm bisexual, and I'm fine with both those things. So why do I carry such a dichotomised view on disability?'

Anon

'LGBT people spend a lot more time working on the acceptance of their own identities before they come out, whereas less time and resources are put towards helping disabled people accept their identities. The spark of the LGBT movement was about "Accept me for who I am." More time needs to be given to letting disabled people do that too.'

Charlie

'We use the word "visibility" a lot in bi activism. It's what we want, what we're lacking, as bisexuals. "Bi Visibility Day" has, in the last couple of years, taken over "[International] Celebrate Bisexuality Day" as the name for what we're commemorating on 23 September. "Bi visibility" is used as an opposite of "bi-erasure" and "biphobia" in our discussions.

Sight is, for most people, their dominant sense. Sighted people get something like 90% of their information about their surroundings from their eyes. Many find it impossible to imagine knowing or perceiving anything without their sight. This failure of imagination is illustrated in the many metaphorical uses of sight in our language. When we say someone is "blind to the consequences of their actions" or "blind with rage", blindness signifies either doesn't know or doesn't care. Conversely, we use "visibility" to mean "care for and knowledge of", which is why Bi Visibility Day is a useful name for a day to highlight the knowledge and care of bisexuals.

(I used to worry that people would think I'm overreacting when I emphasise how important I think language use is in situations like this, but unfortunately Rod Liddle has recently given us a vivid example of this kind of thinking by saying in the *Sun* of a blind trans political candidate, "Being blind, how did she know she was the wrong sex?", which reveals just how crucial some people think vision is to knowledge even of one's own body and mind.)

I am partially sighted, and I am bisexual. Both could be seen as "neither one thing nor the other, but somewhere in between". I learned as a kid of the crushing pressure to gravitate to one binary extreme or the other: to turn yourself into, or at least pretend to be, something most people are more likely to accept and understand.

So, growing up, I pretended as hard as I could to be normally sighted, not even realising all the unnecessary stress this inflicted on me—to no one's surprise but mine, it turns out I'm pretty bad at imitating a sighted person!—because I'd never known life without it.

And even when I finally realised gender isn't a limiting factor in my attractions or relationships, I still didn't call myself bisexual. Most of my relationships had been with people of one gender, and I had even gotten married—surely "bisexual" wasn't the word for me? Just as I'm not the cartoonish blind person, as I don't have a white cane or a guide dog, I'm not the caricature of a bisexual either. It would be years before I met enough other bisexuals to learn that this anxiety about being "bi enough" is common.

It's unsettling when strangers decide my identity is up for debate. Even now, saying "I can't read that menu" or "I'm a bit blind, which platform's the train to Manchester?" is still difficult for me. After decades when I'd have rather died of embarrassment than say anything like that, it's still hard to remember that it's almost always worth it. But as soon as anyone's friendly or helpful to me—and most people are—the relief of not having to struggle in silence is so great that I wonder why I ever did.

But of course I know why. The occasional difficult person who says "But you don't look blind", or seems to resent the intrusion of a stranger asking for information that's right there on some sign, is enough to feed my anxiety for weeks or months. A stressful interaction like that can haunt my thoughts many later times when I consider asking for help, too often leading me to just muddle through, with all the resulting anxiety and the misery of thinking I don't deserve any better.

Just as I expect disablism every time I own up to not being as sighted as I appear, I anticipate a negative reaction I don't always get when I tell someone I'm bisexual—especially if they assume I'm straight because I'm married, or I'm a lesbian because I'm at an "LGBT" event. I don't think anyone's ever actually said "You don't look bisexual," but I'm surrounded by enough biphobia that I've internalised it, so I flinch, I get defensive.

Only when I was diagnosed with an anxiety disorder a few years ago did I realise how pervasive that anxiety was about being both "bi enough" and "blind enough". Turns out, it's enough that I deserve respect, and to respect myself. Enough that I'm both more alike, and more different, from others than they or I imagine. Enough to point out inequalities and injustices I experience, even if they're "not as bad" as what some other people have to deal with. Enough to attempt to articulate the tricky existence between what society falsely sees as binary states: gay and straight, blind and sighted.'

Holly

Finding Community

Some people, especially those who were younger when they came out, have found that the traditional 'gay scene' hasn't been very welcoming or accessible for disabled people. This is especially difficult if you're already having trouble fitting in as a bi person in gay and lesbian spaces.

> 'I assumed the "gay scene" would be [somewhere] where people were largely valued on their personality and contribution, not what they looked like, whether they were cool enough, "gay" enough and shaggable...A gay male friend and I visited the local "gay and lesbian" youth group which he had attended a few times before. I can honestly say I have never been made to feel less welcome, it was like the worst of disablist school bullying with extra added biphobic exclusion. [...] I never went back, and I was devastated.'
> Natalya

> 'Bisexuality doesn't get seen as a "real" sexuality, and doesn't have much of a community in most places. As a result, many people who might think of themselves as bi, or behave as such, blend into local straight or gay social scenes because that's what's there and easy to find. An able-bodied, socially adept person will usually manage this, until such time as mentioning or having a partner of the "wrong" sex causes the acceptance to be cut off. A lot has improved in the last twenty years, but many gay events wouldn't welcome you with your other-sex partner.'
> Hessie

Spaces that are specifically bi can also have trouble with accessibility for disabled people, especially when they take the form of conventional social spaces like pubs and clubs that many people struggle with for reasons of lack of physical access, lack of deaf awareness, difficulties of social interaction, addiction or other reasons. Bi spaces like BiCon lead the way in making their spaces more accessible, for example by banning smoking indoors years before it was a legal requirement. Here, a long-time organiser writes about the experiences that fed into disability inclusion in bi spaces and how that experience is now being fed back into wider communities:

'Boyfriend and I discovered Biphoria, which we went to a few times, but it was difficult for us to travel to and from in the evening. I realised even in a nice group that I struggled to hear a lot of new people, which probably made me socially awkward. I didn't socialise in the traditional ways because cigarette smoke makes me ill, and I don't see the purpose in dark venues with too-loud music. [...]

I was invited by Jen Yockney to join her 2004 BiCon team, which was ideal as they wanted someone to do accessibility like 2003 had successfully had. I knew I was doing the right kind of activism for me when I identified our initial venue bookings as being problematic from an access point of view, and Jen worked with me and the venue liaison to change the booking there and then. Over the course of the BiCon, I ended up doing various other tasks. It was work I could do on my computer mostly and with people who communicated in sensible methods like instant messenger.

In order to reach outside of the comfort of the UK bi community I have been trying to do occasional things outside of it so that I can learn how other communities manage inclusion and intersectionality. I was invited to speak at Feminism in London 2013 about being disabled and bisexual, and while some of my challenge to biphobic and transphobic feminists caused a ruckus, I was separately approached by over twenty women that day thanking me for talking about bisexuality and disability in feminist or women's spaces. I still feel being disabled is a bigger issue for me on a day-to-day basis than being bisexual, but it is a fact that being bisexual is more of a lived experience of constant erasure or exclusion from many mainstream and LGBT spaces. I also did a presentation at the Institute of Equality and Diversity Practitioners seminar about bisexuality with a little splash of disability thrown in. However, as ever, I have to keep managing my energy levels so I can keep doing my job and what activism is most worthwhile.'

Natalya

The Internet

For many people who find conventional social spaces, including LGBTQIA+ or gay and lesbian spaces, difficult to access because of disability or bisexuality or both, the Internet has provided an alternative (but by no means unproblematic) way of finding community.

'From my perspective, the main issue regarding being disabled and bi is that it is much harder to be actively involved in the community, as I don't have the spare energy to attend events that I would otherwise love to be at. It makes it quite isolating and sometimes leaves me feeling that I'm failing the community by not supporting events and not getting more involved. At least these days there is the Internet, so I don't miss out completely.'

Carol

'I first came out as not-straight to someone other than myself when I was sixteen in the mid-'90s on a now defunct Internet forum. […] No one knew I was disabled unless I chose to tell them. I was valued because of the language I used and the ideas I bought to discussions, not how I looked, sounded or what I heard or misheard.'

Natalya

'As a deaf kid I coped fine academically in hearing school, but socially I struggled, finding it hard to follow conversations, let alone being able to jump in and control them. I read lots and played computer games. Then in my gap year working for a multinational company, I was given access to what we now call instant messaging, and an audience of seventy other students. Suddenly, I could sparkle with wit and chat easily to lots of new friends, and when we met up in person we had lots to talk about where I already knew what was going on. It was wonderful. So when I went to university and found I wasn't welcomed at the LBG society by some separatist lesbians (I've since found out they were a minority of two and no one else liked them, but at the time I never went back), it was natural to look online for resources.

[...] Having no money meant [bi] organisers embraced the Internet and marketing via social forums earlier than gay and straight groups.'
Hessie

Bi events

A lot of people have used the Internet or word of mouth to find out about BiCon or other bi events where they have found that disability has been a lot more accepted.

'One month the bi youth group told us about BiCon. [...] I loved BiCon. Here were familiar goths, BDSMers and poly people. No one looked at me weird for being a bit spacky looking. In fact, people seemed downright nice to me and some of them seemed to be flirting with me. There was a British Sign Language (BSL) interpreter in the plenaries who noticed me following him and slowed his sign down so I could follow even though I knew no sign. I went to his BSL workshop and chatted to him afterwards. He convinced me that the narrative that I couldn't learn sign like I'd wanted to all my life because of my hand impairments was untrue because BSL relies more on the facial expression than exact hands. I made friends at that BiCon who are still close people today.'
Natalya

'At BiCon [...] there were a few wheelchair users and people with walking sticks, and people making space for them without any inquisition. There was a Deaf guy and interpreter who ran a couple introductory BSL sessions. There was a wide variety of shapes and sizes of people on the dance floor. [...] The mixture of people—no one getting any derogatory comments—meant I stopped feeling self-conscious about my own stiff wobbly body (not usually apparent unless I'm trying to move gracefully and failing). The structured sessions were also set up for accessibility, as far as possible on a low budget: sometimes roving microphones in an auditorium, but more importantly, speakers repeating questions from the floor to ensure everyone could hear or lip-read. Rooms were rearranged so sessions people wanted to attend weren't in the one upstairs room if they couldn't handle the stairs. Entertainment space was well-lit and, away from the dance floor, quiet. And sessions tended to introduce people, had them sitting in a circle, so easy to lip-read, made one person talk at a time, plus requiring name badges to be worn at all times is great if, like me, you can't recognise faces.'

Hessie

It can be really difficult to find accessible venues, especially for residential events or where costs need to be kept to a minimum. But bi events like BiCon and BiFests have a reputation for being as accessible as possible and often have people on the organising teams who are disabled themselves. Venues where BiCons have been held have been known to approach the team for a copy of its access report so that they can implement similar things themselves.

'Over the years, bisexual events have continued to have accessibility planned in from the start; budgets mean this isn't always apparent to people who find their needs still can't be met, but BiCon organisers specify level access, signage, quiet space, communication via email, not just phone, accessibility by public transport as well as parking, self-catering as well as on-site food to ensure dietary needs can be met, providing seating for the registrations queue, asking about requirements on the registration form so you don't need to contact them separately—all small, cheap things that should be mainstream practice, but sadly aren't.

This positive attitude makes it easier to deal with another aspect of disability that is similar to bisexuality: "I'm not properly disabled/queer, or I'm not disabled/gay enough."'

Hessie

'It was really nice to find out that BiCon made real efforts to make the event accessible for people with disabilities. That was the main reason I felt able to attend. Unfortunately, the uphill walk to the accommodation meant that this year at least their efforts were wasted, and I couldn't avoid spending most of the weekend in pain. It feels like they are at least trying, though.'

Carol

'When I'm at bi events or interacting with people in bi communities, I feel safer disclosing my disabilities. That has become increasingly difficult in the "outside world" in recent years because there is a real anti-disabled feeling from a lot of people. Out in public when I am walking with a stick, I often feel like I'm a breath away from being called a scrounger, pushed over, shouted at or asked intrusive questions. When you're visibly disabled, some people feel they can impose on you with their loudly broadcast views on everything from the welfare state to your choice of shoes!

Bi spaces feel very different to that. I know that I won't be criticised if I move around the room so that I can lip-read, or if I need to stand up or sit on the floor if I'm in pain. I know people won't be rude if I use a walking stick one day and not the next, or even if I put the stick down and hit the dance floor for a bit. There's an understanding of diversity and a respect for setting your own boundaries and saying what's possible for you.'

Julie

'My disability only started noticeably impacting my life after I'd been involved in the bi community for a year or two, and I think that's made my experience of disability a lot easier and less scary than it might otherwise have been.

Bi community events and groups are almost exclusively brilliant around disability. I think there's a virtuous circle (opposite of a vicious one), where some disabled bi activists got involved, so the bi community got better with disability, so more disabled people got involved, and so on.

My disability is an invisible one for the most part, a connective tissue disorder resulting in chronic pain as the main symptom. In bi space, it takes me a couple of sentences to explain it and get the adjustments I need (not to stand up for long periods, not to sit on particular types of chair, opportunities for quiet time off). In the outside world, it seems to

take an awful lot more explanation to get those needs met. The upshot
is that I'm much more likely to be open about my disability in bi space.'
   Fred

It is certainly biphobic of healthcare professionals to assume that
bisexuality is the cause of or a sign of a mental health issue or any
other impairment. Yet research repeatedly shows that there are
much higher rates of declared disability (about twice as high) among
bi people than among the general population. Nobody really knows
why this is. It cannot be accounted for simply by assuming that mental health outcomes are poorer because of bi-erasure and biphobia,
and a lot more research is needed in this area. What we can say is that
bi events try to be welcoming and accessible to people with impairments and to make adjustments for their needs whenever possible.
So it's more likely that people who are visibly disabled will be able to
attend and more likely that people with invisible impairments will
feel it's more okay to talk about. As well as the physical concerns
of finding accessible venues or maybe allowing discounts for carers,
there are also cultural and ethical reasons why bi events tend to be
safer spaces for disabled people. The general ethos is that you should
believe people about their impairments and needs, including about
what they are and are not able to do. And things like variable conditions are very much understood.

> 'I usually find it difficult to be out about my mental health problems, but
> this hasn't been so much of an issue in the UK bi community, as there
> seems to be more of an awareness and acceptance of disability than
> there is in the wider world.'
>   Cat

> 'In bi space, I feel like my disability's unremarkable unless I want to talk
> about it, just like my sexuality.'
>   Fred

8

BISEXUAL BLACK AND MINORITY ETHNIC PEOPLE

Editor: Jacq Applebee

Content note: racism, sexual references, biphobia and hate speech.

This chapter is a series of personal accounts of the bisexual Black and Minority Ethnic (BME) experience. All content is by Jacq Applebee unless otherwise specified.

'When asked about my ethnic and cultural background, I often reply, "Do you want the long answer or the short answer?" Short answer, I'm Scottish-Latina-American. Long answer, I was born in San Francisco and live in Glasgow. My mother is Scottish, Ladin (Swiss Celtic) and Tunummiit (Greenlandic Inuit); my father is Scottish, Irish, Arawak (Venezuelan Amerindian), Berber, Basque, Afro-Caribbean and Jewish. I put guasacaca on oatcakes and listen to American country music on Radio nan Gàidheal and keep a collection of Caribbean seashells in my bedroom; my hair is blonde, but each strand also spins on its axis in a "tortion twist".

For me, all this cultural blending meant that being bisexual didn't seem like a big deal. For many Amerindian cultures, falling outside the "heterosexual and gender-conforming" box is accepted or even honoured. Between this and growing up in San Francisco, I didn't get any negative messages about queerness as a kid. (When I was older, we moved to another part of the United States, and I saw a lot more homophobia and biphobia. However, my response was more being upset that I felt unsafe, not that I felt anything was wrong with me for being bisexual.) I didn't even feel a need to make a big "coming-out" speech to my parents—in fact, I just casually mentioned one day that I was interested in women as well as men.

My cultural background has been very affirming. I can seek out Amerindian narratives about queerness, and fit myself into those stories and ideas. On the Scottish side of my family, I can look back up my family tree to gay and bisexual people from the past. At the same time, being strongly attached to my multicultural heritage means I wasn't really part of "mainstream" LGBT culture. I missed out on a lot of movies, books, music and fashions that gay and bi people I met in university saw as key pieces of their cultural development as queer. Many of these people openly assumed that non-Anglo-American cultures were all horribly homophobic and expressed surprise at the positive attitudes of my parents and extended family (one person even told me that Brazil, Colombia and Mexico couldn't possibly have marriage equality, and only conceded after a consult with Wikipedia). I don't think I'd be as comfortable with my orientation without having that complex cultural narrative to help me form the core of my identity and give me a context for my sexuality.'

Shaylon Stolk

BME Bisexuals and Dress Codes

Picture young gay guys in tight bleached denim and Dr. Martens boots. Older lesbians with labrys pendants and checked shirts. Femmes with 1950s floral dresses, bright-red heels and biker jackets. Older gay leather daddies with moustaches to die for. Androgynous dandies. These are just a few dress codes for lesbian and gay folks. Most of the imagery surrounding these codes conjures images of white people. BME people who are lesbian and gay are often left out of these recognisable modes of dressing in the UK.

Where do bisexuals fit in with dress codes? If one were to have a look at the BiCon dance floor, there would be a whole lot of goths to be seen. But maybe this is an expression of the music that is often played. When I wrote my 'Bisexual Anthem', I included several things that would be instantly recognisable to bisexual people who attend bi events, like purple clothes and New Rock boots. There are other identifiers some bisexual people of all genders wear in bi spaces, such as glitter, fairy/fantasy wear, kinky or BDSM-themed outfits, steampunk and old-school hippy styles. BME people may not identify with many of these themes of clothing; steampunk raises a mass of worries in regards to a glamorised colonial era that impacted negatively on the lives of BME bisexuals and their families. Kinky clothing which includes collars, for example, may shock and bring up unwanted images and memories to some people who have survived abuse and violence; for BME people, this may be even more keenly felt. Hippy or New Age outfits that involve a white person wearing a bindi or sporting dreadlocks may also be offensive, as both of these are religious and cultural items to many BME people. Cultural appropriation is an issue that is often faced in many white-dominated alternative spaces; bisexual spaces in the UK are no exception.

What do bisexual BME people wear? We wear head coverings and do-rags, saris and Punjabi suits, kente cloth, cheongsams, binders, salwar kameez, western everyday skirts and jeans. Some BME people will proudly wear their Sunday best when attending any event.

As bisexual communities are usually very white dominated, some BME bisexuals will not want to stand out by wearing clothes different to the attire worn by the majority. Inappropriate questions about any dress that isn't perceived to be standard is very common. Some BME people may feel comfortable with explaining their outfits to curious white bisexuals, whereas others get sick of it very quickly. Honest enquiry may be fine, but the constant questions can often feel like BME people have to verify that they are in the right place, to prove they are indeed bisexuals and not interlopers. This is something rarely experienced by white bisexual people, especially as questions about clothing are usually followed up by 'Where are you from? I mean *really* from?' Assumptions abound, and they increase the negative and unwelcoming environment felt by many bisexual BME people in these spaces.

My Bisexual Anthem for Bi Visibility Day

Bisexuals.
We're not straight or gay.
Not a silent b
After this great day.
We're out and proud,
Clothed in purple hues;
Smashing fences down
With our New Rocks boots.
Bisexuals.
Going all the way.
Not invisible.
Neither straight nor gay.
Bisexuals.
Let your voices shout.
LGBT
Don't dare leave us out!

Over the Rainbow, through Passport Control

A quick Internet or bricks-and-mortar library search for the words 'black bisexual' or 'bisexual BME people' will result in several results; most of these will refer to organisations in the US and Canada. Porn sites featuring black bisexual men will probably be at the top of the list in an Internet search. You may find publications about men on the 'down-low' too. It will be a rare find indeed to see anything about BME people who live and love in the United Kingdom (even if you use the UK English spelling of 'colour' and not the US 'color'). In the UK, it would be easy to think that every LGBTQIA+ person is white. With the exception of HIV prevention information, it is rare to see a person of colour represented as being LGBTQIA+.

Do bisexual BME people only live in North America? The population there is bigger, but even if percentages were used to calculate these things, the rest of the world would have more of a presence in places where people go to find resources and to end—or at least fight to ease—their isolation. The United Kingdom has made many strides when it comes to protection against discrimination, including sexual orientation and gender identification. However, racism is still alive and kicking, inside and out of LGBTQIA+ spaces. Outright acts of violence may be less common, but threats, dismissal, erasure and a weapons-grade lack of understanding and empathy are regular occurrences in bisexual communities. Anecdotal evidence shows that BME people often go to bisexual events once, and never return because of the environment, and/or the unwelcoming behaviour of other attendees. Sometimes will witness and overtly or subtly endorse these behaviours. BME bisexuals are not scarce in the United Kingdom, but there are often good reasons for them to keep their orientation to themselves and go elsewhere to friendlier spaces. The lack of diversity is an issue that diminishes the potential of bisexual spaces.

According to the *Bisexuality Report*, bisexuals experience the highest rates of poor mental health and suicide compared to gay, lesbian and heterosexual people. There are currently no figures on bisexuals of colour, but these figures are likely to be even higher for them than for white bisexuals. The combination of isolation, biphobia and racism can be a killer, or if not, it can detract from the quality of life for BME bisexuals. BME bisexuals who live in rural areas, are not out to others, are disabled or are older are at particular risk when it comes to isolation. And a quick search on the Internet can leave one sometimes feeling that all the support, social groups and conferences that address our lives are all in a mythical place, somewhere across the Atlantic and over the rainbow.

Bisexual BME people face racism in LGBTQIA+ spaces, and biphobia in lesbian and gay spaces. This is a truth that many white LGBTQIA+ people don't want to admit. 'I can't be racist: I'm gay!' is a familiar refrain. The experience of one oppression does not mean all other oppressions are wiped away from their consciousness. Even if by some chance white bisexuals recognise racism, bisexual BMEs often feel as if not much is being done about it. Bisexual BME people are often left to find ways to solve the problem of racism in their communities. A subtle tactic white bisexuals often use is to ensure BME folks appear in photographs or publicity in order to portray the group or event to the world as being inclusive, when the reality is very different. To rub salt in the wound, white bisexual organisers will often consult a BME speaker from North America or refer to BME LGBTQIA+ activists over there, rather than contact a bisexual BME person from the UK. White bisexuals sometimes ignore the fact that the life experiences of BME people in North America are often wildly different to those of us in the UK. Sometimes the lack of awareness that we are here is the reason, but sometimes the lack of academic publications by UK BME bisexuals is a factor. With the bisexual communities in the UK being very academic, it is somewhat understandable that they will only look to a familiar pool. But this does little to help BME bisexuals in the UK.

The Birth of Bi's of Colour

I came out as bisexual in 1993. My revelation came a year after I ran away from the people I had grown up with. I arrived in my part of London homeless, penniless, very sick, but free to live a life of my choosing.

My first try at becoming involved in anything LGBT was at a black lesbian group in North London. I naively thought it might be an accepting place for me, but I was told in very clear terms that bisexuals weren't welcome. A phone call to the London Lesbian and Gay Switchboard also revealed massive biphobia: I was told that there was nothing for me in England and that I should try going to Scotland instead!

Despite these setbacks, I tried finding and joining one of the bisexual communities, which was a lot more difficult in a time when the Internet was not as widely available as it is now. I went to the London bisexual women's group for almost a year. I was the only black person there, apart from one occasion when there were two of us. Every visit, somebody was guaranteed to ask where I was from, or sometimes where in Africa I was from. (I'm not.) Over time, my annoyance about this turned to extreme irritation. Another issue was the constant emphasis on BDSM; I was to become interested in that lifestyle many years later, but it felt very alienating and scary to me at the time. That only added to my feeling isolated.

It was around this time that I went on my first Pride march. I came up against misogyny and racism from white gay men at the event, which I wasn't expecting; I was treated like a novelty and expected to perform for their amusement.

I felt totally lost with everything to do with LGBT matters. I decided to leave it all behind; I knew I would be lonely, but I also knew that there were worse things than being alone. I longed to be either lesbian or straight. Bisexuality meant I was on the losing side no matter what.

It took me a long time to get over my fear of the treatment I'd received. In the intervening time I found names for other things I was interested in: polyamory, sensation play and more. It was at a one-day polyamorous event, PolyDay 2006, that someone told me about Brighton BiFest, a bi event that would be happening in February 2007 as part of Brighton's Winter Pride. I decided to go along. I was so impressed with the friendly and professional way it was organised that I signed up to attend BiCon 2007. I had heard of BiCon before, but I had always thought it wouldn't be for me.

I had a magical time at my first BiCon in Glamorgan that year. It was without a doubt the best time I'd ever had. On the second day of BiCon I started crying, which surprised me. A man asked me if I was okay, and I responded that I'd been hugged more times in two days of BiCon than I had in my entire life put together.

I suppose I was silly to think that every BiCon would be as wonderful as that. I soon learned in the next two years that racism, sexism and classism were prevalent in the bi communities of BiCon. Things came to a head just before BiCon 2009, when one of the organisers used Islamophobic and racist slurs in a public forum. Only two people initially called him out on his behaviour: the two people who were to form Bi's of Colour. The organiser used standard derailing phrases when he was asked to stop: he couldn't possibly be racist as he had black friends, he was being targeted unfairly, and on and on. After speaking to my friend, we agreed that we would have a session at the next BiCon just for bisexuals of colour. BiCon 2010 would be an international BiCon, so it would be an opportunity for overseas bisexuals to join in. Surely we couldn't be the only ones who wanted a safe space?

BiCon 2010 took place in London. I nervously waited outside the room where we were due to have our session. I was petrified that someone would make trouble, but nobody did. Seventeen bisexuals of colour walked in the room. Each person talked, they cried, they got angry and they laughed. Then the next person did exactly the same. It was an incredibly moving experience. Everyone went off to have lunch together. Everyone was smiling.

A few hours later, at a decision-making session, several delegates got up on stage to complain that bisexuals of colour shouldn't have their own separate session. They said the same thing for trans people too. I sat at the back of the lecture hall, fuming, cursing under my breath as my girlfriend clutched my hand. When a white delegate said we should justify why we needed a safe space—surely BiCon was friendly to everyone?—I finally stood up, walked down to the lectern and addressed the hall.

'Can everyone who's able please stand up?'

I waited a moment.

'Now all the white people sit down.'

I pointed to the small scattering of black and brown faces.

'That is all the explanation you're going to get. It's all you need.'

I sat back down.

We've had bisexuals-of-colour sessions at every BiCon since that time. We've also had sessions at BiFests, and we've given talks about the experiences of BME bisexuals up and down the UK. Bi's of Colour as a group is still going strong. Our online presence is huge, and there is always interest in us when people find out we exist. It feels great that the safe space for us is there; at BiCon 2012 we had our own flat, which was just wonderful! I wish that BiCon was welcoming to everyone, but it isn't. I wish the UK bi communities were a place where racism, Islamophobia and other religious bigotry didn't exist, but they do. Until a time when things change drastically, there will be a need for Bi's of Colour.

Surveys, Research and Bi's of Colour

Finding verified information about sexual minorities probably means looking at academic books and journals. I used to work in a university library, and I had free access to these resources, yet I didn't use them too often, as they felt alienating to me. I am a native English speaker, but academic language automatically puts me on the back foot. I feel as if my comprehension is being somehow judged, even though there is no one else around. Academic writing is important; it's the thing that can sway government policies, it's the work that gets mentioned at conferences that influential people attend. When searching for information on bisexuals in the UK, titles that cover LGBTQIA+ are usually of little use; bisexual and trans people tend to be rarely mentioned, if at all. The scarce bisexual research that is UK-specific tends to be out of date, or behind the journal's paywall, making it hard to access outside of a higher-/further-education setting.

Research on bisexuality in the UK is almost always focused on white people. If I want to find out about BME bisexuals, I have to look at US-based work. That is why, when I see researchers looking for subjects, I try to take part in any calls for participants that I see. The work may take a long time to be written up, and it may forever reside behind a paywall, but I know that if I don't take part, there's a good chance that there may be no other BME bisexuals included in the results.

Taking part in research as a BME bisexual may create problems the researchers had not anticipated. For example, I took part in a photo survey once. The survey was going to be anonymised, but I was the only BME bisexual taking part. I wouldn't have to take a full photo of my face to be recognised, as my skin would give away everything. This was a problem for the researcher that they had not thought of before.

I took part in a face-to-face interview on bisexual people and visual identity a few years ago. The researcher didn't seem to expect to meet a black woman; she looked uncomfortable throughout the interview, and she also used a racist term when I asked her if I was the first black person she'd ever met; apparently there was a black man in her Somerset village called 'Black Bob'.

The biggest research report on bisexuality in the UK is the *Bisexuality Report*, published by the Open University. The report is professionally created and written in accessible language. When I initially read it, I became increasingly excited, until I got to the paragraphs on race and faith. Reading through the half-formed ideas and a mass of assumptions in these sections left me with a feeling of familiar sadness; once again the voices of BME bisexuals had been erased in favour of stereotypes and myths about us. All the authors of the *Bisexuality Report* are white; in the meagre few paragraphs dedicated to race and faith, it reads as if no BME bisexuals were even consulted at all. I cannot imagine this happening to other sections, such as the chapters on health and disability. It remains something that I am very unhappy with.

Thankfully, I've had some positive experiences in taking part in research; experiences where my voice was listened to without bias. It is incredibly important to me to participate at every occasion, to know that when people look back they will be able to see representation of people just like me, and not just a bisexual world where everyone is white.

You've Gotta Have Faith

Jacq Applebee's talk from the Bi Inclusion panel on 25 September 2014

I'm going to talk about bisexuality, ethnicity and faith.
I'd like to start off by asking three questions:
Can you be a Person of Colour and bisexual?
Can you follow a religion or hold a faith and be bisexual?
Do bisexuals really exist?
Well, the answer to all three questions is: yes, yes and HELL YEAH!

Faith and religion have often been used as a stick to beat people with, but they have also been used as a source of hope for oppressed communities for a very long time. My faith doesn't mean I go to church on Sunday, stand when I'm told, sit when I'm told and then go home. It gives me hope when I face multiple discriminations and bigotry on an almost daily basis.

However, I've encountered assumptions held by white LGBTQIA+ people who say that all religious folks hate them, and all BME people hate them too, so they feel justified to hate us back in return. When you're a black person who holds a belief, that's an awful lot of hate to deal with. I've also seen many articles, and heard comments made, that faith groups need to be more accepting to LGBTQIA+ people (which assumes that no religious people are LGBTQIA+). I've only encountered two people who have asked how LGBTQIA+ communities can be more accepting of religious people and BME people. When I've pointed this out in the past, I've been met with the same tired variant of: 'I can't be racist, I'm gay!' I've also experienced mocking, erasure and ignorance as a result of this (sound familiar?).

I've experienced biphobia and racism in most LGBTQIA+ spaces I've attended. Many organisations will happily put 'LGBT' on their funding applications, on their headed paper and above the doors to their offices, but in my experience, the reality is that they are LGGGGG...GGG, very white, and not welcoming at all to bis and BME people. There is an awful lot of racism in LGBTQIA+ communities: Islamophobia is especially bad too, and used as a way to be racist towards BME bisexuals.

I've experienced racism and biphobia at Pride events, being called a 'breeder', which is a racially loaded term, and a very hurtful one as well. I've also been spat on at Brighton Pride by a white gay man who was marching in the parade. No one should have to experience that kind of violation, especially not at a Pride event. It is something that still makes me nervous when I attend events.

I am black, Christian and I am bisexual. These aren't just parts of me; they are me. I cannot stop being these things. And the only time I'll stop is when I'm dead. I want to be here. I want to go on.

I will now end with a little poem:

> Just like sleeping with your tampon in
> being bisexual is not a sin.
> And I don't always shout it out loud,
> but I do like to be out and proud.
> It's hard though, especially when some people insist
> that bisexuality just doesn't exist:
> that I'm trying to be trendy,
> or playing it safe.
> Inviting gays and straights to spit in my face,
> or completely ignore everything I say;

go back in another closet, and pretend that I'm gay.
So I'll tell you all without being too intellectual:
I'm Jacq: black, happy, bisexual!

The Politics of Colour: Being an Invisible Minority within an Invisible Minority

By Yemisi

Bisexuals are not a very visible part of the LGBTQIA+ community. Unfortunately, biphobia is very much alive within the LGBTQIA+ community. This issue has been cause for bisexuals to come together to organise and gain more visibility in the LGBTQIA+ community.

When I moved to the UK in 2009, I was eager to join the LGBTQIA+ community and be part of the bisexual community. I soon realised that although it is easy to have a social life beyond virtual interactions with lesbians and gays activists, it is very difficult to actually meet bisexual activists.

Almost all the LGBTQIA+ events I attended were dominated by gay and lesbian concerns; there was nothing much about bisexuality. I had to raise the question of more bi visibility at these events.

I also noticed that it is one thing to find bisexual events, but it is quite another to find people of colour represented at these events. Unlike most LGBTQIA+ events (which are actually gay-dominated events), where there are at least a noticeable number of people of colour, the few bisexual events I have attended failed in this area.

After making enquiries about bi groups and events in UK, a bi friend who lives outside the UK sent me a link to a bi weekend event organised by bisexual activists in UK. I was glad to attend and was happy that one of the main themes for the weekend was race. The event was held outside London, and I had to travel a bit to get to the destination, optimistic that it was going to be a great weekend with fellow bi activists.

I had, of course, notified the organisers that I was coming. I arrived at the venue at the same time with a white woman, who was also attending the program for the first time. One of the organisers came to get the door to usher us in. I must say, that was the point my bubble began to burst. She was all over the other woman, asking about her journey and all, while all I got was a cursory, suspicious 'Hello' that got me wondering, 'Have I done something wrong?'

When attention was finally directed at me, the question was focused on how I got the information about the event. It seems my answer of 'through a friend' was not good enough; I was prodded to give the name of the friend. I was told that the reason she asked was that some people think the bi activist weekend was a pickup/dating weekend. The alarm bells started ringing because it seems I had to prove I wasn't there to pick up dates but for real activism, while the other woman didn't have to go through that cold reception. I put that down to the colour of my skin.

One step into the meeting room, I realised immediately I was the only black person in the group. The other black-identified person was a facilitator of the race workshop; she was biracial and identified as Irish/African.

I must say as a trainer, facilitator and activist, I enjoyed the workshops, as I had a lot to contribute to the discussions and learned new things. At the end of the workshop, we were asked if there was any instance any of us felt isolated in the group because of our race, and everyone said no except me. Needless to say, mouths were open, aghast, and all eyes upon me, piercingly screaming, 'What the heck do you mean you felt isolated?'

Anyway, I took the opportunity to explain to the group that when one enters a room for a large group meeting and suddenly realises that one is the only black African in that room, there is a tendency to feel a sense of isolation. They probably did not notice I was the only black person in that room, but that wouldn't stop me noticing this important fact. I know I am not the only black bisexual in the UK, and when attending a weekend meeting with an established bi activist's coalition group in the UK, I would expect to see a bit of diversity. Therefore, it came as a shock to me that I couldn't find another of my skin colour at the event. The fact that they did not even notice the absence of that diversity was worrisome, but when some of them put it down to being 'colour-blind', it is irking to say the least.

I did have a good weekend at the event, and when I couldn't get a room at the hotels the other participants suggested (since they were sure that there were available rooms in their hotels, probably my heavy 'African' accent puts off the hotel managers?), a pleasant couple offered to accommodate me for the night.

Unfortunately, I have not been able to attend subsequent meetings mainly due to financial constraints, as they do involve travels and hotel bookings. However, I do also note that as an organiser, if I had a minority attend my program for the first time, I would make an extra effort to reach out to the minority to get feedback and encourage them to attend subsequent programs. This is a way of building diversity. In this case, the organisers did not do this.

I also think many bisexuals in England find it more convenient to identify as lesbian or gay. 'Lesbian' and 'gay' are words that many outside the LGBTQIA+ community are already familiar with, and with this recognition comes legally recognised rights. Bisexuality, on the other hand, often needs to be explained to people, and it does not come with easily recognised rights. For example, I have seen cases of bisexual asylum seekers told to identify as lesbian by their lawyers because it is easier to win a case as a gay or lesbian person than as a bisexual. This unfortunately also promotes invisibility of bisexual cases in the judicial system.

One contrast I have noticed between the UK and Nigeria, where I come from, is the number of people within the LGBTQIA+ community who willingly identify as gay and lesbian. In Nigeria, because of the oppressive laws surrounding same-sex relationships and the sodomy law inherited from Britain during colonisation, the words 'lesbian' and 'gay' are known taboo words. 'Bisexual', on the other hand, is not even a known term to people outside the LGBTQIA+ community.

In the Nigerian LGBTQIA+ community, it is normal to find a self-identified lesbian or gay in a relationship with the opposite sex, as a cover-up strategy to dispel any rumour about their sexual orientation. Because of this ambiguous lifestyle, it is sometimes difficult to know who is really gay, lesbian or bisexual.

In addition, in the UK, I have noticed that in contrast to the ugly situation in Nigeria where members of the LGBTQIA+ community have to operate underground and hide their sexual orientation, this is not much of a problem in the LGBTQIA+ community in the UK. They have rights and can freely identify as LGB or T. Many have chosen to identify with the L and G because they are more recognised and protected by the law. Some who would fall into the bisexual identity would rather identify as lesbian or gay because the LG words are more powerful and inclusive than the B.

It is unfortunate that bisexuals suffer such invisibility within the LGBTQIA+ community, but it is also shameful that the few bisexual groups trying to gain visibility have not really reached out to bisexual people of colour in their community.

I would prefer to be part of an all-inclusive group. When I hang out with my LG activist friends, it is often inclusive in terms of race but not inclusive in terms of bisexual representation. On the contrary, when I hang out with bisexual groups, the non-representation of people of colour is one glaring gap that bugs me. It is sad when one is part of an invisible minority, but it is utterly sad when one becomes an invisible minority within an invisible minority.

This issue of people of colour within a minority is also one that rears its ugly head in some other groups I identify with, for example the atheist community. Atheists are a minority in many countries, and white people dominate atheism as a movement. It seems almost a myth that we have intellectual black atheists. However, there is a growing call in the atheist movement for better representation and visibility of atheist people of colour. While I appreciate this call, one thing that continuously bugs me is that people of colour who are part of a minority group are never contacted unless the group wants to do a feature on people of colour or to promote a PR stunt about its diversity policy.

It seems the only time an activist of colour is contacted to write or speak about a topic in their group event is when the theme is on race or focused on their colour and diversity. People of colour hardly ever are contacted to talk about the main reason they are part of that movement without having to tie it to their race. I mean, I would be very comfortable speaking on topics of bisexuality or atheism, but the very few times I have been contacted to do this, it has been to ask me about my perspective as a person of colour within this movement. This sometimes makes one feel that many people think the only thing people of colour are capable of bringing to a movement is their skin colour to boost the movement's claim to diversity.

I do hope bisexual groups, atheist groups and other progressive groups start appreciating diversity and appreciate the contribution each individual brings to the group aside from skin colour.

My Invisible Skin

How do I talk to you about something that most people think doesn't exist?

How can I stand up for a community that doesn't believe in me?

Sometimes, I feel like an empty chalk line on bitumen, a once-man forever being filled in by other people's expectations and ideas. I try to tell them who I am. I try to show them my depth, my range, the texture and colour of my experience, but I may as well be a passing gust of wind. They see my outline, the most basic sketched detail, and immediately fill it with their preconceived notions.

As a mixed-race bisexual, I cop it both ways (ha, yep, I can joke about it—often, humour is all I have). I'm a half-Lebanese, half-Turkish Australian; I look like your fears. Tall, dusky and bearded, I get it in the sidelong glances on public transport, in newspaper headlines and politics, and the fact that at every checkpoint, be it police at train stations or airports or anywhere, I'm stopped and questioned. It's not always by a faceless white authority figure either, but often by men who look just like I do. They'll hold up their arm with an apologetic grimace, as though saying, 'I know. I do. But I have to stop you.'

Because stereotyping is so pervasive, we're even suspicious of each other. Just a few weeks ago, I was going into work on a cold, rainy day, wearing a nice formal winter coat, and actually thinking to myself, I look so *presentable* today, so officious (read: white), I don't think I'll be stopped. And when I was, it broke me just that little bit more—there's really nothing I can do, no mask I can wear to hide who I am, no way to change how they think of me.

This is my skin.

Which brings me to bisexuality, my invisible identity. Like it or not, it's as much a part of me as my colouring, my racial markers. Sadly, my experience with the latter has informed how I express the former—namely, I don't broadcast it. I'm a big guy, I like watching sport, burgers, girls and going to the gym. I have a lazy masculine attitude, including a general disdain for cleanliness and fashion. You know, the broad caricaturist strokes of your average straight man. It's incredibly easy to play to those elements and let people assume what they will without ever having to speak a lie.

Of course, I'm also a geek, writer, poet, and lover of all things Disney, musical, and theatre. My loves are numerous, my personality multifaceted, and yet, there are so few people willing to accept me as such. Even among my friends—my progressive, left-wing heavily pro-LGBTQIA+ friends—I can count on one hand the people who know and love me for all that I am, and not just a part they find acceptable. Bisexuality, I have discovered, is not just an invisibility I've chosen, but one actively enforced by society—nowhere more obviously than in the community to which I nominally belong.

I thought, naively it would seem, that nobody would be more sympathetic or sensitive to issues of sexual identity than gay people, but I was vastly mistaken. Who better than they would know how it felt to be told, 'Oh, you're just confused', or 'It's just a phase' or any number of clichés outsiders use to enforce their narrow conceptualisation of sexuality onto you? Who better than they to know how it felt to be shamed for who you found attractive, to be told you don't know yourself? And yet, I've faced this and more from gay people, gay friends. I've dealt with rolled eyes and drawled announcements of 'bi now, gay later', that most casual and insulting of dismissals.

I understand where it comes from. I understand that some gay men and women find it easier to use the term 'bisexual' as a stepping stone, a means of getting their homophobic friends or family used to the concept of liking the same sex. They may even use it as a way to consciously get themselves used to the idea, without even realising it. That this is true for some people does not make it true for all, does not make belittling others who identify that way okay. The arrogance in assuming your own experience—your own fear—will be the same for everyone else is staggering. And it's not an idle assumption I've faced, but an aggressive, hostile attack on my personhood by people who may have known me for all of five minutes. Or worse, years.

At a house party once, I had a gay man brazenly declare that I wasn't bisexual (when asked, as I was, I will always answer truthfully), because, oh, how many men have you had sex with? Just the *one*? How many blow jobs? How many women? As if sexuality were no more than the amount of penetrations you've dealt out, or received, the amount of bodily fluids exchanged. The failure here, on the part of both gay and straight communities, is the inability to remove their gendered lenses—their static sexuality is rooted in the gender they're attracted to, who they fuck. Mine isn't. What matters is that I care for the person, that I find them attractive according to the features I like in men and women, that we're both comfortable and enjoying ourselves. That's all.

But it's not only the gay community heedlessly stamping on bisexuality; the straight community is no better—albeit in a different manner. With them, I get lewd drunken grins and exclamations of, "That must be awesome! Any hole's a goal, eh?" or bluntly, "You're just a slut." I've had women just start feeling me up on hearing it, as though I suddenly became no more than a block of meat or a toy to test out. And no, just because I'm a guy doesn't mean I'm okay with being felt up without permission or harassed in any way. That's the best-case scenario, sadly.

Then there's the outright homophobia, as directly applicable to me as a bisexual man as it is to gay men. To bigots, there's no difference. If you like men, you're a faggot. Period. Or there's the straight friend who knows, but will never address it; it's too uncomfortable for them—just ignore it, pretend it doesn't exist, or that it's invisible.

If I struggle this much with my own gay friends, my progressive circle of contacts, can you imagine how I'd fare with my religious Muslim family? From whom I've invariably heard, as I've grown up, 'Gay people should be beheaded', or 'They're all going to hell' or that if I should ever turn out gay, I'd be stabbed, maimed, hurt, hated, disowned—sometimes, this was said with a laugh. Sometimes not. It was always an inside joke, see, that because I was a geek and loved reading books, where my brothers and cousins loved 'sick cars and hot bitches', I would turn out gay. 'Gay' was the catch-all insult used for anything different, odd, out of the norm.

This is why it's so funny to me when gay men suggest that bisexuality is just fear of coming out of the closet, of having to live with homophobia, as though they've gone through things I haven't. I'll say it again: bigots don't see a difference. I've lived underneath the word 'gay' my whole life—and not in the good way, with loving connotations, but as *homo* and *fag*. I've had it branded into my skin so often the letters all run together. I've spent countless nights curled up, wishing I were gay, wishing it were that simple. How beautiful to be part of that great rainbow family, increasingly accepted by the majority, increasingly celebrated. And countless nights wishing I just wanted girls, thinking of the family I want to raise, the wife I want to have, how it will all work out.

I'm stuck between (broadly speaking) two collections of concrete identities, all you brittle-edged people, you sound foundations, you with the unchanging ground beneath your feet, where mine is fluid, is smoke and cloud. My loves are distinct, they are real and they need to be acknowledged. I can't keep fighting in the dark. Just as with my colouring, my features, this is not something I will ever escape. Nor, I think, a fight that I'll ever win. But that's not the point—my mistake has been in letting it go uncontested. Letting the arrogance, the faulty assumptions, the endless bigotry wash over me. Taking it out on myself later.

No more.

My family does not know who I am. They may not for some time. They don't use the Internet much—and if they do, it isn't to read things like this—and I'm too much of a coward to show it to them directly. Coward because, for all their faults, I love them deeply. For all their bigotry, their casual racism, intolerance, superstition and general ignorance—barely a high school diploma among them—I love them so much, and I always will, and I want this to last. But I will lose them as surely as the sun will rise tomorrow, because their love is conditional. Mine is not.

And so I have stayed silent this long. I am, however, so very tired of my heart feeling like a grenade with the pin pulled, so sick of feeling as though I have one foot on a landmine, slowly lifting. Let them see, then. They are not the real audience here, anyway—you are. You, my educated, progressive friends, my obnoxious (and not-so-obnoxious) gay friends, my silent straight friends. You probably have other bisexual friends, or will in future, and you may have said some of the things I've mentioned here. Or acted a certain way towards them (or happily, not). Either way, this is to let you know that we're here, we're real and so is our struggle. Next time you happen to meet a bisexual, should you feel a sneer, or eye-roll or cliché coming on, however jokingly put—just stop.

Hell, indulge me in a little wish fulfilment here—stop, smile and give them a hug instead, would you? (With their consent, naturally.) I think we'd all be much better off, if that were the case. If that's too much for you, or you happen to somehow not like hugs, just stop and think. Put yourself in their shoes. It's never as easy or as simple as you believe.

My name is Omar J. Sakr, I'm an Australian writer and poet of Lebanese-Turkish descent, and this is who I am. This is my skin.

By Omar Sakr, reproduced with permission from the website *Human Parts*.

Contribution

By Ronete

I missed the submission deadline for my contribution. And the next one. I've known what I wanted to write for a long time, but just managed to consistently fail to do so. And then, post-post-deadline, I woke up in the middle of the night knowing why: I was scared of committing my experience to paper for all eternity. I was scared to speak out. And then I thought to myself that this in itself showed that what I had to write was very real and needed to be said.

There is an easy bit: I'm mixed race. I'm relatively light skinned, with dark hair and eyes and what white people consider 'exotic' looks. I get the usual microaggressions that other me, including the infamous 'But where are you *really* from?' I've also experienced some very hurtful and even scary racism. When I'm othered in bi spaces, there's always the safety and sense of belonging of spaces for bi people of colour. And then there's that one thing about me that can single me out even there, and can make even the spaces that should feel safe feel uncomfortable.

I'm Jewish. Atheist Jewish, but I can't hide it because my name is the first one you think of when you try and think of a Jewish name. However much I love Jewish culture and so many other things about this particular intersection of my identity, I sometimes wish it wasn't this obvious. It puts the spotlight on me and makes it easier for people to make assumptions about me. This happens everywhere, including in activist, bi-inclusive spaces. You see, I'm expected to prove my credentials and, before I do anything else, declare my political stance about Israel. I need to reassure people that I do not support Israel and its actions. I could do so now, but I don't see why I have to. I'd like to enter a conversation where I'm allowed to discuss any trivial or serious subject without first placing myself firmly in the corner of 'good Jew' or that of 'bad Jew'. I'd like to just have the same experience as anyone else without having to be dragged into a political discussion. Being Jewish doesn't automatically make me an official spokesperson for the State of Israel. I'm just a person. A mixed-race, atheist, Jewish bisexual woman. I will discuss politics if that's the conversation everyone else is having. I'll even talk about Israel. But I refuse to do so by way of introduction or to have the burden of proving that I'm 'okay' before I'm accepted.

This is probably the hardest thing I've ever had to write. I very nearly didn't, but anything that makes you dread the moment you have to say your name needs to be talked about. Safe spaces should feel safe for everyone.

What's out There for BME Bisexuals?

Social

Bi's of Colour (bisofcolour.tumblr.com)
This is a UK-wide network of bisexuals, with online resources, a Twitter account and a Tumblr feed. The group has met at BiCon every year since 2010, with additional meetings at BiFests around the country.

Rainbow Noir (www.facebook.com/rainbownoirmcr)
Rainbow Noir is a social and community group for people of colour who identify as LGBTQI. It has Manchester-based online resources and group meetings.

UK Black Pride (www.ukblackpride.org.uk)
UK Black Pride promotes unity among LGBT Black people of African, Asian, Caribbean, Middle Eastern and Latin American descent, and their friends and families.

The Safra Project (www.safraproject.org)
This is a resource project working on issues relating to lesbian, bisexual and/or transgender women who identify as Muslim religiously and/or culturally.

Art

rukus! (www.rukus.co.uk)
Rukus! is an arts project that showcases provocative works by Black lesbian, gay, bisexual, trans and queer artists, both nationally and internationally.

Collective Creativity (qtipoccollectivecreativity.tumblr.com)
Collective Creativity facilitates arts-related events in a space that is explicitly created for and by people of different sexualities and genders, and for people of colour.

Health/Sexual Health

Kaleidoscope (kaleidoscopetrust.com)
This group meets once a month and is aimed at black gay and bisexual men who have sex with men of Caribbean and or African heritage, regardless of HIV status. Sessions include discussions, workshops and social events.

Naz Project London (NPL) (naz.org.uk)
This project provides sexual health and HIV prevention and support services to targeted BME communities in London. It provides sexual health and HIV/AIDS prevention and support services to South Asians, Muslims, Horn of Africans, Portuguese speakers and Spanish speakers.

KISS (www.planetkiss.org.uk)
KISS, part of the Naz Project, is a social group made up of women who identify either as lesbian, bisexual or queer and are of South Asian, Middle Eastern or North African descent.

DOST (naz.org.uk/what-we-do-at-naz/naz-men)
This is a support group for South Asian and Middle Eastern gay and bisexual men and men who have sex with men.

Grupo Vidas: Portuguese Speakers (naz.org.uk/what-we-do-at-naz/naz-vidas)
This is a mixed-sexuality social/support group for Portuguese-speaking people who are HIV positive.

Amigos: Spanish Speakers
This is a social support group for Spanish-speaking HIV-positive gay and bisexual men.

Faith and Religion

Sarbat (Sikhism) (www.sarbat.net)

Imaan (Islam) (www.imaan.org.uk)

Rainbow Jews (Judaism) (www.rainbowjews.com)

Gay and Bisexual Men's Buddhist group
(meetup.com/Buddhist-Meditation-for-Gay-and-Bisexual-Men)

Vaishnava (Hinduism)
(www.galva108.org/#!about-galva-108/c24vq)

Various LGBTQIA+ Christian groups
(two23.net/resources/other-helpful-groups)

Black Atheists (www.meetup.com/London-Black-Atheists)

9

LESSER-SPOTTED ATTRACTIONS

Editor: Jamie Q Collins

Content note: mention of rape on pages 175 and 179; mention of transphobia on page 180.

As crucial as it is to explore bisexual issues, it would be remiss of us to neglect other identities which are also erased by heteronormative narratives or can sometimes intersect with bisexuality / biromanticism.

Other Multi-Gender Attractions

Pansexual

Using the Greek prefix 'pan', pansexual means '[sexually] attracted to all genders'.

Hang on—*all* genders?
Ideally, this is the part where you skip back to chapter 4. But if you're pressed for time, a quick rundown is as follows: gender is a social construct—as in, it's been made up. That doesn't mean it's

unimportant; money is also a social construct, and we'd be hard-pressed to do without it.

In the Western world, we ascribe gender to infants based on the appearance of their genitalia, and expect their behaviour and identity to be in line with that assignment, for which we offer two options: boy/man or girl/woman. Infants who present in between this binary are known as 'intersex' and are often given surgery to force them to conform to one of the two options.

Some people find their gender isn't actually what they were assigned at birth. We call this being transgender. Some people might be transgender women (who were assigned male at birth), others might be transgender men (who were assigned female at birth). However, others might not find either category fits—these people are non-binary, and there are many different gender identities within that.

So that's why people identify as pansexual? To include non-binary people?

Sometimes. Though it's worth pointing out that bisexuality *also* includes non-binary people: 'bisexual' means 'attraction to two or more genders'. This definition is used by pretty much every bi organisation, though we do rather have to fight for it. But this isn't down to bisexuality itself erasing non-binary genders: mainstream concepts of gender do that rather nicely for themselves.

This seemingly conflicting etymology is partly due the fact that 'bisexuality', like 'homosexuality', originates as a medicalised term, meaning the term itself was coined by people who pathologised bisexuals—and who didn't grasp the concept of non-binary genders. Whilst gay people have largely rejected 'homosexual', the bi community have reclaimed 'bisexual', changing the discourse around it to more inclusive terms that more accurately define bisexuality.

Georgia says about an old blog post:
'I've never been fond of "bisexual" as a term to suit me, for various reasons: The societal view of bisexuality with the implication of "both" and the need for both at any time. Too many negative connotations there!

Then there's the implication of binary. Man and woman. That's it. Well, what about people who identify as genderqueer? "Pan" seems a better fit, meaning "all, inclusive, every", rather than "bi", meaning "both, doubly". Basically, I'm just a little pedantic about etymology!'

She goes on to explain:

'This is embarrassing to read now, not for the way I identified, but the why—at the time, the only exposure I'd had to bi issues was from main-stream media. I'd just started learning about transgender people and thought I was some sort of amazing ally to adopt this new (to me) term to be "inclusive". I hadn't quite grasped many of the complexities yet.'

Another take on pansexuality is the 'hearts not parts' approach, which focuses on traits beyond a person's gender:

'I don't like the implication that I am attracted to *gender*. I'm not; I'm attracted to the person as a whole. Their personality and who they are as a human being. [Gender] really doesn't matter in my attraction to someone.'
Anon

It's come under fire, however, as many people feel this approach is potentially de-gendering.

'The "I don't care about gender" approach is seriously harmful to the very people it claims to be inclusive of: I have to fight hard to get my gender acknowledged, so I'm less than thrilled when people say, "Oh, it doesn't matter!" Well, it matters to me!'
Anon

Some people, however, use 'pansexual' as a way of controlling the dialogues they have about their sexuality, finding the lesser-known term a boon.

'I use "pansexual", not because I feel "bisexual" enforces a binary, but because a hell of a lot of people do, and I've found "pan" is an easy short-hand to signal to non-binary people that "Hey, I might be attracted to you

too." It also gives me an opening to tell binary people, "Hey, non-binary people" exist.'
Sam

Polysexual

Using the Greek prefix 'poly', 'polysexual' means '[sexually] attracted to many genders'. It's less common than either 'bisexual' or 'pansexual' in the UK, but many people find it has the advantages of 'pansexual' without the linguistic complications.

> 'The bi vs. pan thing does my head in. Both have merits, both have flaws—and identifying either way involves a lot of defending your chosen term. Polysexual seems not to carry quite so much baggage—though I guess it's only a matter of time!'
> Mia

Others find it a more accurate description of their attractions.

> '"Polysexual" works better than "pansexual" does for me, because it allows me to state that I'm not interested in dating women.'
> Ellie

But some people find the term confusing, as it can be conflated with other identities.

> 'I like the term "polysexual". I think it explains my identity well. But it gets confused a lot with "polyamorous" [another term for non-monogamy: being in a relationship structure that allows for more than one partner; see chapter 5] so I don't really use it.'
> Kayleigh

What's the difference between all these terms?
Typically, bisexuality is presented as an umbrella term—attraction to two or more genders—which encompasses other multi-gender

attractions, both sexual and romantic (we'll cover the differences between the two later in this chapter). Pansexuality and polysexuality fall within this umbrella, meaning all pansexual and polysexual people also have access to the term 'bisexual'—*if* they so choose.

Different people have different reasons for choosing different terms: two people may experience their attractions in the same way yet use two different terms; two people who use the same term may experience their attractions in very different ways.

'I've come to dread saying I'm bisexual. I quite often find myself getting a lecture on how transphobic I am for saying I'll only date cis men and cis women, when I've said nothing of the sort. If I can get someone to realise that trans women are women and that bisexuality includes binary trans people, they tell me off for excluding non-binary people. When I say I'm attracted to non-binary people, they say, "So you're PANsexual; that means—" I know what it means. I'm not pansexual—I'm bisexual. I chose the label "bi" because the bisexual movement has a huge history and community behind it, and I really resent people trying to shut me off from that community by telling me that my sexuality and gender erase one another.'

Kai

'If I say I'm bisexual around straight, or even gay, people I get, "Oh, so you like men and women." Or even, "You like both pussy and cock!" But saying I'm pansexual allows me to redefine their understanding of it. So I'm bisexual in bisexual spaces, but pansexual outside of them.'

Alex

Ultimately, define your identity as you choose—just don't do so in ways that force or deny others' taking up that label.

Asexual/Aromantic Identities

Asexual

Using the Greek prefix 'a', meaning 'without', 'asexual' means someone who does not experience sexual attraction. It's also known within the asexual community as being 'ace' and is often represented with an ace of spades.

Aromantic

Whilst we've previously discussed sexual attraction, it's largely been assumed that it goes hand in hand with romantic attraction.

Aromantic people do not experience romantic attraction. This is also known colloquially as 'aro'.

Isn't that just a fancy word for someone who's got serious emotional issues?
People of all and no sexual and romantic orientations—including some but not all asexual and aromantic people—may experience issues regarding intimacy; this is not a prerequisite, cause or result of being ace/aro.

Culturally, we acknowledge many different types of love beyond romantic love. The ancient Greeks distinguished between 'eros' (sexual love), 'philia' (platonic love), 'ludus' (playful love), 'agape' (selfless love), 'pragma' (enduring love) and 'philautia' (self-love). The notion of distinguishing between different types of love is so common, in fact, it's cliché: 'I love you, I'm just not *in* love with you.' Despite its negative connotations, this turn of phrase serves as a case in point: it is possible to love someone—deeply, intimately— without experiencing romantic attraction.

Grey-ace/grey-aro

A term used for those who very rarely feel sexual/romantic attraction to others.

Demisexual/demiromantic

'Demisexual' is a term used for those who experience sexual attraction only to people they have a pre-existing emotional bond with, which is often, though not always, tied in with romantic attraction. For example, a demisexual person will not experience 'lust at first sight' but may develop sexual attraction to someone once they have got to know them.

The romantic counterpart of this is 'demiromantic', someone who experiences romantic attraction only after developing an emotional connection.

Isn't this just not being promiscuous?
Some people may choose not to engage in certain sexual acts with a partner until they have reached particular milestones. But just as someone can be bisexual yet have only had relationships and/or sex with people of one gender, a/demi/greysexuality is not tied to a certain set of sexual behaviours.

Some asexual people may willingly engage in sex: they might enjoy it for its own sake, as an act of intimacy or to pleasure a partner. Conversely, some allosexual (non-asexual) people may have low libidos, dislike sex or choose to be celibate for a number of reasons.

So, what's the problem? Why bother including ace/aro/demi/grey people in the LGBTQIA+ umbrella?
When discussing compulsory heterosexuality, we commonly focus on the 'hetero' part; yet the 'sexuality' aspect is just as—if not more—pervasive in forming our narratives. We're told we will grow up and meet someone and fall in love: as we get older, we're told an active sex life will be part of that. Some of us may be luckier than others and have a more liberal upbringing: we may be told it that no matter what gender we are, or what gender/s we're attracted to, we'll find our happy ending. Allosexuality and alloromantic attraction—that is, experiencing sexual and romantic attraction to others—is taken as read.

'It's hard to unpick what attraction is and isn't. Think about how you learn about attraction: "mummies and daddies" is normally the first introduction—if you haven't processed the little jokes about "Aww, Kitty and Toby are flirting" when you try and grab another toddler's toy.

And you get married to Drew under the slide in year three and then you play kiss-chase and it's just not cool to run so fast, Kitty, or how will you get caught? Then it's all about who you fancy, and you must want to hold his hand and kiss him and when you get older have sex with him.

But then you are older and you don't want sex. Maybe you're gay? But you don't want sex with girls either. So you're kind of—broken. Defective. But the right person will fix that! Maybe you're just a late bloomer? Have you gone to the doctor?'

Kitty

Particularly for orientations defined by a *lack* of attraction, there is a tendency to ascribe feelings to it being 'just a phase'—something a lot of bisexual people can relate to.

'We hear this so often about non-straight sexualities, and particularly about bisexuality, that coming to a new understanding of ourselves can feel like we're just conforming to that stereotype. I think if I hadn't been worried about that, I might have explored ace identities a lot earlier. Maybe it is just a phase. So what? It's still me, and I still expect people to respect that.'

Amanda

There's a pathologisation of asexuality, perhaps more so than other sexualities (note: sexualities and transgender identities are also pathologised), as this approach seems to still be widely regarded as medically sound. Asexual people report being offered counselling, or even medication, when their doctors learn of their orientation; one person who spoke with us even mentioned being offered referral to a sex therapist.

Then there are the more violent aspects of acephobia (the term coined for bigotry against people on the ace/aro spectrum): the

'You'll find the right person' narratives can often give way to sexual assault and rape. Known as 'corrective rape', it's been discussed widely in relation to lesbian oppression, though there is a wealth of anecdotal evidence emerging online suggesting that asexual people—particularly women—are also being victimised in this way.

Of course, not everyone will experience acephobia in the same ways and to the same degree: as with all axes of oppression, it will intersect with and be compounded by other aspects of a person's identity. For trans and/or black and Latina women, there is a likelihood that their asexuality will be disbelieved, in favour of hypersexual tropes. For some people, their asexuality may be assumed, or seen as confirmation of stereotypes.

> 'When people find out I'm ace and disabled there's like this little lightbulb moment. "Oh, so THAT's why you don't do sex!"'
> Phoenix

For people whose a/grey/demisexual identity conflates with a bi identity, or vice versa, the colliding stereotypes can serve to cause confusion—'How can you be both?'—or even self-doubt.

> 'I have only recently come to terms with probably falling somewhere on the asexual spectrum. There are things I still struggle with. I have days when I feel neither bi enough nor ace enough, frankly. But then I ask myself whose yardstick I'm measuring myself against and why. Ultimately, the only yardstick that matters is mine, because no one knows my own experience better than me.'
> Amanda

Challenging the 'Born This Way' Narrative

Thanks in no small part to Lady Gaga's catchy earworm, the 'born this way' narrative has seen a resurgence in recent years. It hits back against right-wing discourses of 'lifestyle choice' and 'abnormal behaviour', tying in with arguments that 'Homosexuality occurs in over [number] species; homophobia occurs in just one.'

However, in recent years, it's also come up against fierce criticism. Some of this criticism centres on efforts to find a 'gay gene'.

'Maybe there is a "queer" gene, but if there is, I don't want them to find it. What exactly would they do with it once they found it? I'd place good money on there being a demand for prenatal DNA screenings. Seems far-fetched? The current level of focus on screening for "birth defects" is terrifying. And we gender kids even before birth, that's how obsessively hung up on this we are as a culture. I'm pro-choice—but as a means of bodily autonomy; not as a means of culling the queer population.'

Lou

But other criticisms have a more political basis.

'"Born this way" was very useful for a time. I have no doubt it still is for some people, in areas where society hasn't quite caught up to progressive thinking. But the liberal focus on it is part of a major problem for LGBTQIA+ society. "We were born this way" suggests "We're just like you except this one small thing." And when you've got marriage all tied up in a bow, what else is there to do? No. "Born this way" lets society off too easily. It lets society pretend the problem is over now. That LGBTQIA+ homelessness isn't a massive problem. That hate crimes are an anomaly. That we can confine sad stories about sad gays to artsy movies about the '80s. No, we're not like you—because for years, you've denied us that opportunity. These problems weren't "born"—you made them this way.'

Jax

Many bi people, as well as asexual and transgender people, said they particularly felt aggression both in and out of the LGBTQIA+ community with demands to 'prove' their gender and/or sexuality.

'It's further worth noting that if a "gay" or "trans" gene was discovered, it'd have implications for people who didn't have it. It's already hard enough for trans people to get medical treatment; what happens if they test negative for the gene? Will doctors, rather than gatekeeping for adherence to arbitrary gender stereotypes, instead start gatekeeping by genetic test?'

Anon

The 'born this way' narrative, and conflating ideas surrounding it, can further this aggression, especially for people who don't conform to a set ideal: bi people who only have sexual or romantic experiences with one gender, for example, or trans people who only came to an understanding of their gender in adult life.

'The LGb(t) movement paved the way for acceptance using this slogan. The asexual movement has followed in these footsteps to some extent, and that's understandable. With asexual people persistently being told that we just haven't met the right person yet, or being asked if we just don't like sex because we were abused in the past, "born this way" can be a useful shield. But here's the thing: I *am* an abuse survivor, and the "born this way" narrative for a long time made the ace community feel unwelcoming to me. I genuinely don't know if I was born this way, or if my experience of abuse contributed to the way I do and don't experience sexual attraction. I needed to come to terms with the fact that I will *never* know who I might have been if I hadn't been abused, and that all I have to go on are my feelings and experiences as they are now. And those experiences can be best described as "bi + grey-a".'

Amanda

So does that mean that sexuality and gender are a choice?

'In some ways I feel it is a choice—not so much how you feel, but what you decide to do with those feelings. Coming out—I don't care who it's to, if they're the world's most accepting person, if they're twenty different forms of not-straight and trans to boot—coming out is a big deal. And I think there's no bigger deal than coming out to yourself. Yeah, you choose to do that. You choose not to ignore it when in some very real ways ignoring it would be so easy.'

Lou

'I think the more relevant question is: does it matter? And the answer to that is no. Of course it doesn't matter. And if you think it does, I'm not so sure you get to say you're an ally. If your support is conditional on it being a choice or being innate or being something that an owl drops off for you on your eleventh birthday—that's not support.'

Jax

However, it is also worth noting that for some people the 'born this way' narrative itself may well be subversive: for people whose cultural backgrounds are at odds with Western gender narratives, or for intersex people who have themselves reclaimed their intersex status, or whose parents fought against coercive regendering at birth, there is the risk of erasure from our refutation of the 'born this way' narrative.

Political Sexuality (or, 'The Threat You Pose Overrides Any Possible Attraction to You')

When discussing political sexuality, it is likely that your first association will be with political lesbianism. This is largely—but not exclusively—derived from the separatist movement that formed a part of second-wave feminism. A simplistic example is that a number of radical feminists rejected heterosexuality as a structure inherent in the upholding of the patriarchy and opted instead to interact solely with other women. Some political lesbians had sexual and/or romantic relationships with women; others remained celibate.

Common criticisms of the movement centre on the treatment of transgender women by Trans-Exclusionary (or Eradicative) (Radical) Feminists (TERFs). They wilfully misgender trans women, and there have been examples of trans women and transfeminine people being doxxed, stalked and harassed by members of this movement, who often do not acknowledge transgender identities as valid. (Doxxing is when someone makes personal information about you, like your address, public.)

Bisexual women are also often targeted by the lesbian separatism movement:

'I've seen radical feminists blame bisexual women for the rape of lesbians, neglecting the fact that bisexual women are raped and sexually assaulted at alarmingly high rates. An incredibly common phrase is "making themselves sexually available to men", or arguing that all man-woman sex is rape. This denies bisexual women their agency in two ways: one, that no woman can ever possibly consent to sex with a man; two, that somehow by dating men, whatever violence happens to us is our fault. And not only are we blamed for men's violence towards us, but we also are forced to bear responsibility for the rape of lesbians too?'

Ania

There are also criticisms which address the appropriation of the term 'lesbian'. There are some complexities here worth unpicking. Women who are exclusively attracted to men and choose to remain celibate do not experience the same oppression as women exclusively attracted to women (or as asexual people, for that matter), and their use of the word 'lesbian' would legitimately be seen as appropriative. However, in the eyes of most modern bisexual communities, a woman who is attracted to men and women (and possibly other genders) and chooses to not have sex with men is still bisexual. It is important to take into account the historical context in which these terms are used as they do evolve, often quite rapidly, as well as respect individuals' own labels — where they are not actively oppressive of other marginalised communities.

So political sexuality is bad?
Not inherently, no. As with any facet of your identity, the key is about exploring the reasons why you feel that way. Some choices are rooted

in bigotry: 'I won't date black women' is undeniably racist, and the thinking behind that choice needs intense and honest self-scrutiny.

> 'A friend once told me, "I'd never date a [transgender woman]. I'm not transphobic, they just have too much emotional baggage and I couldn't deal with penises." She just made the assumption that every trans woman has a penis, and that the emotional baggage of cis people (because we all have it) was somehow lesser or better than that of trans women. Whatever you want to say about that, it's not "not transphobic".'
> Anon

But many people make choices as to who they'll date and/or have sexual interactions with based on axes of oppression.

> 'I sometimes—mostly as a joke—identify as a misandric pansexual. I experience attraction to men, but I have difficulties trusting them in a sexual or romantic context. As a transfeminine person, it can not only be unpleasant to deal with the transmisogyny men often bring, but also actively dangerous.'
> Charlie

Wait, so how come you can say it's fine to not want to date men but not okay to say you'd never date a trans woman?

> 'There's a phrase in anti-oppression activism that sums this up: "You punch up." Choosing not to date someone on the basis of an arbitrary set of traits you assume all [oppressed group] people have? There's probably some underlying bigotry there. But refusing to play Russian roulette in your dating life because of an oppression they exert over you? That's a whole different story.'
> Robyn

(You'll note that our criticisms of political lesbianism *do not* include 'It's unfair towards men.')

Is kinky queer?

BDSM (bondage and discipline, domination and submission, sadism and masochism) is an umbrella term for a variety of (often, but not always, sexual) activities generally considered to be 'kinky'.

> 'I tend to think of the bi and poly parts of my identity as being about the relationships I want to form with people, and the kink part being about sex.'
> Anon

It's a contentious issue: should we include kink/BDSM in LGBTQIA+ spaces? Admittedly, there are some cisgender, heterosexual kinksters who believe that they are entitled to space in the LGBTQIA+ community and acronym by virtue of their kinkiness.

> 'As a member of FetLife [a social media site for members of the kink scene], it's incredible just how many straight people tell me they "totally get the being queer thing" because of their kinks. They like the appearance of being transgressive, the idea of being queer—without dealing with any of the difficulties. The most staggering example was a piece of writing by someone who felt that, as a heterosexual couple, their exploration of the dominant-male and submissive-female roles were so performative, so very heterosexual, it went full circle and ended up somehow queer.'
> Kim

And whilst a number of LGBTQIA+ subcultures are *also* BDSM/kink orientated, the 'oppression tourism' many LGBTQIA+ kinksters highlight requires a nuanced understanding.

> 'Historically, S&M plays a massive role in the reclaiming of queer sexuality. It's brash, in your face, unapologetic. It's why some Pride marches still have kink clubs or dungeons marching with them. Just look at the gay leather scene, or the politics of lesbian S/M scenes, especially in the '80s. But it has context. It's meant to be radical. But you acknowledge the power you have, and if you're part of an oppressing class—and this

means if you're rich, or white, or whatever as well as straight—you own that. You don't jump up for a piggyback on the very people fighting against oppression. You ****ing give the piggyback.'

Jax

Charlie Hale, feminist and BDSM writer, notes that there is a problematic assumption that LGBTQIA+ identities are inherently sexual.

'Even without the added context of BDSM, LGBTQIA+ people are seen as oversexualised, as sexual deviants, or even as dangerous and predatory. It's clear that these perceptions differ between groups within the community—with trans women and transfeminine people often perceived to be a sexual threat by their mere existence—but each group in the LGBTQIA+ umbrella has, to some extent, the issue of being almost entirely defined by perceived-as-abnormal sexual activity by the cishet world.'

Charlie Hale

But haven't there been cases where people have been taken to court or outed in the media for being kinky?

'The overwhelming majority of substantive social stigma is immediately aimed towards LGBTQIA+ people: media circuses surrounding the details of trans politicians' sex lives, court cases attempting to criminalise the consensual sexual behaviour of gay men. By comparison, cishet kink is treated more as a curiosity than an issue of public shame or even perceived danger.'

Charlie Hale

Ultimately, though kink issues often are queer issues, that's not because being kinky makes you queer, but because of the sheer number of people who are both. The kink scene is disproportionately queer relative to the wider population.

However, that's not to say kink can't be a factor in exploration of sexuality and a big factor in queer people's lives. For many LGBTQIA+

kinky people, munches (social gatherings of people involved in the BDSM community that don't involve any BDSM or sexual activity) can be a vital source of community.

'Being kinky has meant that I have met more queer folk, I have learned a lot more about consent and communication, and I feel more comfortable about expressing my interests and nerdiness in general.'
Starling

For some, discovering the distinction between kink and other sexual expression helps them define their own identities:

'I began to feel that the term "bisexual" didn't fit me when I stopped making love with men and started letting them fuck me. Hard. I stopped dating men and began to identify publicly as lesbian. I didn't stop sexual contact with men. I like the gender dynamics at play in our scenes. Kinky sex with women has never had the same kick for me. I love my girlfriend for her own quirks, and BDSM does not have a place in our relationship. Technically I am bisexual—I do sleep with men and women—but I don't use that word. My sexuality embraces men and women but in different ways and in separate contexts. Identifying this for myself has been a positive step in understanding my own sexuality and freed me from a label I never felt comfortable using.

Ultimately, identification is not what others decide, but what you know about yourself. If the words which currently exist are insufficient, find your own label.'
Jenny Guérin

The focus on consent and communication in some kink communities can help people reclaim physical intimacy after abuse.

'For me, kink is about connection and respect. It has a place in my relationships [where the other person is interested] as time together where we are very intently focused on each other. It is a time when I feel really seen by the other person. I enjoy the intense sensations. It can make me feel kind of floaty, and the care my partners take of me in that space makes me feel loved. I know I can ask for what I want, and it always stops when I say stop. Consent in this is key, and the experience of my partner respecting that is affirming to our relationship.'

Anon

And for some, it can help them explore their sexual tastes and inclinations outside of a conventional narrative.

'Creativity is what I think defines queer, nerdy, kinky sex: the ability to experiment and—as is often essential in the case of trans people—improvise. The world outside of cisheteronormative sex is a wonderful one, but the social scripts surrounding sex are so strong that it doesn't really come easily. [But] we can try to offer a dissenting voice [...] Not everyone has to be kinky or queer—or even have sex at all—but everyone should at least be told there are other options.'

Charlie Hale, in 'You Trans-sexy Thing'

When words aren't enough

One of the problems inherent in (Western) LGBTQIA+ linguistics is that almost all of our terminology stems from cisheteronormative language. Whether it's from medical discourse such as 'bisexual' or from slurs such as 'queer', how we speak about ourselves has roots in narratives invested *against* us.

As a result, many of us lack the ability to describe our experiences and feelings with true accuracy.

'I describe myself as bisexual, but my sexuality is actually a bit more complicated than that, and I do not have a label that totally fits. If I was walking down your average high street on a Saturday afternoon, there would probably not be a single man that I saw there that I would be attracted to. All my male partners have been cross-dressers, and that is mainly the type of man I am attracted to. I wouldn't say this was a fetish: I am attracted to the whole person, not just the feminine clothes and make-up (although that image is what attracts me initially). Furthermore, when I started going to lesbian clubs in the 1990s it was also often the case that there was not a single woman in the club that I found attractive; at the time, the majority of women on the "scene" dressed and looked quite "butch", and that does not appeal to me. I would say that, overall, I am attracted to femininity rather than masculinity in both men and women. Is this a different type of bisexuality and, if so, what shall we call it?'

Mary

'Bi didn't feel right because to me it implied sexual attraction to men, lesbian wasn't right because I still had some sort of attraction to men... I dithered over whether or not to identify as "queer" but decided it was useless as a label because no one knew what it meant. LB friends called me things like "basically a lesbian", "close enough". At twenty I was starting to properly fret, starting to worry about my "ethereal and indefinable" attraction to men, and whether it was "continued conforming to societal norms from seven years in the closet". (Never reread your old LiveJournal, folks.)'

Mharie

For some, reclaiming the term 'queer'—which started being applied as a slur to non-cishet people (and initially men in particular) in the early twentieth century and began to be reclaimed in the 1980s—is a solution to this problem.

'I feel I've spent my life kicking back at how other people want me to be: I wasn't straight, then I wasn't gay enough, then I wasn't even doing bisexuality as people expected me to. I don't want to be fobbed off by "but you can get married now", and I have no intention of being quiet about injustice. I've had straight people say that "queer" is too confrontational, too uncomfortable—good. That's precisely what I'm going for.'

Jax

Anyone who is a member of an oppressed group can reclaim a slur used against that group. Slurs should not be reclaimed by people who are assumed to be a part of that group: for instance, men who are read as gay but are in fact cishet cannot reclaim the *F* slur.

Additionally, slurs cannot be claimed on someone's behalf without their consent, even by a fellow member of that oppressed group. A woman should not call another woman the b-word unless she has her explicit consent to do so.

For those reclaiming 'queer', this can cause complications.

> 'I use "queer" as a self-descriptor, but I volunteer with a group run by people who were gay and lesbian activists in the '70s and '80s—in other words, people who've had "queer" shouted at them on marches and used as a form of violence. Because it's got such potential to trigger them, I don't use the word in those spaces, even referring to myself. It's partly a sign of respect to people who paved the way for me to be so completely myself, but it's also basic human compassion: I don't want my words to hurt others.'
>
> Meg

The use of 'gay' as a way of saying 'not straight' is another approach to the problem. As you might expect, it comes under criticism of erasure from both traditional gay and bi communities alike. But with such prolific use of 'gay' as meaning 'LGB' in mainstream media, and the fact that a distinction between the terms with regards to identity is still relatively new (before modern bisexual politics emerged, any woman who engaged in same-gender relationships and/or sexual activity was termed a lesbian), it's little wonder the term still bears some wider credence.

Another term often used by the media is 'sexual fluidity'; like 'genderfluid', it refers to the ongoing shifting of identities. It is often mistaken as a wider and more euphemistic term for bisexuality: a mistake which manages to erase bisexuals and sexually fluid people alike.

> 'I guess I'm bisexual in that I do experience attraction to more than one gender, but I'm also gay because of how my desires and my gender

interplay. I'm not sure which has more of an effect on the other, but basically, if I fancy a woman then I'm in a sort of womanish mode and if I'm in a boyish mode then I fancy men.'
  Katherine/Tom

'I hear a lot of conflation of "bisexual" with "fluid", which riles me because I have experienced my sexual orientation as being pretty static for my entire post-pubescent life. As a non-binary trans bisexual person, I am doubly sick of being called fluid. I am solid! I retain my shape!'
  Fred

With both of the above linguistic approaches, whilst it's crucial to explore the impact of biphobia and bi erasure in a society-wide refusal to say 'bisexual'—especially in the media—it's also crucial to acknowledge individual autonomy. We may apply one set of rules to scrutinising fictional characters and media discussion of bisexuality (see chapter 13) and quite another when discussing an individual's choice of language.

Perhaps the most flexible solution is the 'pick 'n' mix' approach to language: mixing the '-sexual' and '-romantic' roots with various prefixes. And frankly, if one of the most famous queer writers of all time can establish approximately two thousand new words into the English language, we can certainly follow in Shakespeare's footsteps and coin a few new terms to more accurately describe our experiences.

'I still find the intricacies of aesthetic, romantic and sexual attraction too complex to untangle, but I have adopted the label "bi + grey-a" for myself, which in slightly longer words I use to mean "attracted to people regardless of gender in the rare instances when I can be bothered to be attracted to people at all".'
  Amanda

And whilst many advocate for a 'labels are for soup cans' approach, there's no denying the power of finding the terminology that fits you.

'I could finally describe what I felt. And what's more, I could describe it using existing words, which made it easier for others to understand what I meant. Now don't get me wrong, people still don't understand, because [...] if you don't experience romantic and sexual attraction separately, then they feel linked together, and people don't seem able to imagine them apart. But some people understand, thanks to that terminology.'
Mharie

From being able to explain your identity more clearly, to having access to communities of similar people, to the feeling of 'Others feel this way? That means I'm not broken', the language we use, personally and in wider spaces, has real impact.

'Having taken the step of expanding the label I use for my sexuality, I think we need to find more ways of opening up possibilities for people to do that. We as people grow and change. Our understanding of the world and ourselves changes. We develop and acquire new languages to talk about our feelings and experiences, and the expectation that we will work out what our sexuality is in our early teens and it will remain fixed for the rest of our lives just seems unrealistic to me.'
Amanda

10

BISEXUALS AND FAITH

Editor: Symon Hill

'I remember the rush I got when I first gave thanks to God for sex in prayer,' says Natalie. 'It was like a massive weight had been lifted from me, and I no longer felt guilty about who I was or what I was into.' Natalie is bisexual and kinky. She is now training for the priesthood in a major Christian denomination.

It's an odd thing that discussions about sexuality and religion usually begin with questions framed in negative terms. We tend to ask: Is being bisexual compatible with being Muslim? Or Christian? Or Hindu? What are the tensions between your faith and your sexuality? Debates in religious circles often ask whether bisexuality and homosexuality should be 'tolerated'.

Assumptions about religion and sexuality lead many religious bisexuals—as well as other religious LGBTQIA+ people—to speak in defensive terms. We start with responses to the criticisms of religious 'conservatives' and the surprise of secular liberals. We talk about how our faith and our sexuality are 'compatible' as if the most that we could hope for is that they don't contradict each other.

But there is another set of questions we could ask. How does our faith affect our sex life? How does our sexuality inform our image of the divine? Is our relationship with God anything like our sexual relationships? How does our experience of bisexuality affect our religion's teaching on gender? Are our sexual ethics rooted in our faith, and do we manage to stick to them?

For some people, sexuality and spirituality are not distantly separated aspects of life but integral parts of each other. The links are deeper, stronger and more entangled than can be conveyed by words such as 'compatibility' and 'tolerance'. Many religious people say that their faith informs the whole of their life, including their sexuality. Others explain the link differently. This is not a new thing. Medieval Christian mystics spoke of their love for Christ in terms that border on the sexual. The eighth-century Muslim writer Rabiah took a similar approach to God in her poetry.

Being Religious, Sexually

In the midst of recent controversies about religion and sexuality, there has been an increased emphasis in many circles on celebrating sexuality as a gift from God. Natalie says, 'I know God loves me and created me to be bisexual and kinky and smiles upon that part of me, providing I don't abuse it.'

Others point to religious teachings that emphasise love and treating others as we wish to be treated, a principle common to virtually all religions. 'My spiritual practice affects everything I do,' says Alice Fleabite, who is Jewish. 'When I follow my religious practice, I think it makes me a better person in all areas of my life, including my relationships.' Ozge, a Muslim teenager, points out that Islam teaches love for all. She says, 'The day I finally accepted myself as who I am didn't change my relationship with God. I still practise my religion as I would if I were heterosexual.'

Faith-based ethics are central for many religious bisexuals when it comes to living out their sexuality. Amaranta Lily quotes the Pagan idea that our actions will rebound on us three times over. She therefore seeks to treat others as she wishes to be treated, in sexual contexts as well as others.

> 'The biggest way that it manifests for me is that I am absolutely militant about consent. I consider it when I'm in any sort of interaction, any sort of romantic or sexual interaction. For me, freely given enthusiastic consent is the bare minimum, that's the starting point.
>
> And in terms of the wider community, I try to campaign for greater awareness of consent and how to treat each other in a way that honours and respects that. And I think being a feminist has a big part in that as well.'
>
> Amaranta

Amaranta also cites the Pagan principle of 'do no harm', a phrase also found in other religious traditions. 'Buddhism is very much based on moderation—the middle path—and "do no harm",' says Qing, a Buddhist. 'In that vein, as long as I don't kill anyone, lie to anyone—and this includes cheating—or cause anyone harm, then my sex life is ethical.'

There are uncountable other ways in which faith and sexuality can inform each other. Julie, a bisexual Christian and former Pagan, told me that 'being around conversations in bi spaces about how sexuality can change and be fluid over time (and that's okay) has made me more okay with the fact that my faith and spirituality have changed over time too.'

Keisha, a bisexual Seventh-day Adventist, rejected the homophobic and biphobic teachings that came from her church when she was growing up. But she explains that her faith has deepened, not lessened, and that it continues to inform how she understands her sexuality.

> 'I've learned not to stop at surface rules or teachings but to look for the higher principles that the rules are based on or point to. As far as sexual ethics go, I use themes like mutuality, respect, compassion, pleasure, beauty, communication, commitment, loyalty, trust, integrity, honesty and intimacy as my touchstones. My faith teaches me that both I and my partner are the children of God, and we merit respect on that basis...

I'm still pretty private about my sexuality; for me that's an expression of respect for it and the sacredness of the space partners can create with each other. A sanctuary is different from a hiking trail! I think that that sense of difference comes directly from Adventism's distinctions between the "common" and the "holy".'

Keisha

Natalie found that her sexuality and her theology began to inform each other more after she started blogging on the links between them.

'My sexuality didn't really affect my faith until I started blogging about BDSM and theology recently. I suppose BDSM, particularly the psychology behind it, can give me new ways of looking at the scriptures and understanding our relationship with God as well as offering new language to describe this relationship.

Whilst I do hold a more liberal view on sexual ethics than most Christians, my faith does still inform some of it. For example, I believe that marriage should be monogamous between those who have been married; if you can't or don't want to be monogamous, don't get married. I also believe that sex is a holy thing and should not be treated lightly or rushed into. I would say that a one-night stand or going out "on the pull" would be ethically wrong, as they tend to see sex as a quick fix and the other person as disposable. This is where my faith informs my ethics most; it is in how we see the other person rather than the act of sex itself. Of course, I'm still working this out, and my views may change in time.

I have never doubted that alternative sexualities and gender expressions, be they gay, bi, kink, poly, trans, are not sinful or against God.'

Natalie

Of course, many non-religious people also seek to live by high ethical standards in sexual relationships. Religion has no monopoly on morality. Some religious bisexuals find that the way they make ethical decisions is affected by their faith. S, a bisexual Quaker, says, 'Quakerism involves guidance by the spirit, a belief if we wrestle with the angel we will find a guidance that brings unity between us, and rules need to be read in that light.' He adds, 'This applies to discerning how we live in the social and economic world as well as to particular sexual behaviour.' For some, belonging to a faith community provides strength and guidance when it comes to living ethically. Fred, also a Quaker, says, 'Being part of a religious community that shares my values helps strengthen those values and my ability to live them.'

The Context: Religions Divided

It would be naive to overlook the reality that many bisexuals experience challenges about their sexuality from within their faith communities, as well as doubts or fears as to whether they are behaving ethically. At times, they encounter bigotry and vile treatment. Qing says, 'When my mother couldn't get me to deny I like girls, she tried to exorcise me.' There are numerous accounts of bisexuals and other LGBTQIA+ people being driven to suicide by social prejudice, often linked to a religious community.

Attitudes to bisexuality vary to some extent between religions. Even more so, they vary within them.

Traditionally, sexual relationships between people of the same gender have met with the strongest hostility in the Abrahamic religions (this family of religions includes Judaism, Christianity and Islam as well as smaller faith groups such as the Bahá'í faith). It can be argued that there has been less hostility in the Dharmic religions (this group includes Hinduism, Jainism, Buddhism and Sikhism). Religions deriving from East Asia are also sometimes presented as relatively tolerant, although faiths such as traditional Confucianism place a strong emphasis on observing family roles.

The problem with summaries of this sort is that each religion is extremely diverse. Groups within a religion may have different teachings. At the same time, some official teachings are enforced more than others. 'Pretty much all Jews in the UK are not going to have problems with my sexuality, even though according to the Law, they should have,' says Alice.

'In the UK, most Jews are Orthodox Jews. Even though the words that we speak are homophobic, I don't think many attitudes are homophobic, in the way you might find in some Christian communities. Everybody is aware that they don't keep the Law absolutely. It would be different among ultra-Orthodox Jews.'

Alice

Alice's comments on 'some Christian communities' are significant. Some decades ago, while most British Christians disapproved of same-sex relations, it was not an issue that they singled out. Things have changed. A number of conservative Christian groups are frightened of the widespread social and cultural changes that have come about since the second half of the twentieth century. Such changes are varied: a rise in immigration, the growth of a multifaith society, the decline in nominal Christian affiliation, the growth of abortion. But it is the rapidly changing attitudes to same-sex relationships that some of these people have latched on to. Right-wing Christian commentators such as Andrea Williams, director of the lobbying group Christian Concern, identify 1967 as the date when everything really started to go wrong. This was when Parliament legalised sex between men over twenty-one in England and Wales.

Opposition to LGBTQIA+ rights has become an obsession for hard-line Christian conservatives in Britain. This has embarrassed more moderate conservatives, even those who have a problem with same-sex relationships (but don't bang on about it all the time). Growing up in conservative Christian settings places an extra level of confusion and guilt feelings on teenagers struggling with their sexuality. Keisha was brought up as a Seventh-day Adventist by Jamaican parents in the UK.

'I grew up in the UK under Margaret Thatcher's tenure, and so I also grew up under Section 28 [the law that prevented schools from presenting same-sex relationships as acceptable]. I had heterosexual sex education in my secondary school but, as the law intended, I didn't learn any content regarding orientation or different kinds of marriage. Even when

I heard slurs like "bugger", "wanker" or "poof", they didn't have any substantive meaning to me. I only knew that they were vaguely sexual, that they were intended to hurt, that they were always aimed at boys, not girls, and that they seemed to be attacks on the boys' gender and/or masculinity. Beyond that it never occurred to me to dig deeper.

Part of that ignorance was class and culture—I seriously didn't know that [one of] the Monty Python gang, Elton John or Boy George were gay; I thought they just bent gender for entertainment and it was something they could do but the rest of us could/would never do. No one who looked like me or came from where I came from was openly different, so I never knew it was possible.

The other part of the ignorance was faith training. At church, there was only talk about "marriage", which involved a man and a woman; dating, which was preparation for marriage; and "sex before marriage", which interfered with education and would mean destroying one's life. Nothing else existed.

I'd say that my faith conspired with society to raise me with a completely inadequate language for my sexuality. I had to look beyond the church to get a solid, healthy self-understanding, and I think that's a shame.'

Keisha

Religious Biphobia

Several people told me that they found an apparent acceptance when coming out as bisexual in a faith community, only to find that the acceptance did not go as deep as they had expected. Ozge, a Muslim, felt happier after accepting that she was bisexual when she was seventeen. She started dating a woman and told two of her Muslim friends. Initially, they were positive, saying, 'As long as you're happy.' But over time, she noticed that they were not entirely comfortable with her sexuality.

'They told me things I did not want to hear, such as "You can't marry a woman. You're gonna marry a man, right?"

I came out to another Muslim friend, who is also part of the LGBTQ+ community, and obviously she was totally okay with my sexuality. I've decided that I would never come out to my family (who are Muslim too) because I don't think they would get it, and they would probably stop talking to me. They believe that as a woman, I am supposed to marry a man and have children.

Don't get me wrong, though; I know many Muslims don't think like that. Islam teaches to love and accept everyone. Some people just don't get that part.'

Ozge

Clearly, many of the problems faced by bisexuals in religious communities are the same as those experienced by their gay and lesbian counterparts. Nonetheless, there are some prejudices that are aimed at bisexuals specifically. Luke Zalman Griffiss-Williams was open about his bisexuality when applying to train as a Church of England priest. He was in a monogamous marriage with a woman, so did not expect his sexuality to be an issue. He was surprised when it was raised.

'I was sat down by a senior priest and asked about how I would deal with my bisexuality. What would I do if I really felt an urge for some cock?

As we seemed to be getting pretty personal, I asked the priest concerned whether his wife had big or small breasts. He told me she had small breasts. I asked him how he deals with the urge when he is really in the mood for huge breasts. I explained to him that it really is the same thing, that whether you are bisexual, heterosexual or homosexual, if you are in a monogamous relationship, the gender of people that you are attracted to does not mean that you suddenly become unable to overcome your desires.

Luke Zalman Griffiss-Williams

Biphobic attitudes are often linked to assumptions that bisexuals cannot be monogamous. Many religious communities have little understanding of polyamory, but this is not the issue here. Even monogamous bisexuals have to deal with an assumption that they will cheat on their partners. In 2015, I wrote a comment piece in the *Church Times* to mark Bisexual Visibility Day on 23 September. Two weeks later, the letters page included a letter from a reader who said that 'Homosexual behaviour may be tolerated' in an exclusive relationship, but that 'Bisexual behaviour cannot be anything other than promiscuity.' He asked, 'Is the author suggesting that the Church advocate sexual promiscuity?'

Since coming out as a bisexual Christian, I have found a number of Christians who are okay with people being gay but less okay with bisexuality. This is partly because of this prejudicial assumption about promiscuity. However, there are other reasons too. Within Christianity, 'conservative' Christians have often dictated the terms of the debate, putting the pro-equality wing on the defensive. Thus, debates get bogged down in contrasting interpretations of the tiny number of biblical passages that can be interpreted as forbidding same-sex relationships.

One of the most bizarre 'liberal' arguments is to claim that the apparent condemnations of homosexual behaviour in the Bible are not condemning gay people but were aimed at heterosexuals who were also interested in sex with people of their own gender.

I am surprised how often this argument is made. As a bisexual, I struggle to make sense of it. Who are these 'heterosexual' people who are interested in sex with people of their own gender? I can suggest a word for people who are sexually attracted to both men and women; it is not 'heterosexual'. The logical conclusion of this argument is that these passages are not condemning gay and lesbian people; they are condemning bisexuals.

Leaving, Staying, Joining

In light of all this, it is necessary to emphasise that many bisexuals do have a positive experience of belonging to a religious community, whether it be one in which they have grown up or one they have joined in adulthood.

Fred grew up in a LGBTQIA+-friendly Baptist church, was baptised at the age of sixteen and remained a Baptist until attending university. Fred describes what happened next.

'In terms of my choice of religious community, my sexuality had quite a significant influence: when I left home and the liberal, LGBT-friendly church I'd been involved with there, it was very important to me to find an equally welcoming church to settle at as an adult. After some deliberate exploration and some flailing, Quaker Meetings fitted my requirements in that area very well...

Quakerism's a good fit for me in lots of ways, but being able to be open about my whole life, including my sexuality and my gender (I'm trans), is vitally important.

I'm lucky: LGB (and more recently T) people have been welcomed in British Quakerism for a long time, and my religious community has done a lot of work to seek equality for us in society more widely.'

Fred

Not every religious bisexual was religious before coming out as bisexual. Some have joined a religion as openly bisexual adults. Amaranta says she was drawn to the Neo-Pagan community partly because she found it to be 'a fairly progressive space in terms of being accepting of all different sexualities and sexual and gender identities'. She explains: 'There's a lot of crossover between polyamory and Paganism in particular, and Paganism and kink.'

Others go in the other direction, leaving a religious community because of biphobia. This does not necessarily mean that they abandon their faith. Amy is a bisexual Christian who no longer goes to church.

'I know many Christians that I've come out as bisexual to, but I've not found a church where I've come out as bisexual and found accepting attitudes.

I've had nice door-to-door preachers come by who I always let in, because I like talking about the Bible and that sort of thing, who have then been quite pushy in trying to save my soul because they've found out I'm bisexual. Because that, not all the other sins that are sins, is obviously the thing that's going to send me to Hell!

I don't go to church. To be honest, I don't see going to church as a thing that is essential to my religion at all due to the fact that Jesus kind of tore down the Temple and said that, you know, you don't need a priest to be an intermediary to me, you can speak to me directly by prayer. So a priest is not an essential part.'

Amy

Many bisexuals have left one faith community to join another that is more affirming. Julie left a Christian denomination with a poor track record on acceptance of LGBTQIA+ people, and for a long time she felt 'as though being queer meant I didn't have a place in the church'. She then deliberately sought out faith groups with a reputation for being more accepting, such as Unitarians and Quakers. She spent several years as a Pagan. However, she says that none of these groups was her 'forever home'. Things then took a surprising turn when she became interested in High Church Anglicanism.

'Some friends of mine invited me to their (very "high") Anglican church over Easter and I went on Good Friday and again on Easter Sunday. This seemed like a good point in the year to start going regularly, and I thought I would do a year and see how I went.

I sat down with my cousin (who was raised in the same denomination I was but who is now a priest at a fairly high Anglican church elsewhere in the country), and we decided on a local church for me that we thought would have the level of music and liturgy that I was looking for but that also had a priest who was well known to be gay.

I've settled in, joined the choir, been baptised and am going to be confirmed. I even gave myself queer-friendly middle names when I got baptised, ones that are relevant to my personal spiritual path. I don't think there's any doubt that I'll stay beyond the year that I initially gave myself. I sometimes worry about finding somewhere else equally suitable if I ever have to move. But for now I am very happy in a church where, for example, my priest publicly refers to my baptism as an LGBTQIA chris-tening and is careful to use gender-neutral language when talking about sending bras to Africa.'

Julie

There are many people who remain in faith groups that are less than accepting. Sometimes they seek to change them from within, or they may consider that, apart from its attitude to sexuality, the group in question reflects their beliefs and spirituality. Alice says, 'In some ways it would be easier if I wasn't an Orthodox Jew. In London there's a Reform synagogue that has a lesbian rabbi. I wouldn't even have a woman rabbi in the Orthodox tradition, let alone a homosex-ual woman rabbi!' But Alice has chosen not to join Reform Judaism. 'I feel spiritually drawn towards Orthodox Judaism in a way that I don't to Reform Judaism,' she explains. 'Orthodox Judaism meets my spiritual needs.'

Increasingly, 'conservative' religious groups include members who are seeking to change attitudes to LGBTQIA+ people. Keisha remains in the Seventh-day Adventist Church while being bisexual and living in a same-sex relationship.

'Shortly after I came out to myself, I got in touch with a local region of Seventh-day Adventist Kinship International, which serves and sup-ports LGBTI current and former Adventists. Connecting with that group of people when I did helped to save my faith and my relationship with the wider denomination...

I feel more spiritually coherent than I ever did before, and I didn't realise I would. I actually blame my spiritual growth for prompting me to be more open and intentional about my sexuality. And I'm grateful for it.

My local ministers know who my partner and I are to each other. I also shared a resource on bisexuality, faith and improving congregational support with one of my pastors a couple of months ago, but following up with him about it hasn't been high on my priority list. When my partner faced cancer a couple of years ago, two of the ministers checked in with us and one visited us at the hospital.'

Keisha

Others who remain active in their religious communities feel the need to keep quiet about their bisexuality. For some, this may involve a lifetime of suppressing the truth, or else being very selective about who they choose to be open with. I interviewed a bisexual Muslim (who wishes to remain anonymous) who is open about himself on-line, allowing him to meet other gay and bisexual Muslims on the Internet and to discuss issues of faith and sexuality. But he is not open in what he calls 'real life'. On the Web, he hides the details of his identity.

I have often heard bisexual members of 'conservative' faith communities express their admiration for those religious members with a reputation for acceptance. However, even 'liberal' groups have their prejudiced members, or those who avoid controversial issues for the sake of unity. S is a bisexual Quaker.

'Since becoming a Quaker, there have been many other issues, identities and challenges, so my sexuality is not the most important. One issue, however, is that Quakers who are happy to sound off about complex issues like advancing the Middle East peace process, re-engineering our economy for a green future, etc. tend to keep their heads down on sexuality.

The Quaker campaign for same-sex marriage was driven through Quaker unhappiness about being told what to do about our own marriages by the state. Straight Quakers tend to see sexuality as a pastoral issue, not a justice issue. But more and more Quaker Meetings openly support their local Pride, etc. I still have more good stories about acceptance than bad stories about stupidity.'

S

Coming Out Twice: Telling Bisexuals You're Religious

Many religious bisexuals have to 'come out twice'. They have come out as a bisexual in their faith community, and as a religious person to other bisexuals. Some find bisexual communities to be affirming or at least accepting of their religious identity. At other times, there is hostility. A Sikh told me of the prejudice he had encountered in LGBT pubs in Brighton. On one occasion, he met someone at a bar who, noticing his turban, asked, 'Are you wearing that for a bet?'

Most of my interviewees say that anti-religious reactions in bisexual spaces are in the minority, but are not unheard of. Amaranta describes a mixed experience.

'You say in a bisexual space "I'm Pagan" and someone will say, "Oh, me too", which is really nice.

There is a corner, there is a community that's fairly, I guess, militantly atheist. And that also has a lot of crossover with queer/poly/kink space. And some of the attitudes within those circles seem to be that anyone who has any kind of religious belief is stupid and deluded and living in cloud-cuckoo land or whatever. So I do find that off-putting in some ways because I think it could be hard to tell until you know people quite well, within the bi community and so forth, whether they kind of fall into that camp who are likely to say "Oh, you shouldn't believe in mythical beings in the sky, you should believe in science." So, yeah, that can be tricky sometimes with there being a lot of crossover there.

But mostly it's been fairly positive. I think when people are open-minded about one thing they tend to be open-minded about everything. Which is probably why there's so much queer/bi/poly/kinky/ Pagan crossover.'

Amy has also had mixed experiences when coming out in queer spaces, in her case as a Christian. She says, 'Some people are very interested in how you can be both. You'll speak to other people who were Christian and have left the faith and would not ever consider ever going back.' She also finds that some bisexuals expect her to be 'really judgemental'. Others have assumed that conservative Christians are accurate in their statements about the Bible forbidding same-sex relationships, leading to conversations in which Amy explains that this is based on 'digging out passages' from their contexts.

Julie has told her bisexual friends that she is no longer Pagan but has become a Christian. 'Some people who had a horrible time coming out to their own faith communities have been concerned for my welfare,' she explains. 'Mostly, though, people have been hugely supportive, even when they don't understand it.' She was unsure what to expect when inviting them to her baptism.

> 'When I was baptised, a big group of LGBT friends came, of various faiths and none. They were invited to join in the service in various ways, and it was a really beautiful day. I had had my fears about mixing the various bits of my life in one place (my queer friends, my family of origin and the congregation at my church), but it all went really, really well!'

Natalie initially built up friendships with other bisexuals and kinksters without revealing that she was training for the Christian priesthood. She then decided to tell them.

> 'When I first entered the kink scene, I kept it [her Christian identity] hidden because I didn't want people to look down on my faith or think I was some sort of prude judging everyone. However, I also knew that part of my keeping it secret was because I didn't want to run the risk of the church finding out and kicking me out, so even though I was keeping it a secret from the LGBT+ and kink scenes, it was because I was more concerned of Christians finding out.
>
> I eventually made the decision to "come out" as a priest-in-training to the kink community, as I wanted to find a way of bringing the two sides of me together and (ironically) knew that the kink community would be far more welcoming, accepting and loving than the church would be if I came out as kinky and queer to them.
>
> A few of my friends were completely shocked; they had no idea, and I think one was hurt, though more that I'd kept a secret from them

rather than what the secret actually was. Most people I tell in both the LGBT+ and kink scenes are surprised but genuinely interested. Though it's mostly an interest in why I'm training to be a priest rather than how I wed my sexuality and faith together. It seems to be a non-issue with most people. I've never had any grief from anyone about it, thankfully.'

My own experiences of coming out at as Christian among bisexuals have been largely positive but have led to surprising results. When I decided to accept my own sexuality, I determined that I would not lead a double life. I would be open about my Christian faith in queer contexts. It has not always been easy to have the confidence to do this.

As an author and activist, I have found myself speaking about religion and sexuality to churches and to Christian groups. This is what I expected. What I did not expect was the number of secular LGBTQIA+ groups, and non-religious individuals and queer conferences that wanted to hear what I had to say. I have felt privileged to be part of absorbing discussions about the Bible at BiCon (the annual bisexual convention in the UK) and at LGBTQIA+ societies at universities. Leading a workshop on Christianity in a fetish club is an experience I am unlikely to forget.

In other words, I have found myself not only talking with Christians about sex but also (as it were) telling queers about Jesus.

What Now?

How will things develop in the future? What are the expectations of the people we have met in this chapter? Natalie hopes that she will one day be able to be open as a kinky, bisexual Christian priest. Ozge fears the pressure to marry a man rather than a woman: now nineteen, she says, 'I feel like there will always be a part of me that will feel guilty.' Alice is confident that most Orthodox Jews in the UK will continue to be okay with bisexuality regardless of official teachings; her hopes for change in the community are focused on other issues. Keisha seeks change within her own denomination of Seventh-day

Adventism. Julie seems confident that she has found her spiritual home in a pro-LGBTQIA+, high Anglican church.

I will give the final word to Kathleen Jowitt, who demonstrates that poetry can sometimes convey more than prose. Her poem is called 'Circles'. Here it is:

> *I wear a ring, no collar; hurried through*
> *the controversial sacrament aware*
> *of having failed to knock upon that other door,*
> *scared, fearing finding tasks impossible,*
> *and dreading how I might hear 'No';*
> *not brave enough to strip my soul bare, then;*
> *at last turning myself away from service—*
>
> *And now I know: I might have swapped these rounds,*
> *ensnared myself within the confines*
> *of a different circle, and be fighting now*
> *a different battle—one that I fight yet:*
>
> *For all the women that I might have been—*
> *the pilgrim, pedant, poet, priest—and those*
> *I might be yet, lie coiled within my soul,*
> *not lost, but sleeping—and*
> *the one whose love she cannot bring*
> *into the sanctuary: for her I write:*
>
> *Dear Editor, dear Bishop, I,*
> *a member of this Church of which*
> *I am ashamed, write to express*
> *the disappointment, dolour and disgust*
> *with which I greet the Church of England's stance*
> *on same-sex marriage, and the way*
> *the clergy's treated. I, lay and married,*
> *bear witness still in such small ways as this,*
> *telling you: I'm queer, here in the pews,*

and here I'll stay (can do no other), till
the Church can demonstrate it knows
the meaning of its greatest message, love,
Just so you're absolutely clear that
I remain,
Yours,
Mrs. A. Bisexual (one of many)

—And though I walk the gentle path,
still this I know: it might have gone
the other way, and so I fight.
I fight in guilt and gratitude for having
had it easy—for my friends
hurt deeper in the heart than I could claim
—but most, for this: it might
have fallen so to me, and still it might.

11

BISEXUAL THROUGH THE YEARS: LIFE EXPERIENCES

Editor: Kate Harrad

Content note: mention of suicide on pages 209, 211 and 231; references to bullying on pages 207–208, 210–211, 217 and 221.

Here we look at what it's like to be bisexual at different stages of life, mostly through people's personal experiences.

Biphobia in Schools

'A large 2006 survey found that 65% of young LGB people had experienced direct bullying in UK schools (75% in religious schools), and 98% had heard LGB-specific insults (notably 'That's so gay' used pejoratively)....58% of people never reported the bullying. For those who did, 65% reported that nothing was done about it.

...The UK reports on LGB experiences in schools do not address bisexual experiences specifically, and internationally bisexuality in schools has been a neglected topic due to bisexual invisibility. International studies which have addressed the experience of young bisexual people specifically tend to find that, in response to the stigma they face, they have higher levels of identity confusion and lower levels of self-disclosure and community connection compared to lesbian and gay peers. Participants in one qualitative Australian study which did explore the experiences of young bisexual people specifically found mention of many of the forms of biphobia listed above, including the assumption that bisexual girls would be sexually attracted to everybody and would want to engage in threesomes; pressure to identify as gay or lesbian and "prove gayness" so as not to be further ostracised; as well as physical and sexual attack.

...Recently in the UK, a school student spoke out publicly about his experience of biphobic bullying in school after he came out as bisexual at the age of fourteen. He was bombarded with abuse on his social networking site and started self-harming. Through the Manchester Lesbian and Gay Foundation he is now part of a campaign challenging such bullying through presenting to assemblies in local schools. It is also important to remember that these issues may be faced in schools by children of bisexual parents, as well as those who are bisexual themselves. Suggestions for tackling bisexual issues in schools can be found in some recent US research, but have yet to be translated into a UK context.'

From the *Bisexuality Report,* p. 23

My harmful heteronormative education
I was born the year before Section 28 was introduced, so with two exceptions, nothing LGBT+ was ever shown or mentioned by teachers at school. There was nothing in the syllabus either. Before I write about these two exceptions though, let me take you through a brief history of my education...

In primary school nothing LGBT+ was ever mentioned. We had sex-education lessons in Y6 (10–11 years old), but this was mostly about how our bodies changed during puberty. We watched videos that explained that one adult woman and one adult man could have sex, and that having sex made a baby. I remember having to draw pubic hair on sketches of a naked man and woman (!). I also remember the act of sex itself being shown by a cartoon of two cats rubbing vigorously against each other (!!). The video understandably left me feeling confused and gave me more questions than answers.

I didn't know what I was at the time, I didn't even know there was a word to describe it, but from a very early age I knew I liked more than one gender. From the age of about 8 I had posters of Jet from the Gladiators on my wall along with several female characters from Baywatch. When an attractive, female teacher in training gave everyone in the class a Christmas card, I kept mine for a long time afterwards because I liked her so much. I kissed boys I liked. I never felt like I was wrong or disgusting, but by the time I finished primary school I was keenly aware of the fact that no one else was apparently like me. Sex ed taught me that I must grow up and have sex involving penises and relationships involving one man.

At secondary school sex education classes re-enforced these ideas. Again nothing LGBT+ was ever mentioned. We learned about some STDs and some forms of contraception. So I now knew that women were supposed to have sex with a man, and sometimes that man's penis might be a bit diseased so I had to be careful. (But I gained the scarily false assumption that two women having sex was always safe.) I was frustrated by the fact that no information was provided at all if you wanted to have sex with someone of the same gender. Whilst I now had a rough idea that sex involved putting a penis in a vagina (rather than two cats rubbing against each other!), I had no idea how I would have sex with a women. I certainly wasn't able to put my hand up and ask.

Thank goodness for Google and Scarleteen!

One of the two exceptions where anything LGBT+ was mentioned was during my A-Levels (16–18 years old) as we were studying *A Streetcar Named Desire* by Tennessee Williams.

(SPOILER ALERT ——— In the story the husband of the main character commits suicide, partly because of her inability to accept his homosexuality. ——— END OF SPOILER.)

So there was nothing positive for me to take away there, just another reminder of what I already knew from my own experience. Homophobia (and bi and transphobia) makes people feel suicidal and in some cases it kills.

I knew this from my own experience as I came out to a few close friends at 13. Naturally at this age it was hardly going to be a secret for long. One girl was drunk at a party and told everyone there. The next few days it went round the school and soon everyone in my year group knew. Whilst I was constantly teased, humiliated and questioned about it, I felt lucky because it only turned into physical violence on one occasion, when I was shoved against some lockers and had some rubbish thrown at me.

This leads into the second exception of when something LGBT+ was mentioned at school. From the age of 14–16 I had this amazing teacher who would sit and talk to us for a bit when he had some time left before the end of class. One day he mentioned Section 28 and explained what it was. He added that it meant a teacher couldn't even say it was OK to be gay. It was one of the most important things I'd ever heard. In a few sentences he managed to convey the message that for most of my life I'd been living under a law that resulted in a harmful, heteronormative education, without actually breaking that rule. His tone of voice made it clear that he didn't think Section 28 was OK (and he was married to a woman who also taught at my school, so to have someone who I assumed was straight say it made the message stronger for me). From that day on I knew I had an ally who I could turn to if "things got really bad". (Bullying was so normal I never thought things were already "really bad".) I will always be grateful to him for that. I will always remember him.

What angers me about the education system is it lets everyone down, not just LGBT+ people. For example, no one gets a decent sex education. One result of this is that STD rates keep on rising. Teenagers don't get taught what they need to know, where to go to get tested, how often they should get tested, what happens when you go to a GUM clinic, etc. They feel scared, confused and isolated when something happens. This carries on into adulthood.

Any LGBT+ students don't get the relevant sex education they need. We are also asked questions like, "How do you have sex with a women then? One of you must wear a strap on," a lot. Imagine if everyone was taught the answer to questions like that at school! Imagine a world where we weren't constantly being made to act as the educator and explainer.

Imagine a time where we aren't bullied or harassed or discriminated against because of our gender or sexuality. Where young people don't have to suffer at school, and endure depression, self-harm and low self-esteem. A life so painful suicide seems like the only way out. I never thought about telling a teacher what happened after I came out, because I believed it was normal and to be expected because I was bi. That it was my fault for being different. Plus I was terrified the teachers would disapprove or bully me too. Again, all of these issues of discrimination and bullying continue on into adulthood.

Societies' norms and values are taught and instilled into us through our education. We must be straight. Anything else isn't normal or acceptable or worth mentioning. We must be vanilla and monogamous. No mention of open relationships or polyamory. No mention of BDSM. Hell, there wasn't even any mention of fun! Sex was never presented as something that could be enjoyable or pleasurable. I just thought it was something that you had to do... Consent was never spoken of. Never mentioned. Never explained. Why the fuck not?! It's absolutely vital. This is one of the reasons we have rape culture.

Again, we all suffer the effects of this limited, piss-poor education as adults.

I never understand why we have to even campaign for sex-positive, consent-based, accurate, LGBT+-inclusive sex education. For the education system itself to be LGBT+ inclusive. It should be the norm. How long is it gonna take?

By Hannah Bee. Reproduced with permission from *Hannah Bee's Bisexual Blog*.

Changing Sexualities

'What's interesting, says [Dr. Lisa] Diamond, is that transitions in sexual identity aren't "confined to adolescence. People appear equally likely to undergo these sorts of transitions in middle adulthood and late adulthood."'

Keira Cochrane, 'Why It's Never Too Late to Be a Lesbian'

One of the most common narratives around LGBTQIA+ sexuality is the woman in her forties or fifties who's been married to a man for years, then realises she's a lesbian, leaves her husband, and spends the rest of her life with a woman. The *Guardian* article quoted above lists a number of celebrities who've lived heterosexual lives and then switched to lesbianism: Cynthia Nixon, Portia de Rossi, Mary Portas. A 2014 article in the *Telegraph* printed interviews with several women who experienced this process. The dominant story is of someone who ignored or repressed their lesbian impulses for years, either because they fell in love with a man or because of cultural homophobia, or both. Then they meet and fall in love with a woman, and it all comes bursting out, the previous life is rejected, and the new life is embraced.

Have these women always been lesbians, but closeted? Or have they actually changed their orientation from straight to gay? Or are they in fact bisexual? Can bisexuality include the idea of 'attracted to men, then attracted to women' if you don't experience both at the same time?

Dr. Lisa Diamond, who's an associate professor of psychology and gender studies at the University of Utah, studied changes in women's sexual identity over fifteen years. From the same *Guardian* article: 'The women she chose at the start of the study had all experienced some same-sex attraction—although in some cases only fleeting-ly—and every two years or so she has recorded how they describe themselves: straight, lesbian, bisexual, or another category of their own choosing. In every two-year wave, 20–30% of the sample have changed their identity label, and over the course of the study, about 70% have changed how they described themselves at their initial interview.'

Dr. Diamond found that it often wasn't the case that women had been completely repressing their same-sex attractions: they'd 'always thought that other women were beautiful and attractive' but 'without the context of an actual relationship, the little glimmers of occasional fantasies or feelings just weren't that significant.' The experience of falling for a specific woman crystallised the feelings into a definite identity.

On the one hand, we very much support the position that people's sexual identities are theirs to define. So, to define as straight and then gay is of course perfectly okay, and so is defining as 'always secretly gay but repressed it for a long time'. But it's interesting to wonder how things might be different if bisexuality were more of a standard item on the sexuality menu (instead of a special you have to ask for): would there be another narrative where the story was 'woman identifies as "a bit bisexual but mostly into men" early in life and later identifies as "a bit bisexual but mostly into women"'?

> 'Every one of the women I studied who underwent a transition experienced it as being out of her control. It was not a conscious choice. ... I think the culture tends to lump together change and choice, as if they're the same phenomenon, but they're not. Puberty involves a heck of a lot of change, but you don't choose it. There are life-course transitions that are beyond our control.'
>
> Dr. Lisa Diamond

Bisexual Life Stories

My Coming-Out Story

Until two weeks ago, this was going to be a very boring coming-out story. To set the scene, I'm a thirty-one-year-old man, and for most of my life I have hidden the fact that I am bi from friends, from family, even from myself. Any thoughts towards guys were repressed and locked away in that part of the brain one puts things that don't bear thinking about. Why all this repression? For the same reason as everybody: fear. Fear of being different, fear of not getting a girlfriend or wife, and fear of people not understanding. I felt pressured into 'picking a side' and, as I've always been more emotionally drawn to women, lived as a straight man for most of my life.

Then one night on a dark drive home last January, I came out to my wife. I say 'come out', but it was more a case of me blurting, 'I sort of like guys but not sure what to call it, please don't leave me!' Happily, she didn't, and we became stronger than ever. With some therapy I came to the conclusion that I was bi, and for a little while everything was great. My best friend greeted the news with a high five and a shrug, work colleagues didn't even blink when I brought it into conversation, and the most controversial reaction was a surprised 'Oh!' from a friend of my wife.

I was on a roll. I didn't realise how much this repression was affecting my self-esteem, and the anxiety I so often felt in social situations (a feeling of being 'different' or hiding something) began to melt away. The last mountain to climb was my parents. Very friendly, outgoing suburbanites from North London, they were certainly old-fashioned in some of their views, but I knew that after some discussion they would accept it regardless. I told Mum first, then Dad. Both times were met with surprise, but support. 'You're still our son' was the general message, and I couldn't be happier.

After about a week, however, the tide started to turn. Fear crept in, and I had several uncomfortable conversations trying to ease my parents' worries. Was I tempted to cheat on my wife? Would I be hanging out in gay bars now? Do we have to talk about it all the time? Will I change how I talk? Hurtful questions, but nonetheless sincere. My wife and I became a team, fending off questions with the calm demeanour of a government spokesperson.

We thought the worst was over, and then one Monday I came to my parents' house, and was greeted at the door by my dad. My wife was already there, as I was meant to meet her and have dinner with my family, but unfortunately my dad had other ideas. 'We've got to talk about your "little surprise package",' he began, and it just got worse. He angrily called me 'half gay', didn't understand why I'd come out with it now, and said I'd hurt his family by coming out. He seemed convinced that I would cheat on my wife with a man, and generally acted like a bully. I'll save you the blow-by-blow account, but I left in complete shock, having called him a 'dinosaur' and stormed off (that was the most restrained word I could think of). My wife stayed for another hour, standing up to this bully, before leaving, in tears.

Devastated, we didn't talk to my family for a week, bar the occasional text message from my distraught mum. The poor woman was caught in the middle. I sense (or maybe just hope) that she knew my dad was in the wrong, but knew, as I did, that this anger was a reaction caused by fear. He was worried for me; he just showed it in the crappiest way possible. We stuck by our guns, saying we wanted an apology, and then my sister turned on me too, accusing me of cutting off the family. I argued my case, but eventually she replied with 'So are you two the only ones who are allowed an opinion?'

Suddenly it all became clear: there was to be no resolution to this. I'm sure my sister said what she said to just try and get the family back to normal (or maybe it's just that 'hope' thing again), but it became clear to me that these people were self-centred, ignorant and very afraid. I wrote a long email to the family, apologising to my mum for putting her in the middle and asking my dad to apologise for the way things were said. His account of things was already so airbrushed with his hidden good intentions and, most confusingly, stating that 'It's nothing to do with your sexuality', that I knew in his mind the meaning justified the method. Still, I wanted an apology, and I got one. A quick phone call cleared things, and we have peace.

The thing is that, and I like to think they know this, in gaining peace they've lost me. I still love them, and I forgive them for all of this, but I'll never forget. They will never be the people I trust with my secrets again, they will not be the first people I call when good or bad news comes. The closeness I had with them before has gone—they're still my family, they will still be a part of our lives, but they'll never get the best of us. Most harrowing of all was the loss of who I saw my dad to be, which was nothing short of a superhero. He was the best man at my wedding, and my very best friend. That day, the cape fell off, and I just saw a confused old man, frightened at the world that was rapidly changing around him. I still love him, but he'll never be the person he once was to me.

As strange as this may sound, this story does have a happy ending. I'm hurt by what happened, and I lost something very important, but I gained something vital. I gained pride in myself, and the knowledge that my sexuality did not make the sky fall in. I have friends and extended family who have stood by my side throughout, my marriage is closer than ever, and after I get over what's happened, I know I'll be able to walk into a room confidently, knowing that there's nothing to hide.

If you're reading this and thinking of coming out, please do not be put off. Your experience may be better, it may be worse, but as long as you can do it safely, it is always worth it. I may have lost a hero, but I gained myself.

Jack

I was born in Belfast in 1979 to a Catholic father and a Protestant mother. We moved to England when I was three, eventually settling in Yorkshire when I was six. I first became aware of there being such a thing as bisexuality when I was nine, from a book that I got out of the library. I started identifying as bisexual when I was fourteen, when my teenage hormones began rampaging. I was lucky that my close friends seemed to be quite accepting, and I started dabbling sexually with boys and girls in my teens.

I started going to indie and rock clubs when I was fifteen (without my parents knowing, natch) and found a world that played the music I loved and where my sexuality was accepted. It's also where I first started meeting other queer people and hanging out with them. I could kiss boys, I could kiss girls, I could kiss people who weren't boys or girls, and it was okay. It meant that I never really tried to seek out a queer scene; on the rare occasions where I did venture out to gay pubs and clubs it never was somewhere I was very comfortable, as the music wasn't stuff that I liked and the scene was very lesbian and gay focused.

I didn't really get involved with any type of queer scene until I was in my twenties and went to my first BiCon in 2003. It felt like belonging in a way that going to gay clubs had never made me feel. It's a place that I always enjoy coming back to (so much so that I even helped run it in 2012!), and I've now been seven times in the last ten or so years. I'd have been more often, but I have children now, which makes it difficult to attend as often as I'd like; also, before I had kids, I was a fairly isolated bisexual geographically. I tried to start a local bi group which failed spectacularly, so made do with getting my fix of the bi community by travelling to visit friends and going to events like BiFest.

Now I'm in my mid-thirties and have a couple of kids. Because I have a male partner and children, people often assume that I'm straight, and I feel that recently my bi identity has been erased a bit by my largely heteronormative lifestyle. This isn't helped by living in a small city where there isn't really a bi scene as such (though I hope to change that soon, and hopefully I've learnt from my earlier mistakes when it comes to running a bi group). Getting out is also difficult because of the kids, but I'm lucky in there being a small pub around the corner which is truly LGBT friendly and having some bi friends around here, so I'm not totally isolated.

To be honest, I don't know what the future will hold. I'm hoping that my current partner and my children will still be in it, but I'd like there to at least be a bit more bi community interaction in real life day to day.

Cat

Early life

I was born in Solihull, West Midlands, in 1977, and grew up in a tiny village called Earlswood. My family are pretty middle class, but my dad was made redundant in 1984 and my mum became pretty much the sole earner. I grew up on credit. Mum did a fantastic job of making us look as normal as possible to the casual observer.

I was a pretty happy child. Not really a tomboy, or a girlie girl. I was encouraged to use my imagination at every opportunity, and to 'show off', but to do it in an 'acceptable' way (being clever was acceptable, but not too clever, and nothing controversial).

I think I first heard about bisexuality as a concept when I was sixteen in my school's health-ed class. That's certainly when I started to realise that I liked girls and boys. I knew I was different to my peers; we would talk about sex stuff, and I worked out that I could *never* tell them what I liked.

How was school?

School was hell. I was bullied throughout secondary school and had been bullied from year four in primary school. I went to a private girls' school (I had an assisted place), and wasn't rich enough to fit in. I didn't care about clothes, hated sport, wasn't allowed to wear make-up, was too weird and too different. My teenage years were spent knowing that I didn't really fit in anywhere, and being desperate to leave home and get away from my father.

I don't know if I had any LGBT role models. I adored Madonna, Sandra Bernhard, was very into '70s glam pop and '70s punk (OMG, '70s punk was like coming home). I fell in love with *The Rocky Horror Picture Show* and *Grease* (I wanted to be Rizzo or Kenickie). My clothes were 'chosen by Mum', who, whilst wonderful, was more into how long things would last versus how cool they were, so I didn't really have a personal style statement for most of my teenage years. I was big on jumpers and jeans, or T-shirts and jeans with boots. Mum did buy my first pair of boots with heels at seventeen, and I haven't worn flats since, really.

Dating

My first boyfriend was thirty-four (I was seventeen); he was married with two kids and was quite possibly the worst first boyfriend anyone could have. I wanted to rebel against my father desperately, and I'm pretty sure that's why I did it. Plus, he was the first person to pay me any attention in that way, and then Dad hit the roof and it turned into this whole 'you and me against the world' rubbish that happens when you're seventeen and have read far too many trashy romance novels.

This boyfriend always said that he never had a problem with my sexuality, but he also told me that it made me so weird and so bizarre that no one else would ever love me. I never felt that I fitted in with the LBG society at uni because I wasn't a 'real' bisexual (having never done anything with a woman), so it was a thing I kept sort of quiet and sort of secret. I always told boyfriends, but never really did anything about it.

Adult sexuality

I do think my sexuality is a positive thing. I've had a bit of a weird relationship with it for the past few years, but I think I'm getting into a better headspace with it. I've lost some of the confidence from my twenties, and it would be nice to get that back.

As for stereotypes, I now class myself as poly, I identify as kinky, I'm a goth and I'm femme, so I probably tick a few bi-bingo boxes there. I don't think it matters: to be honest, it's very easy to get into a knee-jerk 'I'm not like that' when people start with biphobic bobbins, but we shouldn't have to justify aspects of ourselves just to make other people feel better. Also. it sets up this false dichotomy of 'real' and 'pretend' bisexuals, which hurts everyone.

A lot of my friends do identify as bi, whether they are part of the bi community or not. I can occasionally feel isolated, but that is down to the fact that the majority of my friends are all over the country, and geography is a pain. I like to date people with the same sexuality, mainly because there is less explaining. Some straight guys tend to regard bi women as a threesome waiting to happen, and I've no desire to be that again.

I do consider myself part of the bi community: I've run two BiCons, run a Coffee Meet, write for *Bi Community News*, and have run sessions at BiCons and BiFests. I also have a lot of friends in the bi community, which makes it a pretty comfortable place to be.

As for being out, I'm out at work, and out to my friends. I'm not out to my parents (although I think my mum has sort of worked it out), and I doubt I will ever be out to my father.

Bi-friendly spaces

Goth (and alternative) spaces are in my experience very bi (and queer) friendly. Certainly, the goth scene in Birmingham was very inclusive (I've not been part of the scene for some time, so can't comment about its current incarnation). I know of several people who are part of the goth scene whilst not being goths because they were too different for the LGBT scene.

Being a part of the goth community has been incredibly important for me. Without it, I would never have gone to BiCon, and I certainly wouldn't be as comfortable with my sexuality. Also I wouldn't have had the courage to wear amazing clothes and fabulous shoes. I have never come across biphobia in goth space (this could just mean I know the right goths), and generally people don't attach huge importance over the gender of the people they may snog. Most of the guys I know have kissed at least one guy, regardless of how they identify. The lack of condemnation or becoming freak of the week is rather fabulous.

I don't feel comfortable in L&G space, and really don't feel like I fit in at Pride, so it's great to find a space where I can be myself, and that's what I get from goth spaces.

Oddly, the largest collection of bisexuals that I've found outside of goth and bi space was at *Torchwood* conventions. I'm very pleased that the Hub (a *Torchwood* convention) was my first con, as other experiences have been rather more 'straight'. Having people get excited over the fic you read and the pairings you love prepares you for the expression of horror that you get from some fans when you dare to ship anything that isn't het *rolls eyes*. I would have been a lot more reticent had that happened the other way around. *Torchwood* fans in my opinion are one of the most accepting, queer-friendly, warm and welcoming groups of fans in the multiverse. I've watched people in their early teens grow and become the person that they want to be with the full support of their friends who believe that there is more than gay/straight, or male/female. It gives me a warm fuzzy feeling in my heart.

Jules

About

I'm in my early thirties, from Lincolnshire, where I grew up with my two mums as an only child. I was an absolutely horrid child, with emotions that were always turned up to eleven. From being a colicky baby to a belligerent child and a depressive teenager, my parents didn't get a break from day one. My parents never came out to me—I had to figure out their relationship for myself. This almost certainly fed a lot of discomfort with my own sexuality. My birth mum is bi, and her not coming out made me distrustful of the label.

Early ideas about sexuality

I was always different in a can't-put-your-finger-on-it sort of way. I was completely oblivious to my parents' sexuality until I was a teenager. I deduced their relationship from clues, realising that my non-biological mum was gay much earlier than realising she was in a relationship with my biological mum. That said, I don't really remember finding out that there were orientations other than straight, so however I found out, there was no big revelation. I probably just sort of absorbed it from the world at large. I definitely knew before I turned thirteen, because that's when Ellen came out in her sitcom, and that was a pretty big moment for me; it was the first time I questioned if the way I liked girls was like the way she liked girls. I came out within about eighteen months of that, and I identified as lesbian from shortly after turning fifteen.

School

I was bullied at middle and upper school pretty mercilessly, until I fell in with the alternative kids.

In middle school, at about age eleven, I got picked on every single day, by people both within my friendship circle and outside of it. My friends, I realise now, were not really my friends, they were just mean to me *less*. But I so wanted to be liked that that was enough for me. This was all to do with my undefinable difference, but also had a lot to do with being poor. In a school where most of the kids were reasonably well off, we were decidedly poor.

After year nine, the first year of upper school, I got into music and joined the alt. crowd. Goths, metallers and music nerds. I came out (as gay) when I was in the first year of my GCSEs, and, while there were a handful of gay men (boys?) out in my peer group, there were no women. People used to whisper about me in corridors, but it was something I had controlled. Many years later I'd watch *The West Wing* and learn about controlling the story, and that's exactly what I was doing. I came out. They couldn't drag it out of, and they couldn't use my shame against me because I clearly had none. From then I was pretty untouchable. I had developed a real fuck-you attitude, dying my hair, getting a face full of piercings and building a reputation as a hard case (even though I wasn't, but that didn't matter. No one would start on someone they thought could hit harder than them.), which extended to making out with girl-friends in the school hallways.

The irony is, I wasn't gay. I was bi and I knew it. And that shame did exist. I couldn't tell anyone I was bi because insert pathetic stereotype here. It was all bravado.

Both androgyny and hypermasculinity were really big in the *Kerrang!*-reading crowd of the late '90s, but sexuality wasn't much discussed. We read into the androgyny of people like Brian Molko and Marilyn Manson what we wanted to, and it was considered very cool for women to choose the same hypermasculine nu-metal style of big hoodies and even bigger jeans. But bisexuality was only theoretically okay. In practice the make-your-mind-up trope was pretty common, which meant I hid my different-sex attraction until long after I'd left school.

Dating

I started dating at fifteen and dated women exclusively until I was twenty-two. My crowd was exclusively lesbian, and they had some pretty strong views about bisexuality. When I confided in them that I might sort of maybe fancy a boy, I got a lot of grief for it. I was persona non grata for even considering being with a man. At the time I was heartbroken. I felt like I was too weird for the weirdos, losing my friends and my identity. Now I realise how sad that was. I don't need friends like that.

I didn't have a 'relationship' with a man until I was twenty-nine, but I'd sown a lot of oats by then. I always thought men were just for sex, not relationships, and I continued to think that until I'd been in a relationship with a man for a good few months. Cognitive dissonance. I definitely felt pressure to stick to women, like if I dated a man I was letting the side down. This is despite having a very supportive network of friends who would never undermine my choices. It's all from within; I've internalised biphobia I experienced from lesbians and kept it with me even after dumping that toxic crowd.

Adult sexuality

I find my sexuality to be completely neutral, neither a negative nor a positive influence in my life. That's not to say that I'm totally over the difficulties I have with it, just that I can recognise the intrusive thoughts for what they are.

Bisexual stereotypes are so confusing. I'm feminine, so I sometimes worry that people will think I'm just putting on a show for attention. But I wouldn't think that of anyone else, so why do I judge myself by a different standard? My sexual history is strongly in favour of women, so I don't feel any need to prove my queerness, usually. I'm least confident when I'm in LGBTQ spaces, where there can sometimes be pressure to prove you belong.

Most of my friends are bi, but that's not surprising, since I met most of them at bi events. I've still got one foot in the closet in my professional life, but I'm working on allowing myself to come out entirely. I don't make a point to come out to people, but I'm direct if the matter comes up.

I am not a big activist, but I do try to be involved with the community by helping out where I can. I've volunteered at bi events and written on the subject online and in the queer press, so I've met activists through that, and many of them have become friends. Being involved with events like BiCon makes me feel I'm part of a movement as much as a community. It's a very secure place to be.

Elinor

Am I Too Old to Be Bisexual?

By Sue George

Bisexual feelings and behaviours are obviously nothing new. Nor is calling them 'bisexual'. In the 1970s, when I first gave a name to my feelings, there were already at least a few people who were talking publicly about being attracted to more than one gender. So where are they now? And why are bisexual individuals over a certain age—let's say fifty—just not around?

In brief, it is because of the stereotypes around bisexuality and the hostility that they provoke. A bi identity is commonly considered to be temporary, a product of psychological confusion, something that is bound to change. It is a temporary state that will stabilise. Lesbian, gay or heterosexual identities are, by contrast, assumed to be permanent, even when they aren't—sexuality is not fixed for everyone, and if it changes, it can be at any age.

But many people don't agree with or like this. The disparaging comments and microaggressions directed towards many younger bis become that much more contemptuous when they are directed to older people.

Bisexuality is so often seen as something that belongs to the more or less young—to not deciding, to a period before answering the question who will you 'end up with?' But a lifelong monogamous relationship is not something everyone wants, or experiences. Even for those who do have such a relationship, monogamy is rarely the end of all other desires, intimacies, fantasies.

In particular, the disconnection between bisexuality and older age is due to the overwhelming conflation of bisexuality and sex. For much of mainstream society, bisexuality is *only* about sexual activity, and lots of it—not any of the other things that encompass sexuality.

This stereotype also says that when we are older—and how old depends partly on the age of the speaker—we should be 'past it' and no longer particularly interested in sex. If we refuse to be 'past it', then we are somehow disgusting, dirty old men/women. This applies to older people of whatever sexuality, unless they are part of a stable heterosexual monogamous couple, in which case sex is acceptable as part of 'ageing well'. Alternatively, older people may be seen as some kind of fetish. Google 'older bisexuals' and you get many pages of specialist porn.

For some people, as they grow into older age, sexual and romantic relationships do become a little less important than they were. But even when that is the case, identifying as bisexual is not simply to do with sexual behaviour, or romantic feelings, now or in the past. Bisexuality can encompass a person's desires, fantasies, relationship to mainstream society, history, community, interests, friendship networks, and their place in the world at large. For me, my bisexuality is about my whole self, and my whole life. It also means that whether I am in a relationship with someone else or not, I have an entirely different relationship to mainstream society than someone who identifies as straight or gay.

Because of these stereotypes, the erasure and invisibility of bisexuality that exists for people of all ages is so much stronger for older bisexuals. And because bi erasure is so strong for older people, they may consider that they can't be bisexual because such people don't exist. The older a person is, the stronger the invisibility. For instance, all the interviews of older people that follow this introduction are of bisexuals in their fifties. Where are those in their eighties? They will have very different perspectives.

Older bis may have different priorities and challenges from those who are young. For instance, older bis may find it harder to find new partners if they want them; they may be caring for frail partners, parents, siblings or friends; they may be less able to travel to social events and feel those that are available are not meant for them. A youth-oriented bar scene may actively discourage older people, whether they want to go to those bars or not. These issues aren't confined to older people, of course, but they are likely to affect more of them.

All older bisexuals are not the same. For instance, people who come out in their sixties will have different perspectives to those who have been out since their teens. People with an activist framework or a supportive queer poly community will not have the same experiences as those who live more conventionally. Similarly, while ageing happens to everyone, the way it impacts on any one bi individual will change depending on the intersections of race, class, gender and religion. This will affect the way people see their own sexuality and their ageing, and the way that others see them.

There is another difference between younger and older bi people too: individuals are shaped by the time in which they grew up and by their personal and political histories, which all interact with how things are now. For instance, older people are likely to remember a time when any kind of same-sex behaviour was treated with outright disgust. When AIDS was untreatable. When lesbian and gay reactions towards bi people were overwhelmingly hostile. They will also remember 'queer' being an insult, not a way of disrupting accepted ways of being. Many of us fought back against all of this, too. It has formed our personalities and our politics.

Many older people who consider themselves bisexual are not out about it, though; it has faded into the background of their lives. They may indeed have 'settled down'. They may be unsure if they can call themselves bisexual, because they are not intending to 'do anything about it'. But if they want to, they can. Like many who are very out, I have often been the recipient of confidences from people who want to tell me about their bisexuality. Often, now, these people are my age or older; they are pleased, surprised and frequently moved that there are out bisexuals who are not young.

So, am I, or you, 'too old' to be bisexual? No. There is no one alive who is 'too old' for that.

Interviews with bisexual people over fifty

Sue George has been conducting interviews with bisexual people over or near fifty. She and her interviewees have kindly given us permission to reprint those interviews here.

'Call me Butch. I am fifty-one years old. I am a white bisexual queer woman, and I present as butch. I am a college-educated creative who worked in publishing for many years, and currently works in the public sector. I live in the New England region of the US, and have been married to a hetero cis male for eighteen years. We have a young child together, who is our biological offspring created the old-fashioned way!'

How did you come to think of yourself as bisexual?

'I realized when I was fourteen that I was attracted to both binary sexes in a very fluid way. I heard the term "bisexual" in my twenties and knew it was me. Over the years, my attraction has remained fluid, although my preference will settle for fairly long periods of time on one side of the gender binary; yet even so, the attraction to the other side of the gender binary remains. I am attracted to female-bodied queer women and male-bodied hetero men. I have had no experience with transitioned individuals with regard to relationships.'

What does being bisexual mean to you?

'For me, it means having the ability to love both men and women, sometimes at the same time. That is the perceived dirty little secret about being bisexual: the ability to love two people of differing genders at the same time. Personally, I find it liberating, amazing and utterly natural. I think that many in the bisexual community regard the existence of polyamorous bisexuals as counterproductive to the task of giving legitimacy and respect to the term "bisexual", but I'm not the only one out here in the world.'

Has this changed over the years, and if so how?

'I was strictly monogamous when I was younger. But now I have a secondary relationship with a queer woman who is also hetero-married. I was fully open about my bisexual orientation with my husband-to-be, although I thought at the time I would remain monogamous indefinitely. My husband remains my primary partner, and I am devoted to him.

As I aged, it became impossible for me to suppress my version of bisexuality (in which there are two partners of differing genders), and both my physical and mental health eroded severely. In order to stay a sane and productive member of society, and to hold at bay the overwhelming depression that was pervading my life, I opened up my personal ethics to include limited polyamory. All parties involved are aware of each other's presence. I have no more than one partner of my two preferred genders, and STI testing was done before initiating a relationship outside my marriage and required of my proposed female partner.

My secondary relationship is kept private to all but my husband and a few of the closest people in my life; my secondary partner also keeps the relationship private in the same way. We are each well known in our community, and it would cause some serious ripples, both personal and professional, if the true manner of things was revealed. To the world, she and I present merely as very good friends. Do we hate that it has to be that way? Yes. But society is not yet ready to openly accept polyamory, even in this very liberal part of the country.'

What do other people in your life know about your bisexuality and how do they react?

'When folks meet me, I'm sure it is pretty obvious that I am not straight. I present as butch, and I have a decided butch headspace. There have been times when I passed for straight, mainly for a previous job and when I was not feeling good about myself, but mostly I've looked fairly obviously queer. I have never hidden the fact that I'm not straight, and when asked if I am a lesbian, I have responded firmly that I am bisexual, although my being married to a hetero male has confused a good many people. I came out to my siblings early in 2014, and I was surprised that they were surprised. I guess my marriage to a man threw them.

When I was twenty, my mom figured out I was not straight (I was with another woman during that time), and she outright rejected me. Those were very dark days of my life. She was the only parent I had, and she didn't talk to me for a long time. I think it wasn't until I was dating a guy in my mid-twenties that she felt comfortable around me. Last week, I came out to my mom, again. She is eighty-one and has dementia. Her reaction was completely different than her reaction thirty years ago. It was nice to be accepted by her at last for what I am. It was a long time in coming, with many tears along the way.'

Looking back over your life so far, is there anything you wish you'd done differently?

'I wish I had recognized my potential need for polyamory before I was married. Revealing it to my husband eighteen years into the marriage was very rough on both of us, but most of all on him. He is an incredible person and is relearning to accept me for who and what I am.'

What about your hopes or fears for the future (regarding bisexuality)?

'I can only hope that bisexuality, in all its permutations, will gain the wide acceptance it deserves in the greater LGBTQIA community. We are not even close to there, yet. The louder we are, the more we will be heard.'

Any words of wisdom for younger bi people—or older ones?

'Be who you are, despite all obstacles real and perceived. Be out, and be proud. Be loud in your LGBTQIA community. Find other bisexuals, and be there for each other. Everyone probably knows at least one bisexual already, but they are often hidden. If you stand up as an example of bisexual pride, it will give others the courage to stand up, too. Be brave, and be kind to yourself. You are amazing, at any age!'

'I'm Lou Hoffman, fifty-sex, white, cis female. I live in Minneapolis, Minnesota, USA, and I'm legally married to Martin Quam. He's also bi and fifty-six, and he's Native American and white, cis male. We live with our two kids, Arthur and Tristan, who just turned twenty-two. We're poly, and I have a girlfriend who is also bi.

I currently work part time at Target, though I am semi-retired due to disabilities. I've had quite a few different jobs over my lifetime and also a lot of experiences outside the ordinary, as my philosophy is that if I haven't done something before that's a good enough reason to try it!'

How did you come to think of yourself as bisexual?

'When I was twelve or thirteen, I realized I was attracted to both men and women. I first heard the word 'bisexual' when David Bowie came out as bi, and I was so relieved, not only that there was a word for it but also because if there was a word for it, that meant there were others like me. They wouldn't have made up a word for just Bowie and me! It's funny now, but I grew up Catholic and on a dairy farm in rural Wisconsin: *very* isolated. I didn't come out to anyone until I was twenty-four.

When I went to college, I finally met people who were out as lesbian and gay, though comments and jokes about bisexuality ensured I stayed closeted. But I was rumoured to be lesbian and was openly an ally. It was after college that I moved to Minneapolis, met people who were trans, realized that my attractions were all across all the spectrums, and then met my partner Martin. We were both closeted but soon came out to each other, and shortly after that joined a local bi support group. I've been coming out and being active since then: thirty-two years now that I've been out, and forty-three years since I started identifying as bi. Some phase, huh?'

What does being bisexual mean to you?

'Up until that point (coming out and joining a bi group), I hadn't thought out a definition of bisexuality and what it means to me, but it was through talking with others that the idea solidified for me. I was part of the discussion back then on what we, as an organisation, meant by the word, and for me it's an attraction to people who are similar to and different from my own gender identity.'

What do other people in your life know about your bisexuality?

'Since I am very active and out, I can't think of anyone who doesn't know I'm bi. Most people are accepting and supportive, but the more conservative family members just ignore it. This is not to say I haven't been harassed for my identity, but I've been lucky to live in one of the best cities to be bi in the United States. I have not experienced sexual or physical harassment or violence; unfortunately I do know a significant number of people who have. I maintain many connections to people in the rural communities and have a great deal of sympathy for those who are isolated. While it isn't perfect, thank technology for the Internet, so people can find others! That is the biggest, most significant change in the years I've been out and active!

I'm pretty satisfied with my life so far. I've had a lot of fun! I may not be rich in dollars but I'm rich in experiences, friends and family. It would be nice to win the lottery so I could financially support the non-profits I'm involved in, but hey, I contribute my time and energy, and as I retire I hope, health permitting, that I can continue to do so. Being part of the bi communities has enriched me beyond any measure.'

What are your hopes or fears for the future?

'I hope that in the future the bi communities get funded! Though I may be experienced at working on a shoestring, it's so much easier to work on stuff when your organization has funds! We really need to do outreach to the celebrities that are coming out as bi! And I absolutely support people identifying as whatever speaks their truth, but I hope we don't fragment into competing identities. I hope all non-monosexual people work together!'

Any words of wisdom for younger (or older) bi people?

'I don't know if I have any advice to give to anyone. Keep open to new ideas and experiences, but don't be gullible. Be kind. Get involved. You can make a difference.'

'My name is Lynnette McFadzen, and I live in Portland, Oregon, USA. I am a fifty-seven-year-old single white cisgendered woman with three daughters and four grandchildren. I am single and, at the moment, celibate.

I am disabled but have had many occupations in the past, from nursing to chainsaw-chain packaging. The packaging job is where I lost most of my hearing, but it really started way before then. After the death of my estranged husband and my mother, I had my biggest breakdown and attempted suicide. That time I sought help. I spent the next ten years healing and figuring out why my life was so dysfunctional. There was no room for relationships during that time.'

How did you come to think of yourself as bisexual?

'Last year I had finished my second round of chemo for hepatitis C, which I probably contracted as a nurse in my twenties. Not that it is important where I got it—hep C is non-discerning. The first round failed, so I spent a total of two years in treatment. That's a lot of downtime to think.

At the end I felt ready to try dating and my old demons re-emerged. I found women attractive. I always had. My first crush was on Audrey Hepburn, and I had a series of 'girl crushes' throughout my life. But I truly believed all the lies I had been told about bisexuality. I spent the best part of my life proving to myself I was heterosexual and somehow broken and wrong inside. I know that was a contributing factor to my depression and suicide attempts. I really believed my loved ones would be better off without my evilness. What saved me was realising I could not leave the legacy of suicide to my children and grandchildren. My father had done that to me.

I had never really acted on my same-sex attractions but once, and it was a disaster. But with the help of good friends and family I began to learn bisexuality was not what I thought. I turned to the LGBT community and was met with disdain, coolness or outright hostility. I was shocked and disheartened.

So I searched for a bisexual community and eventually was able to find it online. I made good supportive friends with similar stories and similar struggles with internalised biphobia. Through this I was able to accept that, yes, I am bisexual. But it took some searching, and the search engines at the time were not much help.

It also spurred me to help others like me who felt lost and alone and confused to find and build their support, and realize they can be proud.

And have a community of their own. Since I am limited physically, I decided to learn to podcast. And with friends and volunteers we created *The BiCast*, a podcast for the bisexual community.'

What does being bisexual mean to you?

'It means being a complete whole person with no internal shame or feeling of wrongness. Of understanding myself. It means being at peace with me. It has really nothing to do with sex and everything to do with self-love. And knowing that just because I am bisexual it doesn't alter my moral compass at all.'

How has this changed over the years?

'I just came out last year. Doing that to myself was the biggest issue. The climate is changing for the general public perception of bisexuality. But the biggest reason I could not accept sooner that I was bisexual was because of what most people believed as I grew up and many still do. That it is a lifestyle choice, that you are shallow, indecisive, hypersexual, liars and all round morally bankrupt. It is changing, but not fast enough for me.'

What do other people in your life know about your bisexuality, and how do they react?

'Everyone knows I'm bi. It's part of being on a podcast about bisexuality. My family and friends are totally supportive. I am blessed with a diverse and loving family and have been fortunate to find amazing people as friends. I am a lucky one. I am in a really safe place.'

Looking back over your life so far, is there anything you wish you'd done differently?

'I wish sometimes I had come to terms with this at a much earlier age. [I worry] that I may have dismissed a good relationship as a possibility based on gender. [I wish] that I had not tortured myself for no reason at all.

I get a bit melancholy but then remember it gives me a better appreciation of the happiness I have now.'

What about your hopes or fears for the future (regarding bisexuality)?

'Truthfully, I want to see how all bisexuals are treated change, and help others understand they are okay.'

Any words of wisdom for younger bi people—or older ones?

'For both, really. Don't believe what you are told. Find out your own truth. Stay strong.

You are not wrong. You are not broken. You deserve respect. You are a human being. You are bisexual.'

'I am Laura, forty-eight, female, chronically sick from Ehlers-Danlos, living in the USA since February 2013, in the Netherlands before that.

I am married to a woman, since May 2013. From 1986 till 2005 I was with a man and had two children with him.'

How did you come to think of yourself as bisexual?

'I have always had crushes on boys *and* girls. Sexuality in the Netherlands is not a taboo and certainly not in my family. When I told my mother that I was seeing a girl, my first sort-of-relationship when I was sixteen, it got accepted without any word of surprise. When I got my first real relationship with a boy at eighteen, that was no subject of discussion either. I don't even remember when I started calling it bisexuality; I do know that when I dated that girl, it was not a word I used. And it did not change for me during the years.'

Has this changed over the years, and if so how?

'After my first girlfriend, I had a few sexual experiences with girls, but after that I met my boyfriend, later husband, and stayed with him for almost twenty years. After that I started dating again, but by then I had a chronic illness and the responses of the men I dated were horrifying. The last date ended with the guy asking, 'But what if I want to go out on Friday evening and you are tired?' and that's when I decided I'd had it with men. So I contemplated: how about dating women. And that was quite a step. Because I knew I was interested sexually and I knew I could fall in love, but having a relationship with a woman? And I didn't want to date women and then have to tell them, 'No, sorry, I'd like a night with you but a relationship, no thanks...' But I took the step and never looked back. I met my present wife, by the way, very unconventionally, via FarmVille on Facebook. She was a new neighbour, saw my pic, thought "hm ho", asked me if I needed something for FarmVille, and after the second talk we were both hooked.

When I was dating, many lesbians had atrocious statements on their profiles, like "If you're bi, don't even bother dropping me a note, I won't even write you back." The bi-hate is so big in the lesbian world. That was very, very hurtful, and still is. They try to make it sound like just one of the many preferences they have, like preferring tall women, but it boils my blood. So let's not go there today.'

What do other people in your life know about your bisexuality, and how do they react?

'Here in the US I don't know a lot of people, and since being gay is hard enough, I refrain from taking it one step further. When I started dating women after my divorce, though, there were people who were sort of offended that they didn't know that about me. Well, when I am with a man, you can't *tell* that I am bisexual. And if the subject doesn't come up...'

Looking back over your life so far, is there anything you wish you'd done differently?

'Not in regards to my bisexuality, no.'

What about your hopes or fears for the future (regarding bisexuality)?

'I hope that the biphobia and bi-erasure will stop, certainly from within the LGBT community.'

Any words of wisdom for younger bi people—or older ones?

'Don't let others tell you what your bisexuality means for you. People like to think that they know better, but there's only one person who knows you best: you!'

'I'm Jan Steckel, fifty-one, white, female, writer and former paediatrician. I live in a house in Oakland, California, USA, with my husband, who is also bisexual.'

How did you come to think of yourself as bisexual?

'I'd had boyfriends since the eighth grade [aged thirteen] and assumed I was straight. Then, the summer before I turned eighteen, I sang in a band. I was falling in love with the lead guitarist, a man, when the drummer, a woman, asked me out. I made out with her that night and realized that I was bisexual, even though I ended up with the young man.'

What does being bisexual mean to you?

'It means I am sexually attracted to some people who are the same sex as I am and to some who are of a different sex from me.'

Has this changed over the years, and if so, how?

'Not much since I realized I was bi. It's my gender identity that has changed instead. When I was a kid, I thought I was a boy and that some mistake had been made. In college I wished I was a man. I was pretty dysphoric about my body's curves, such as they were. I wanted the hard planes of a man's body, and I wanted to love a man as another man. Almost all the fiction I wrote then was first-person male, and my closest friends were male, too.

Now I'm comfortable with being female. As an adult, I was always more sexually attracted to women but had a tendency to fall in love with men. Since my recent menopause, I think I've become more attracted to women as well as to trans and non-binary people and less attracted to men, though my attraction to my husband has remained constant.'

What do other people in your life know about your bisexuality, and how do they react?

'Most people who know me know that I'm bi. I'm pretty out and loud about it, and have been for decades. Since my poetry book *The Horizontal Poet* won the 2012 Lambda Literary Award for Bisexual Nonfiction, I pretty much lead my literary bio with that. One of my older female relatives told me angrily that by putting the fact that I was bisexual on the back of my book I had disrespected my marriage to my husband, but most of my family has been pretty cool.

When I first came out to my mother, she was worried that if I ended up with a woman I wouldn't have children, or my children would be screwed up. She got over that well before I was out of my childbearing years, I think, though in the end I didn't have kids. My dad was probably more uncomfortable at first than my mum, but he's pretty cool about it now. My brother's always been fine about it.

It was definitely not cool, though, with many of my fellow physicians. That's part of the reason I'm not in medicine any more. Poets and writers are a lot more accepting.

My husband is bisexual, too, and it's a pretty big part of our lives. We march every year in the bi contingent of the San Francisco Pride parade, and he hosts a social group called Berkeley BiFriendly, where we met. We've both been published in bisexual anthologies and periodicals. I just had a short story come out in *Best Bi Short Stories*, and he has a painting being reproduced in a forthcoming anthology of work by bi men. Many of our friends are queer, so we get a lot of support from our community around it.'

Looking back over your life so far, is there anything you wish you'd done differently?

'I wish I had dated more women early on and had longer-lasting relationships with them. I was a little passive at first, waiting for people to pursue me instead of taking the initiative.'

What about your hopes or fears for the future (regarding bisexuality)?

'I belong to an online writing critique group where some jackass keeps attacking me every time I mention writing for bi periodicals or any honour I've got for bi writing. He accuses me of playing identity politics. My answer to that is that I'd be delighted not to need identity politics any more. When discrimination against bisexual people goes away, then if people don't want to label themselves according to their sexuality, fine. Until then I'm sticking to my label and making sure young people see plenty of bisexual characters in literature. I want young bisexually inclined people to see themselves reflected in what they read. I want them to have a peer group of other bisexual people, unlike me when I was coming up.'

Any words of wisdom for younger bi people—or older ones?

'Find a peer group of other bi people, even if it's only online. Get support from them. Try to find a safe way to come out, even if it means moving to a city with a visible bi population.'

12

BI IN THE WORKPLACE

Editor: Milena Popova

An exploration of the issues facing bi people at work and what can be done about them.

The Actionable Bisexual: Why Is Being Bi at Work Different to Being Bi Elsewhere?

As we've seen elsewhere in this book, being bisexual can mean many things for us: our sexuality can bring us joy and fulfilling relationships, it can expose us to bigotry and prejudice, and it is often ignored or erased by others to the point where we feel invisible. Ultimately, though, for most of us our sexuality is an inalienable part of us, not something we can give up or just stop being. It is part of who we are and informs how we approach the world in even the most basic of ways.

It is therefore unsurprising that, no matter how much we try to keep our work and personal lives separate, our sexuality follows us even into the workplace. How we feel about that, and how our employers treat us as a result, will have an impact on our performance and happiness at work.

There are a few factors that make workplaces particularly tricky ground to navigate for bisexual people. One is that they remain one of the more conservative institutions in our society, dominated by heterosexism and monosexism despite recent progress in tackling some lesbian and gay issues. In addition to that, workplaces are all about *doing things*. Discussions of identity aren't a natural fit in an environment dominated by delivering results.

This creates a double trap for bisexual employees. There are some of us for whom our bisexuality is primarily an issue of identity: we may be in long-term monogamous relationships, so people assume we are gay or straight, or we may be single and not looking. This does not make us any less bisexual. We still want to be able to take our whole selves to work but find ourselves having to explain how this matters in a workplace context. There are others for whom bisexuality is a practical day-to-day matter, either temporarily as we end a relationship and begin a new one with someone of a different gender to our previous partner, or ongoing as we have multiple partners of different genders. These are situations where our workplaces could do a lot more to support us. They could ensure our new partner is welcome at the Christmas do regardless of their gender or our relationship history; more radically, they could extend benefits such as pensions and parental leave to our multiple partners. This is, however, where we run into that conservatism that makes some of our community too edgy for even the most progressive of workplaces.

Most of us end up negotiating a fine line between being an actionable bisexual and a 'respectable' bisexual. Where that line is will vary with your workplace culture and your own experiences, situation and comfort zone. This chapter is intended to help you think about some of the most common issues you are likely to encounter as a bisexual person in the workplace and thus determine—or possibly even redefine—where your own line is.

The Legal Context

Please note that the *Purple Prose* editors are not lawyers; this is intended as a starting point, but please consult a lawyer before you take up a case with your employer.

The UK has reasonably good equalities legislation which protects you in the workplace. Here are some highlights. If you need further details on anything, your HR department should be able to help, or check the end of this chapter for further resources.

Discrimination

Your employer should not be discriminating against you *directly* or *indirectly* based on your sexual orientation. An example of direct discrimination would be not being offered a promotion because someone thought as a bisexual you would be too indecisive for such a senior role. Indirect discrimination is when policies or rules which are in effect for everyone put one group at a particular disadvantage. An example of indirect discrimination might be having a strict promotion requirement to have worked in a country where being lesbian, gay or bisexual is illegal.

The anti-discrimination rules also cover *perceived sexual orientation*, meaning people should not be discriminating against you based on what they *think* your sexual orientation is, regardless of what it actually is. Your employer should ensure they are not discriminating on the basis of sexual orientation in the way they recruit and hire, determine pay and promotion, provide training and development opportunities, or apply their grievance and disciplinary procedures.

Harassment and victimisation

Your employer should be providing a workplace that is free of bullying and harassment. They should have proactive strategies in place to prevent bullying and harassment, as well as effective procedures to address instances of harassment or bullying reported to them. Both *intentional* and *unintentional* harassment are covered under the law: it is how a comment or action is received that makes it harassment, not necessarily how it was intended. Examples of biphobic harassment include unwelcome comments or jokes around your own or someone else's sexual orientation, intimate questions about your personal or sex life, assumptions about your sexual orientation, or perpetuation of biphobic stereotypes. It may be 'just banter', but if it makes you feel uncomfortable, it counts as harassment and should be dealt with as such.

If you do report an instance of harassment or bullying, you are legally protected from *victimisation*. That means your employer should not be treating you unfairly because you have made a complaint (including taking a case to court or employment tribunal) or helped someone else make a complaint.

Benefits

The simple way of thinking about benefits is that any benefits your employer offers to unmarried heterosexual employees and their partners should be offered equally to unmarried or not civilly partnered LGBTQIA+ employees and their partners, and any benefits offered to married heterosexual employees should be offered equally to married or civilly partnered LGB employees. There are some differences between civil partnerships and marriage that specifically affect survivor benefits for final-salary pension schemes. If you think this may affect you, speak to HR, an accountant or a lawyer, or check the additional resources at the end of the chapter.

What the law does not protect

There are a few areas which don't affect just bisexual people but do tend to have important intersections with our community which the law does not currently protect.

Polyamorous relationships of any kind are currently not protected. An employer should still not discriminate against you or harass you based on your being polyamorous, but there is no legal recourse against such actions. Additionally, any partner benefits your employer offers are generally only available to one partner.

The legal definition of bisexuality currently speaks of attraction to 'same' and 'opposite sex'. This means that if you yourself are non-binary, or you are dating someone who is, the legal waters get rather murky.

Coming Out/Staying In

There have been several studies internationally which suggest that LGBTQIA+ people who work in environments that are supportive and inclusive, and where they can bring their whole selves to work, are up to 30% more productive. To put it simply, if you're not spending time and energy playing pronoun games and trying to work out if you're safe, you're spending that time and energy doing your job. It is in every employer's best interest to create the kind of environment where employees can be themselves and thrive. This is sometimes easier said than done, and for bisexual people in particular, coming out and staying out in the workplace brings its own challenges.

The UK LGBT rights charity Stonewall found that bisexual women are up to eight times less likely to be out in the workplace than their lesbian colleagues, and bisexual men up to ten times less likely than gay men. Gay-friendly workplaces are not automatically bi-friendly. There are many factors to consider when making a decision to come out at work, and many tactics employers can use to ensure their workplaces are safe and inclusive of bisexual employees.

In some ways, coming out as bisexual at work is similar to coming out as gay or lesbian. You have to consider your safety from physical attack and harassment, as well as the safety of your job. While the law does protect you from harassment and discrimination, filing complaints or taking your employer to court or tribunal can be costly in both money and time, and can cause you infinite amounts of emotional and mental stress. You also have to consider who you want to be out to: your manager, colleagues, clients and business partners may all react in different ways to you coming out. Some people we spoke to found it more difficult to be out in their particular lines of work. Being self-employed in childcare, for instance, may bring a pressure to conform to the expectations of parents; working in an international context with countries where being gay or bi is illegal can also be difficult, as can client-facing roles or non-permanent contracts.

There are, however, also challenges in coming out at work that are specific to bisexual people. Being out to lesbian and gay colleagues, for instance, can be just as fraught as being out to straight ones. When I was running my employer's LGBT network group, I had both gay and straight colleagues ask me why. 'You're not,' they said, 'lesbian, gay or...' You could see the penny drop. Bringing a partner of a different gender to the LGBT night out can get you just as many glares as bringing your same-gender partner to the work Christmas do.

Another common frustration is that to be truly out as bisexual you have to educate people over and over again. In many workplaces now no one would bat an eyelid if you told them you were dating someone of the same gender, but the information that you are not monosexual still takes a while to sink in. You have to educate everyone you meet, and often educate the same people more than once. A proactively supportive workplace should not place this burden on a single individual. An organisation truly inclusive of bisexual employees should cover bi issues as well as other types of invisible diversity in their general diversity and inclusion training.

While being out at work carries some risks, staying in is not without costs either. Even if you believe in maintaining a strict separation between your work and personal life, sometimes it is difficult to draw that line. When colleagues talk about their weekend plans in the middle of Pride season, or you don't want to share that you spent part of your summer holiday at BiCon, you can seem distant and aloof. You are also much more likely to hear homophobic, biphobic and transphobic language around you, as people say things like 'Tom Daley still likes girls too, eh? I bet he's just too scared to properly come out' and 'That jumper looks a bit gay, doesn't it?' We've all been there. Such 'banter' makes the workplace feel much less safe, and challenging it if you're not out can often draw attention to you and raise questions you may not want to answer.

If, like many of us, you are active in the LGBTQIA+ community outside work, you may want to showcase some of the skills you've gained through your activism on your CV. Many people we spoke to felt that was a two-edged sword: on the one hand they were worried about possible discrimination and difficulties in finding a job, but on the other they felt it would help them weed out potential employers for whom their sexuality would be an issue. Equally, not showcasing those key skills can be just as detrimental to your job prospects. Many of us have two versions of our CV: one 'queer' and one less so.

If you do decide to come out at work—whether to your manager, to everyone or to a select few trusted colleagues—the next big question is how to do it. Revealing a current same-gender relationship will generally lead people to the assumption that you're gay. Past same-gender relationships, if you have them, may get written off as 'just a phase'. Using casual chat about 'hot' celebrities to come out, or more likely to *remind* people that you're *still* bi, can sometimes be helpful, but some feel uncomfortable with objectifying people in this way. Personally, I am very open about my long-term relationship with someone of a different gender, but also about my involvement with the LGBT network. My desk is covered in rainbow flyers, posters and magnets, which hopefully creates a safe space for others and opens up opportunities for conversation. You may also want to think about a few key phrases you can use to come out, and practise them with friends. Sometimes you just need a little time to get your head around the words that you are most comfortable with.

Here's what some of our contributors said about coming out or not coming out at work

'I also worry that if I say "I'm bi", people won't grasp what I'm talking about [...] but if I say "I'm bisexual", that makes it sound all about sex. [...] I think I do have the advantage of "looking queer" to mainstream

people, so I'm more telling them I'm not gay than telling them I'm not straight.'
Fred

'Not being out annoys me, because I'm a bi activist and I really want bi people to be out! But I don't seem to be able to do it in a work context.
Reasons I'm not out:
→ I've been there over six years; it feels too late now.
→ I have a husband, so it's easy not to be out as bi.
→ I work in a big open-plan office, so coming out to one person means coming out to everyone at once.'
Joanne

'I still haven't mastered the nonchalant reveal.'
Linette

One particularly tough coming-out conversation to have can be the one with your manager. Coming out to them may help you build a better relationship, but it may also put them on unfamiliar ground that they struggle to deal with. Sometimes you will want to come out because there is something specific you need from your manager: time in your work plan to get involved with the LGBT network, support as you go through a relationship break-up or at the start of a new relationship with someone of a different gender to your previous partner, or maybe even help in addressing homophobic or biphobic language in your team. This approach has the advantage that you are having a very factual and actionable conversation. You use a genuine workplace need to disclose a piece of information about your identity. At the same time, your manager may feel 'ambushed', particularly if you're asking their help with a serious issue like bullying or harassment: they have to process the information you have given them and address the problem at the same time.

If you genuinely want to come out to your manager in order to build a better relationship, and you feel you would be safe doing so, your best bet may well be not to wait until there's a crisis you need help with. That conversation can feel more uncomfortable in a workplace setting: you are sharing something about yourself and your identity with no immediately obvious action or work impact resulting from it. This can make both you and your manager feel vulnerable.

There are a few ways to mitigate this. Being open about your motivation is a good starting point. Say that you want to build a good relationship, maybe even share some of the statistics about supportive workplaces, and explain that you would like to help ensure that your work environment is inclusive. Make it clear to your manager that you would not be coming out to them if you didn't feel safe; this tells them they are doing something right already. Finding something small but actionable for your manager to go away and do after your meeting can also help. Ask them about the wording of a policy, or whether they would help you celebrate the next Bi Visibility Day in your team. This will bring the conversation back firmly into workplace territory and help with some of the discomfort. Do also remember to be clear on how out you want to be with the rest of your team and company. You don't want your manager making assumptions and accidentally outing you.

If you do decide to come out in the workplace, you will probably find it is only the first step on a journey. *Staying* out as bisexual continues to be a challenge for many of us in the face of constant erasure and invisibility. Despite bisexual people being the largest demographic within the LGBT community, very few of us have the privilege to be out and visible. This puts those of us who are out in the spotlight, so the next section will help you think about the next steps on your journey as an out and proud bi role model.

Being a Bi Role Model

Because of the many challenges involved in coming out and staying out in the workplace, it can often feel—even in organisations with thriving 'LGBT' networks—like you're the only bisexual in the village. It is possible that you are, but more likely that there are at least a few other bi people around you struggling with the same invisibility and erasure, or trying to make the same judgements as to whether it is safe to come out, as you are.

No one has an obligation to be out, in the workplace or anywhere else. In a society that often still treats us with bigotry, prejudice and erasure, every bisexual person needs to make their own judgement as to what level of exposure is right for them. Furthermore, the onus should always be on the employer to create an environment where we feel safe to bring our whole selves to work, and even then coming out is a very personal choice that we need to make for ourselves. However, being out has the potential to benefit a lot of people.

Having even a single out bisexual person in an organisation can drastically change the environment. Straight and gay colleagues may start taking their cue from that person as to what is and is not acceptable in terms of banter and workplace conversation, and other bisexual people will be looking to gauge the reactions and determine whether it is safe for them to come out too. Effectively, simply by being out and bringing your whole self to work, you become a role model—and this is true no matter what level of the organisation you happen to be at.

This realisation can be tough to deal with. Being a role model is a position of both power and responsibility. It is not something you necessarily asked for or aspired to, and it is not a position that everyone feels comfortable in. There are nonetheless a few tactics you can use to cope with and make the most of your unexpected new role.

First, you should be aware of what others will be looking for from you. Straight (and gay) colleagues might have questions about being bisexual. The way these are asked can range from friendly and respectful to downright harassing and abusive. It is worth thinking about where your boundaries are: what you will and won't answer and how, or when you will seek support from management or HR. People may also look at how you react to certain things: do you ignore homophobic or biphobic comments; do you challenge them publicly or take a colleague aside? There isn't a 'right' reaction for all situations, but it may help to be aware of your options up front and to have thought about different scenarios. It is easy to get flustered in the heat of the moment, so having a few key phrases prepared that you can use to challenge or diffuse a situation can be incredibly useful. Both closeted bisexual colleagues and straight or gay colleagues may come to you for advice, for instance on coming out or on creating a more inclusive workplace. It is important to be open and honest about your experiences, but particularly when talking to straight and gay colleagues, ensure that they understand that yours is only one point of view and that you do not speak for all bisexual people.

Once you have a rough idea of what you are letting yourself in for, you need to consider your personal safety and well-being. Being a role model, even in a low-key way, can be hugely mentally and emotionally demanding. You need to ensure you are looking after yourself as much as you are looking after others. This might mean that some days you just don't have the energy to be the out, proud bisexual in the village; it might mean that you prioritise what issues and activities you get involved in. Most importantly, it is vital that your organisation supports and empowers you as a role model. You need to know that management, HR and your LGBT network will have your back, and ideally that your work on bisexual issues in the workplace will be recognised and rewarded.

Perhaps the biggest challenge of being a bi role model in the workplace (and arguably elsewhere) is the amount of internalised biphobia we all invariably carry with us. It is easy to fall into a habit of putting lesbian and gay issues first because we ourselves have come to see bi issues as less important, less immediately actionable, or essentially the same. It is easy to decide that your sexuality has nothing to do with the workplace—and that may well be the right decision for you and your particular situation. It is easy to fall into a pattern of only presenting the 'respectable' (i.e. most straight-like) side of the bi community even if you do engage in bi issues at work.

In my experience, being an out bi role model in the workplace tends to bring those tensions and that internalised biphobia to the surface. Like with so many other things, there isn't a single right answer to how to best deal with these internal conflicts. You have to find a way that keeps you safe and that hopefully still enables you to serve the wider community. With any luck, and with the right support, that process itself will be an enriching experience for you and those around you.

Intersections at Work

There are a few intersections with issues of gender and relationship type which, while not affecting all bisexual people, are nonetheless sufficiently common in our community to warrant some discussion with regards to the workplace. Non-binary bisexual people, those in polyamorous relationships and those dating non-binary people may find that their bisexuality is one of the identities they are more comfortable with being open about in a workplace setting. While campaigns on bisexual workplace issues still lag behind those on lesbian and gay issues, they are considerably more advanced than discussions of polyamory and non-binary genders in a work context.

A key challenge in all these situations is the lack of legal protection. UK law does not currently recognise genders outside 'male' and 'female', and this affects the legal definition of bisexuality where the law speaks of attraction to the 'same' and the 'opposite sex'. We are not currently aware of any legal precedents in this area, but this wording certainly seems to put non-binary people and people attracted to them on shaky legal ground with regards to protection from discrimination or harassment in the workplace to the point that your only legal recourse may be to misgender yourself or your partner.

Another issue is that there is relatively little public awareness of non-binary genders and polyamorous relationships. Public perceptions in these areas are even more dominated by myths and stereotypes than when it comes to bisexuality.

The lack of public awareness combined with the lack of legal protection significantly changes the safety assessments you need to make to decide whether to come out at work. Non-binary people we spoke to reported watching out for hints of transphobia from colleagues and using the mention of non-binary celebrities like musician CN Lester to gauge reactions before they came out. Unfortunately, if you are polyamorous or non-binary and you do want to be out about these parts of your identity, you will almost certainly have to do even more educating and explaining than 'just' about bisexuality.

Some of our contributors found that being polyamorous was also a barrier to coming out as bisexual at work even if they would have been happy to do so otherwise. They were worried that coming out would eventually lead to discussions of polyamory, which they didn't feel comfortable with. The intersection between common stereotypes of bisexuality and polyamory (greedy, cheating, dishonest) is particularly unhelpful here.

Living at the intersections

Here is what some of our contributors had to say about the experience of living at these intersections at work.

> 'I'm out as poly and out-ish as genderqueer. With poly, I just drop more than one partner into conversation from time to time, and at staff social things I answer (friendly) curious questions about how it all works. It's a bit harder to drop genderqueer into conversation, but a few of my colleagues follow my public Twitter account, so they know I use that word to describe myself. Generally I just let colleagues take clues from my presentation, my preference for the all-gender toilets, and so on, but occasionally I'll refer in passing to "not really being in either category", if it comes up.
>
> I do get questioned about my relationships more than most of my colleagues! Usually in a very friendly way.
>
> I'm sometimes concerned that I'll be pigeonholed as "the radical one" and that I might miss out on more senior jobs because of that, but I don't know how realistic a worry that is. I don't think it affects my prospects with my current employer.'
>
> Fred

'Coming out as bi might also end up coming out as poly, and I don't know if I want to have those conversations.'
Joanne

'Most issues I face are to do with misgendering. Because I'm not out professionally (even being out at work is to colleagues on a personal level, not to students and not on the systems), I'm recorded as Miss/Ms. [...], not Mx. (students complain about Ms.—how they'd take Mx. is beyond me); I get called "Miss" well over a hundred times a day (registers "yes Miss", or students addressing me. Even colleagues!), am forced to use "female" bathrooms, have "Miss" in my email title, etc. I'm also unable to bind on days when I have chest dysphoria.'
Allie

Ultimately, in much the same way as gay-friendly workplaces aren't necessarily bi-friendly, LGB-friendly workplaces aren't necessarily trans- or poly-friendly. Our contributors' experiences ranged widely, from workplaces where they felt happy and safe to bring their whole selves to work, including non-binary and poly identities, to ones which subjected them to countless microaggressions on a daily basis.

There is still a long way to go for employers who want to become truly supportive of non-binary and polyamorous employees, bisexual or otherwise. Not making assumptions about employees' gender and relationships and not forcing people into binary gender boxes in their day-to-day working environment were some of the top things our contributors wanted their employers to do in order to support them.

Some Practical Things You Can Do to Help Your Employer Be More Inclusive

⇨ Offer to share your story in team meetings or through the company newsletter. It will send a strong signal that yours is a bi-friendly workplace where bisexual issues are discussed openly and honestly.

⇨ Join your LGBT network—and challenge them to become more bi inclusive if they aren't. You may need to start with the basics: help them ensure their materials don't just speak of 'lesbians and gays', and even if it feels petty, mercilessly persecute that hyphen in 'bi-sexual'.

⇨ Help HR get the language in policies right. One key area where this is important is the bullying and harassment policy. Calling biphobia out clearly as unacceptable behaviour and giving concrete examples of what it looks like can make a huge difference to the daily lives of other bisexual people at your workplace.

⇨ Help HR improve their diversity and inclusion training. Ensure the introductory training mentions bisexual issues and biphobia as distinct from homophobia and lesbian and gay issues. Training for people managers which covers bi issues will also have a significant and lasting impact on your workplace.

⇨ Help your organisation understand the business case for diversity and particularly for being more bi inclusive. Increased productivity, better recruitment and retention of top talent, and better services or products for customers and service users can all result from having a diverse and inclusive workplace.

Quick Tips for Employees

⇨ Take some time to get to know your workplace and decide how out you want to be and to whom.

⇨ Prepare a few key phrases you can use to both come out and challenge homophobia and biphobia around you.

⇨ When coming out to your manager, tell them one thing they can do to support you. It will make them feel more comfortable.

⇨ Get involved with your LGBT network group. You have every right to be part of it and be supported.

⇨ Help your workplace get it right: volunteer as bi rep, talk to HR about the wording of policies and diversity training, be a bi role model if you feel comfortable.

Quick Tips for Employers

➯ Be proactively and obviously inclusive: get the wording right in your training materials and policies, celebrate Bi Visibility Day, make sure your LGBT network group is bi (and trans!) inclusive too.

➯ Train your people managers on invisible diversity and bi issues in the workplace.

➯ If you have out, engaged bi employees, give them the support they need to become role models in your organisation, regardless of what level they're at.

➯ Make sure your harassment policy specifically calls out biphobia and gives examples of what it looks like.

➯ Provide gender-neutral toilets for non-binary employees.

13

FICTIONAL BISEXUALITY: REVIEWS AND REFLECTIONS

Editor: Milena Popova

In this chapter, we will examine positive and negative trends in the representation of bisexual people in fiction, and our contributors will share some of their most- and least-liked fictional bisexual characters.

Why Representation in Fiction Matters

I learned to pick up signals on whether it was safe to be out before I knew I was queer. I am as startled by this realisation as anyone, but that doesn't make it any less true. I remember the first time I heard the word 'homosexual'. I had no idea what it meant at the time, but it sounded like a dirty secret. I remember my father disapproving of a particular music video because it had women kissing in it. I don't remember anything from biology class except this: our teacher explaining (incorrectly) how anal sex between men led to HIV transmission. All this between the ages of seven and twelve. Later, there was the teacher who was sacked for being gay, and being taught *Where Angels Fear to Tread* without reference to Forster's sexuality.

I grew up in an environment where the only images and narratives of queerness authority figures gave me were negative ones. As a teen, I fled to pulp sci-fi and, later, fan fiction to find positive or even just neutral representations of bisexual and other queer people, to reassure myself that I was 'normal'.

Seeking such reassurance from society and our external environment is very common, regardless of who we are. Finding this kind of validation in media, fiction and the people around us can be a great source of personal comfort and confidence. For those of us on the margins of society and culture, on the other hand, the constant misrepresentation or erasure can cause a deep disconnect between our lived experience and what society tells us is acceptable or desirable.

Having a range of well-rounded bisexual characters in fiction would therefore be immensely helpful to many bisexual people. It would allow us to see the diversity of our experience reflected in the stories our society deems important enough to tell and give us the feeling that we are valued and included. Unfortunately, we are still way off the mark here. Bisexual representation in fiction continues to be rare and plagued by tropes and stereotypes. In many cases, characters' bisexual identities are deliberately erased, for instance in TV or film adaptations of books. A recent example of this is the *Constantine* TV series, an adaptation of the *Hellblazer* graphic novels, the protagonist of which is canonically bi.

The BBC adaptation of D.H. Lawrence's *Women in Love* and the 2008 film of Evelyn Waugh's *Brideshead Revisited*

By DH Kelly

Both adaptations, as far as I saw them, wound me up in various ways, but there was one thing they had in common. Both books have a major bisexual male character (Rupert Birkin and Charles Ryder), and in both adaptations, their sexuality was changed. Birkin becomes a homosexual who dabbles with women, and Ryder becomes a hetero-sexual who dabbles with (horribly caricatured, camp) men. It is as if, in the early twenty-first century, we are less able to cope with sexual ambiguity than in the mid-twentieth when these books were published.

Neither Lawrence nor Waugh used the word 'bisexual', but the characters of Birkin and Ryder both had deep romantic and sexual feelings towards both men and women. Ryder has a romantic affair with a man and later has a romantic affair with a woman, whom he wants to marry. Birkin is somewhat in love with his best male friend and gets a tremendous kick out of physical contact with him (as does his friend) as well as other men. But he is also properly in love with a woman, even if he is a bit sexist and will insist in overthinking it all.

When making adaptations of sixty-three- and ninety-one-year-old books means simplifying and sanitising sexual matters, then I think that we're not nearly so sexually progressive as we imagine we are.

Sometimes such erasure of identity doesn't only happen to characters but to authors too!

On how Shakespeare is taught in schools

By Kaye

I get very frustrated about the way that Shakespeare is taught in schools. Back when Shakespeare was being set up to be the national poet, it was seen to be very important to portray him as straight, even though identity labels like gay, straight and bi didn't exist when he was alive. So the plays and poems that had any hint of same-sex activity were played down or ignored. Of Shakespeare's 154 love sonnets, 126 are addressed to a man, but in the past this has been explained away or hushed up, and at one stage they were even rewritten with feminine pronouns and given titles to make them sound straight. If the same-sex desires in these texts are acknowledged, which is often not until people have got to university (assuming they haven't got bored by then and studied something else), people usually reframe the poems as homoerotic rather than acknowledging that the desires for other-sex partners in the texts are just as valid, let alone that gender was a lot more fluid when Shakespeare was writing than modern audiences and critics usually give him credit for.

It may sound like heresy, but there's nothing particularly special about Shakespeare. However, because he has become this huge cultural figure, a lot of his words and phrases, like 'if music be the food of love', are used in everyday speech. Ideas like the star-crossed lovers in Romeo and Juliet have entered into our collective understanding of what love means. If bisexual people can't see themselves reflected in Shakespeare's work, because of this drive to sanitise him as 'the Bard', then they are being culturally excluded from something very significant. The obsession with Shakespeare also obscures other playwrights from the same period, like Christopher Marlowe and John Lyly, whose work is even more easily seen as reflective of bisexual desire in the Renaissance period.

One area where representation matters even more is in fiction aimed at children and young adults.

Mary Sue pieces, and what they tell us about LGBTQIA+ youth

By Allie George

As an English teacher, I mark a lot of Mary Sue pieces. I'm fairly confident of my abilities to hand back creative-writing pieces which lack students' names with a high degree of accuracy. Students reflect themselves in their protagonists: the daredevil always in trouble at school; the shy but brilliant scientist; the isolated, brooding poet. Small details may change: the general character rarely does.

It's not just as-yet-undeveloped writing skills. And it's not teen narcissism. It's the desperate desire to see ourselves reflected in fiction. Young people will automatically create this for themselves. In order to make sense of the world, what better way than through a fictionalised advocate?

Reading is crucial: most English teachers would agree that they can easily identify a reader from a non-reader simply from students' writing. Schools are bending over backwards to implement DEAR

(Drop Everything And Read), Reading For Pleasure, Accelerated Reader, Active Reader, and oh-dear-God-please-just-read programmes. And the recent popularity of young adult film adaptations is a firm indicator of the influence of fiction in young adult culture.

For LGBTQIA+ teens, it's difficult to find sufficient representation of that facet of their identity—and we must remember, LGBTQIA+ people are not a monolith; no teen will identify with every LGBTQIA+ character they are presented with, nor enjoy every LGBTQIA+ book. And yet, of the 2013 *New York Times* Young Adult Best Sellers list, only 12% of books featured LGBTQIA+ characters. Whilst at first glance this may seem statistically comparable with the percentage of LGBTQIA+ people in the population, when we count *characters*, this percentage dramatically falls.

What is more, only 17% of school libraries stock any kind of LGBTQIA+ fiction. And a scan of the books available in that lucky 17%—even there, hardly in abundance—tends towards the 'safer' forms of representation. One librarian told me of her fondness for Patrick Ness's *More Than This* because the protagonist 'just happened to be gay. It wasn't made into a big deal'. Another even told me that she felt *Harry Potter* was representation enough.

This simply isn't adequate. LGBTQIA+ teens deserve space in fiction, to be told that they too are valid. Yes, they deserve protagonists whose sexuality and gender do not drive the story, heroes who are LGBTQIA+ without issue; but they also deserve to see protagonists struggling with the same issues they themselves are struggling with. They deserve advocacy. They deserve to not have to rely solely on their self-penned Mary Sues.

YA fiction recommendations with bisexual protagonists

By Allie George

David Levithan's *Every Day* features A, who occupies a different body, of different genders, each day. Levithan touches on non-binary identities, and A is canonically multisexual.

Malinda Lo's sci-fi series *Adaptation/Inheritance,* and *Ash,* her retelling of *Cinderella,* both feature bisexual protagonists, whose sexuality is a central part, but not the sole main theme, of the plot.

Pink, by Lili Wilkinson, addresses a lesser-explored side of bisexual representation: coming out as bisexual having previously identified as a lesbian.

Laura Lam's *Micah Grey* series explores gender as well as bisexuality. The eponymous Micah is coercively assigned female at birth: something which sits uneasily with the genderqueer, intersex protagonist.

Sophie, the protagonist of *Far From You* by Tess Sharpe, is something of a rare find in bisexual young adult literature: a bisexual character who explicitly states her sexuality, and isn't made into a trope of confusion or deceit.

Some Common Pitfalls

Given the scarcity of bisexual characters in fiction, the ease with which we can find examples of just about every negative trope and stereotype associated with bisexuality is staggering. Many bi characters are in fact simply a collection of such tropes, so there is significant overlap between the categories below. I have tried to pick one or two examples to illustrate each one, but I am sure you can come up with more.

The 'it was just a phase' bisexual

Willow Rosenberg from the TV show *Buffy* is the Marmite of bisexual representation in fiction. For all his alleged progressiveness, series creator Joss Whedon definitely missed a trick in the way he handled Willow's sexuality. Through the series, Willow is shown to have meaningful romantic and sexual relationships with men and women. Her famous line, 'Well, hello! Gay now!', however, deliberately erases part of her sexuality and identity. Willow remains a hugely popular character with fans of the show as well as with at least parts of the LGBTQIA+ community, but for many bisexual viewers her 'turning gay' was a deeply painful reminder of just how marginalised our own identity is in popular culture.

The 'anything but in name' bisexual

There are a lot of things that the critically acclaimed Netflix original series *Orange is the New Black* does brilliantly. It deals with issues of race, class, crime and punishment, gender and sexuality, and institutional abuse, and generally it does so in a sensitive and enlightening manner. Yet there is one word that frustratingly does not seem to feature in the writers' vocabulary: 'bisexual'. Piper Chapman, the main character, is based on Piper Kerman, a self-identified bisexual woman whose experiences in prison serve as the inspiration for the series. The fictionalised Piper is shown in relationships with a man and a woman, but even three seasons in, the closest she comes to discussing her sexuality on screen is to say she is 'a former lesbian'.

The 'honestly, they're bi, we just can't show it in the text' bisexual

Fans of *Harry Potter* will recognise this one. After seven books, J.K. Rowling finally announced in an interview that Dumbledore was gay. Clearly, there was no time to mention this in the actual text, in between the detailed descriptions of exams and waiting around in tents. Bisexual characters, too, suffer from this 'not in the text' syndrome. Princess Bubblegum from the popular animated series *Adventure Time* may or may not have dated Marceline in the past, depending on which comment from the show's cast and production team you trust. And they say bisexual people are indecisive! (This is also known as 'queerbaiting', and we will talk more about it later in this chapter.)

Similarly, the relationship between Korra and Asami in the popular Nickelodeon show *The Legend of Korra* is only hinted at in the very last scene. Both women were shown in complex, well-written romantic relationships with one of the male leads, and talking about feelings is one of the key features of the series. Yet when it comes to the blossoming romance between Korra and Asami, all we get is a plan to go on vacation together and some hand-holding that parallels a previous scene in which two characters—a man and a woman—get married. The redeeming feature of Korrasami (as the pairing has become known among fans) is that the show's producers very clearly stated that both characters are bisexual and definitely in a relationship. The tragedy is that this could not be shown more clearly in the series because Nickelodeon execs did not deem it appropriate for the younger audience the show is aimed at.

The 'what do you mean not only women are bi?' bisexual

Particularly on screen, bisexuality seems to be reserved almost exclusively for women (and by extension catering to the male gaze). The occasional man we see all too often conforms to the 'too scared to come out as gay' stereotype. For instance, Andrew in the US TV show *Desperate Housewives* tells us, 'Look, I love vanilla ice cream, okay? But every now and then I'm probably gonna be in the mood for chocolate.' Andrew has a series of flings and relationships with men. However, the only relationship with a woman he is ever shown in is called into question by his mother and the woman he is dating as being for money alone. Andrew is never really shown to call out these biphobic assumptions, and his sexuality seems to conform more to the 'too scared to come out as gay' trope than reflect a bisexual experience.

This is just the start of fictional bisexuality's gender woes. The notable absence of non-binary genders from the vast majority of cultural output means that we hardly ever see either non-binary bisexual people, or binary bisexual people attracted to people of non-binary genders. This lack of representation is clearly harmful to non-binary people in much the same way that lack of bi representation is harmful to bi people. In addition, it reinforces the 'bi equals two' and 'bisexuals are transphobic' stereotypes, and doesn't reflect many bisexual people's lived experience.

The 'OMG, don't make them kiss on screen!' bisexual

Fictional bisexual women of the past share something with fictional bisexual men of the present: their mysterious inability to kiss same-gender partners on screen. In the '90s cult sci-fi show *Babylon 5*, Commander Susan Ivanova is portrayed as bisexual, with several tragic romantic entanglements with men and one (equally tragic) with a woman. Yet just before Susan and Talia get to kiss, the camera pans strategically away, leaving us gnashing our teeth in frustration.

Frank Underwood, the lead character in the Netflix original series *House of Cards*, is similarly afflicted. At one point he is shown tongue-deep in the vagina of a woman half his age, yet when it comes to kissing a man, Frank proves remarkably camera-shy.

The 'blink and you miss it' bisexual

I first read Guy Gavriel Kay's historical fantasy novel *The Lions of Al-Rassan*—which remains a favourite book to this day—in my teens, at that vulnerable time when I was clutching at even the tiniest straws of bisexual representation I could find. This is the only explanation I have for how I walked away with the firm conviction that one of the lead characters, Ammar ibn Khairan, was clearly stated to be bisexual in the book. On further readings, Ammar's sexuality is barely even alluded to in about four sentences throughout the book, and every single one of those is ambiguous and open to interpretation. More on 'headcanons' later.

The 'sexy villainess' bisexual

Catherine Tramell, the female lead in the '90s erotic thriller *Basic Instinct*, is everything you ever wanted for your bisexual trope bingo card: hypersexualised, manipulative and deceitful; bisexual for the male gaze. There are considerably more sexy bisexual villainesses on film than in real life. This trope is often defended with arguments around the character's personal choices, which might even be valid if it wasn't nigh on the sole form of representation bisexual women get on screen. This gives an extremely limited and unrealistic view of the experiences of bisexual women and reinforces biphobic stereotypes. Misrepresentation like this often leads directly to harassment of or discrimination against bisexual women, such as being assumed to be sexually available and asked for threesomes, or being assumed to be manipulative and deceitful, potentially leading to direct discrimination in the workplace and other spaces.

The 'gay because the straight character says so' bisexual

LGb(t) representation has become quite fashionable in mainstream comics these days (after webcomics had been doing it for over a decade). Superheroes come out left, right and centre. In *All-New X-Men* it was the turn of a young Bobby Drake, also known as Iceman. Except he didn't so much come out as was kicked out of the closet by his friend Jean Grey, along with every biphobic trope you can think of. Seriously, you might want to get your bingo cards out for this one. 'Bobby...you're gay,' says the telepathic Jean. This being Marvel, and involving time travel and continuity issues, apparently the writers felt the need to explain away the character's long-established history of relationships with women. Maybe, young Bobby speculates, his older self couldn't cope with being both gay and a mutant. Look how all those relationships failed, says Jean helpfully. One of his exes doesn't even live on Earth any more!

'Maybe I'm bi,' says Bobby.

'They say everybody is,' Jean continues in her helpfulness. 'But I think you are more...full gay.'

It's almost like writer Brian Michael Bendis had consulted the biphobia handbook for this one.

And Sometimes They Get It Right

In between all the tropes and stereotypes, very occasionally a bisexual character leaps off the page or out of the screen at us, and all we can feel is a sense of deep recognition and euphoria, an ecstatic 'YES, yes, *this one*, this one's an actual human being, a bit like me!'

The 'not suddenly gay' bisexual

Captain Jack Harkness of *Doctor Who* and *Torchwood* fame is another Marmite character to the bi community. Many love his openness about his sexuality, while some object to his 'would fuck anything that moves' attitude. Regardless of how you feel about Jack himself, his flamboyance makes an excellent counterpoint to the much subtler characterisation of his partner, Ianto Jones. We first meet Ianto early on in *Torchwood* when he has infiltrated the organisation to try to save his girlfriend, who has been turned into a Cyberman. Once that fails, however, Ianto develops an intimate relationship with Jack. There are a couple of Ianto's interactions with friends and family which particularly stand out.

In *Torchwood: Children of Earth,* Ianto's sister and her family confront him about his relationship with Jack. Ianto doesn't dismiss or diminish past relationships with women and explains that he hasn't 'gone bent', but that he does love Jack.

In the radio play *Torchwood—The Lost Files 2: Submission*, Ianto has to work together with an ex-girlfriend, Carlie. During a quiet moment in the action, Ianto and Carlie have a brief heart-to-heart. They acknowledge their past relationship, but also Ianto's feelings for Jack. Ianto makes it very clear that what makes Jack different for him isn't gender but the fact that, despite the love they share, Jack's immortality means that one day he will have to leave Ianto behind.

Ianto's characterisation and story arc are far from perfect. Many fans would prefer not to remember his tragic death in *Children of Earth*. He is, however, portrayed as unapologetically bi, and we get to see how his sexuality affects his relationships with the people around him. These conversations are generally treated sensitively and respectfully by the show writers, and Ianto often tops lists of favourite bisexual characters.

The 'biphobia is a thing, and I deal with it' bisexual

The groundbreaking Channel 4 series *Sugar Rush* follows the misadventures of lesbian teenager Kim. Once she gets over her unfortunate infatuation with her straight friend Sugar, Kim starts dating Saint, a young bisexual woman and owner of a sex shop. Kim is constantly worried that Saint will cheat on her, and particularly once she meets Saint's ex-boyfriend, she has doubts that Saint will be able to remain faithful and not be tempted away by men. Ironically, Kim is the party in this relationship who is perpetually indecisive and even caught cheating once.

Through all this, Saint makes it consistently clear that what she's interested in is a monogamous relationship with Kim. She is assertive about her feelings and her needs within the relationship, while also seeking to reassure Kim and find compromises that work for both of them.

In an ideal world, I think Saint would have explicitly called Kim out on her biphobia. Saint's portrayal does, however, mirror many bisexual people's experiences of biphobia in their own relationships, and the series handles the subject maturely and insightfully.

The 'smoking hot' bisexual

Erotica is, unfortunately, not a genre that is immune to biphobic stereotypes. Yet here, too, there are some gems worth talking about. I spoke with author Aleksandr Voinov about his approach to writing bisexual characters in erotica:

AV: Bi characters are the most natural for me to write.

MP: I loved what you did with *Gold Digger*, particularly with Henri being supportive of Nikolai's sexuality.

AV: I figured he's seen it all and is confident enough in being gay/himself that he doesn't feel threatened by loving a bi guy. Though my favourite couple/throuple (?) is Stefano/Silvio/Donata—genderfluid bi menage. And hot as hell. #DarkSoul

MP: That's the other thing I like: you show a range of different bi characters.

AV: Well, we are all people. :) Sexuality is not WHO they are, though I love writing sex and am sex-positive. Most of all, I want to get away from usual bi clichés: kill off the other partner so they can be with same/different sex partner... I also loathe the 'Evil Bi'—people so screwed up by conflicting desires they destroy other people. Thirdly, I hate them coming out on one side of the fence and emotionally disavowing previous other-sex relationships. I try to write characters who are largely at peace and mature in how they deal with desire and conflict... after all, I have to spend weeks and months in their heads and want to be able to like/relate to them.

Purple Prose contributor Jules also cited Chris Parker from Laura Antoniou's *Marketplace* series of BDSM erotica as a favourite bisexual character 'because it is *so* rare to find a well-written, three-dimensional bisexual trans man in smut'.

The 'bi the way' bisexual

Sometimes it's refreshing when a character's bisexuality is an integral part of them but not a big deal. Gwendolyn, in the graphic novel series *Saga,* travels across the galaxy in pursuit of her ex-fiancé and now fugitive, Marko. Yet we also learn—with the help of the wonderful Lying Cat—that Gwendolyn lost her virginity to a woman. In the sci-fi show *The 100*, Clarke finds herself in a terrible position, having to kill her boyfriend Finn. When Lexa later kisses her, Clarke does not deny she is interested, but says she is not ready for another relationship so soon after Finn's death. And in *Warehouse 13*, Helena G. Wells refers to her past and present relationships with men as well as women. One of her colleagues does a brief double take, but that's about all the attention Helena's sexuality gets. Gwendolyn,

Clarke and H.G. are well-developed, complex characters with their own stories. Their bisexuality is a facet of their personalities in the same way as Gwendolyn's protectiveness, Clarke's leadership, and H.G.'s brilliance.

The 'I'm just another member of a diverse cast' bisexual

Video games may have a bad reputation, particularly after GamerGate, but they *can* be a medium for risk-taking, exploration of complex social issues and representation. There are independent games that deal with issues like depression, migration, gender identity and sexuality. And even the occasional big blockbuster game does a good job. Developers BioWare are noted for their representation of diverse sexualities in role-playing games like *Mass Effect* and *Dragon Age*.

Romance options are a key game mechanic in both game series: the player character may choose to flirt, or have sex or even a long-term romantic relationship with one or more of the companion characters. BioWare caused a stir when they included two characters available as romance options to both male and female player characters in *Dragon Age: Origins*. When challenged by a self-identified 'straight male gamer' for neglecting their 'main demographic' in *Dragon Age II* (where four out of five romance option characters are bisexual), BioWare writer David Gaider publicly defended the decision, stating that the romances in the games were 'for everyone'.

While the first two *Dragon Age* games feature characters who are either straight or bisexual, *Dragon Age: Inquisition*, the latest release in the series, also features two characters (a man and a woman) who will only engage in same-gender romances. This is a significant statement from BioWare: bisexuality is no longer just a way to make diverse romance options available while saving yourself writing a whole other character; it is a sexuality distinct from gay or straight.

There *are* diverse and well-written bi characters out there, in mainstream media and genre fiction alike, but it does take effort to find them.

What Our Contributors Thought

We asked our contributors to tell us about fictional portrayals of bisexual characters which they found notable. Here's what they thought.

Chasing Amy

In this 1997 Kevin Smith movie, comic book artist Holden (Ben Affleck) meets another comic book artist Alyssa (Joey Lauren Adams) at a convention and falls for her. When he finds out that she's a lesbian he still insists on pursuing her and eventually they get together. Holden thinks that he's special in some way in getting together with Alyssa—as far as he's concerned, he's the only man that she's ever been with.

Holden's friend Banky (Jason Lee), who he writes comics with, is jealous of the relationship and tries to dig up dirt on Alyssa. He discovers that whilst at high school Alyssa participated in a threesome with two guys, which gave her the nickname 'Finger Cuffs'.

Despite seeking advice from friends over the situation, it comes to a head when Holden angrily confronts Alyssa over her past and the relationship ends. Holden then makes things even worse by suggesting a threesome with Alyssa and Banky to try to show Alyssa that he accepts her past and to repair his friendship with Banky, who he now realises is in love with him. He loses Alyssa for good as well as his friendship with Banky.

Holden does eventually realise that he was in the wrong, and the film ends on a bittersweet note with him trying to make amends with Alyssa and Banky after they have gone their separate ways.

Throughout the film Alyssa faces hostility for her sexuality: from lesbian friends who see her as tainted from sleeping with a man; from Banky, who uses her sexuality as a reason to not like her; and also from Holden when he discovers her past. The film is classic Kevin Smith, so if you enjoyed other films of his such as *Clerks* and *Mallrats,* then you'll love this. However, the biphobia towards Alyssa in the film is very accurately portrayed and can cut a little close to the bone at times.

Cat

The Stranger's Child

By the time I'd read the first few pages of this novel by Alan Hollinghurst, I knew why my friend had recommended it to me: all suppressed early-twentieth-century homoerotic undercurrents and (at least behavioural) bisexuality.

It generation-hops every few chapters, ending up in the first decade of the twenty-first century, and uses that opportunity to explore reliability of memory, subjectivity and interpretation of experience among the central group of characters, leaving a surprisingly satisfying uncertainty even when the book ends.

It gives a sideways picture of how the experience of male homosexuality and/or bisexuality has changed over the last century in the UK, for queer/gay/homosexual/bisexual men and to a certain extent for those around them.

The characters are rounded and human enough to be engaging without being especially likeable—just enough good points to keep me reading—and the fact that we only get a partial portrait of each one adds to the deliberate sense that we're only being given part of the story. Several of the characters are or might be bi; the lack of clear sexuality labels is consistent with the book's themes of partial information, unreliable narration and uncertainty.

Overall, it was very enjoyable: a queer page-turner.

Fred Langridge

Lost Girl

Lost Girl is a Canadian TV show about Bo, a bisexual succubus who refuses to choose a side between the worlds of the dark and light fae.

When I first heard about the concept, I was wary, as it sounded like it would be playing on tired stereotypes of bisexuals being sexually voracious and unable to choose, and I feared the character's sexuality would be used for shock value. I've been very pleasantly surprised. Bo's sexuality is written well and consistently. Her serious relationships are given equal stakes, regardless of gender. She has a strong female friendship in which there is no sexual tension at all (it's sad that I find that remarkable for screen depictions of bisexuals). In fact, I wish the other characters and plots had been written to the same standard!

If you can get past the 'weird and wacky fae of the week' plot device which is used repeatedly, I'd say this is one of the best depictions I've seen of bisexuality on the screen.

Linette

Fixing It for Ourselves

As we have seen, the representation of bisexuality in fiction can often be problematic. To add insult to injury, many writers and producers of popular culture deliberately engage in 'queerbaiting': implying either in the text or in commentary same-gender desire between characters, but never following through on it by depicting a real relationship. The intention behind queerbaiting is to attract certain audience demographics (the LGBTQIA+ community and allies, women of various sexualities who enjoy male/male romance) while still retaining more conservative viewers by never outright showing queer relationships. The US horror/fantasy TV show *Supernatural* has become among fans synonymous with queerbaiting, with the sexual tension between rugged, macho Dean Winchester and the angel Castiel never leading to anything more than snide, borderline homophobic comments from the cast.

The problem with queerbaiting is, of course, the message it sends. What creators are telling their LGB audiences (trans representation is even more problematic) is effectively that they will happily throw us a bone in order to take our money, but that at the same time we are not deemed respectable enough to warrant full representation.

Fortunately, readers and TV and film audiences have long stopped taking canon—or even commentary from creators—as the word of God. Many of us will simply pick and choose the parts of a show or book that we like and add bits of our own to create a 'headcanon': a version of the story or the character that lives in our heads and loosely fits within the original story but also better reflects our own desires and sensibilities.

Sometimes we simply take creators up on their queerbaiting. Often, we read between the lines, attaching more significance to certain lines than people not starved for representation would. I did this many years ago with *The Lions of Al-Rassan*. The beauty of bisexual headcanons in particular, though, is that unless a character goes out of their way to specifically identify as straight, gay or aromantic asexual, a bisexual and/or biromantic reading is impossible to disprove. (And, of course, sometimes even characters who specifically state their orientation may have good reason to be closeted, or may not have had opportunities to explore their sexuality.)

Our contributors mentioned some of their favourite bi headcanons:

⇨ Steve Rogers (Captain America) in the Marvel Cinematic Universe. In *Captain America: The First Avenger*, Steve is shown in a romantic relationship with agent Peggy Carter. However, his relationships with both Bucky Barnes and, in *Captain America: The Winter Soldier*, Sam Wilson can also be read as romantic. The bi community in fandom has firmly claimed Steve Rogers as one of our own.

⇨ Dean Winchester in *Supernatural*. Throughout the series, Dean is shown flirting and occasionally sleeping with a number of women, but fans attach significance to his relationship with Castiel and more casual encounters with other male characters too.

⇨ Sam Tyler in the BBC time-travel/cop show *Life on Mars*. Sam has a girlfriend, Maya, in his original timeline in 2006, but also pursues Annie in 1973. Many fans also read more than friendship into Sam's relationship with the gruff Detective Chief Inspector Gene Hunt.

⇨ *Everyone* in Canadian-American sci-fi show *Stargate Atlantis*, especially Dr. Rodney McKay and Colonel John Sheppard (with a hefty side order of Dr. Elizabeth Weir and Teyla Emmagan). Both John and Rodney express attraction to women, but their joint dynamic is the most homoerotic thing on television since the original Kirk and Spock! The timing of Elizabeth and Teyla's respective on-screen relationships with men conveniently allows them to have developed a romance with each other off-screen in between.

⇨ Remus Lupin and Nymphadora Tonks in *Harry Potter*. Both Remus and Tonks are very commonly read as gay in their early appearances (and Remus is often paired up with Sirius). So strong is this fan reaction to both characters that their eventual relationship with each other is often dismissed. Bi fans, however, have another option open to us: recognise their love for each other in the same way as we see Remus and Sirius's relationship and identify with Tonks's queer presentation.

Of course, once a version of a story or a character is in your head, you might as well write it down and share it with others—which is what many fans do in the form of fan fiction. Much of fan fiction depicts same-gender relationships between men, often erasing canon different-gender relationships for these characters. It is therefore not always a bi-friendly place, but bi representation (and general diversity) in fan fiction has improved significantly over the years. It is definitely a space open to bi fans to play in.

Ultimately, it should not be fandom's or the wider audience's job to fix a lack of representation of bisexual and other queer people in popular culture through headcanons and fan fiction. They are great workarounds in the crisis of representation we are currently faced with, but in an ideal world we would see a wide range of diverse, three-dimensional bisexual characters across our media and cultural output. This would allow us to see our own lived experiences reflected in the stories our society tells, and help do away with all those hurtful biphobic tropes and stereotypes we currently have to deal with on a daily basis.

14

ALLIES IN THE BISEXUAL COMMUNITY

Editor: Elizabeth Baxter-Williams

Not every person you find in bisexual spaces, either in real life or online, identifies as bisexual. Monosexual-identified people who are invited into our spaces and communities might be our friends, partners or members of our families, or someone with a professional interest in bisexuality, like a health worker or researcher. They might even be someone who is just curious to learn more. People with a supportive interest in bisexuality are usually called allies.

When bisexual community organisers meet, they often use the word 'ally' as a shorthand for anyone who might be in a bisexual space who does not identify as bisexual, but in practice allyhood is more complex than that.

What Is a Bisexual Ally?

An ally to any marginalised identity is someone who does not share that identity but nevertheless engages in actions designed to uplift those who do. For bisexuals, that means a person who supports bisexual individuals and stands up for the rights of the bisexual community. From helping a friend come out of the closet to participating in lobbying campaigns, allyhood can take a lot of different forms.

Primarily, though, it consists of two overlapping strands: the interpersonal and the political.

'A lot of being a good ally is just being a good friend and a decent person.'
Avalon

Most people are introduced to the notion of allyhood because they know somebody who identifies as bisexual and they want to be supportive. That might mean going with them to an LGBT or bisexual social group to steady their nerves, or listening and sympathising if they describe the biphobia they have encountered. It could mean baking them a coming-out cake or giving them a pep talk before a date.

It is not enough to be supportive of the bisexual people you have relationships with and those who live a similar lifestyle to you; you must also lend your voice to support bisexual people from outside your peer group.

There is not a single social group that does not include bisexual people. You will find us across all genders, classes, religious affiliations, nationalities and races. You will find us across all age groups, professions, and levels of income and education. Some of us have physical and/or mental disabilities. Some of us have criminal records, histories of abuse or a fluctuating immigration status. Being a bisexual ally means standing in solidarity with *all* bisexuals. Even, or, indeed, especially, those with experiences that you do not recognise or share. To be an ally only to those who present a tasteful or assimilationist version of bisexuality is to do a disservice to the entire community.

Why Does the Bisexual Community Need Allies?

We live in a biphobic society. The negative stereotypes and stigma surrounding bisexuality mean that it is the least understood of the basic models of sexuality. Despite having been at the forefront of what was once known as 'gay liberation' and is now called the LGBT rights movement, bisexuals are marginalised and still lack visibility and respect from both 'mainstream' and lesbian and gay communities. Bisexual people who also identify as a person of colour, transgender and/or working class are marginalised further still. It is our unavoidable responsibility to make those voices heard. This book is full of both hard data and personal anecdotes that demonstrate that our struggle towards an equitable place in our own society is far from over.

Allies have a key role to play in this struggle. They may have access to resources and assets at platforms frequently denied to bisexual people, and they have voices that are harder to ignore and more opportunities to use those voices. Even by simply adding to our number, allies can make a difference: the more people we have, the more we can do.

A note on LGT and queer-identified allies to the bisexual community

If you fall under the LGBTQIA+ umbrella, you might think this chapter is not about you. Well, it is and it isn't. This is definitely the page that you casually leave open, hoping that your father/sister/best friend/aunty/girlfriend will pick it up, but it's important to remember that in the LGBT community we have got the opportunity to be allies to each other. Our identities as members of an oppressed or disenfranchised group do not give us a 'pass' on perpetuating the oppression of other groups.

It is a bleak fact that bisexual people are sorely in need of allies within the LGBT community. There is a culture of biphobia among lesbian and gay people which means bisexual people have difficulty accessing the spaces and services that are nominally for them. This includes vital health and community services.

Being Straight in the Bisexual Community

By David Matthewman

Monosexual people fall into bi space for many reasons. In my case, it was because most of my friends were bi. I've always found it a very welcoming place, whether it's an informal night down the pub, or the full-on immersive experience of BiCon. It's so friendly, and so lacking in anyone gatekeeping who gets in that it's easy to miss something important: it is a bi-majority space, and those spaces are rare and precious to bi people. Monosexual allies who are used to having spaces where they know they'll be welcome—straight people hardly need to think about it, gay people may need to seek them out but they're relatively common—can take this for granted, and we need to respect that this very comfortable space is not ours, and that it can be fragile.

It's also important to remember that bi spaces are so used to (usually) straight men arriving in them looking for a threesome that they've coined a term for it: 'unicorn hunter'. Don't be one of those, and don't be insulted if you're suspected of it; they have good reason to be suspicious. Also, don't expect praise or 'cookies' for not being biphobic; it might indeed be noteworthy among monosexual people, but it shouldn't be.

That aside, if you come to bi space as I did for the people in it, and try to find your place in it rather than shaping it to fit you, you'll do just fine. I fell into bi space because most of my friends were bi and, over fifteen years on, I'm still there and most of them still are too.

How Do I Become an Ally?

Asking that question is the first step.

Learning how to be a good ally can feel like it's a long list of 'don'ts'. It can feel like you're being told off for something you haven't even done wrong yet. It requires an amount of honest self-reflection that can make us defensive. But just like anything else, it takes practice to get it right. Think of it as driving a car: putting the key in the ignition is easy, but mastering a three-point turn takes a while.

At the end of this chapter, you will find some suggestions of positive actions you can take as an ally-in-training. But first you need to do some groundwork.

Just like a house, for our allyhood to be strong, it must be built on firm foundations. Here are four no-nonsense, harsh realities that potential allies must understand:

⇨ It's hard. When you decide to become an ally, it means opening the door to sometimes feeling a little uncomfortable. Learning about other people's experiences can be rewarding and enlightening, but it can also be upsetting, angering and deflating. But allyhood is not just about learning, it is also about acting, and that means making mistakes and being criticised. You may want to give up and walk away. Remember: while you have that option, bisexual people don't.

⇨ There's no such thing as a self-appointed ally. Anyone can claim to be an ally, but true allyhood is reflected in your actions. It is helpful in this respect to consider an ally as something you aspire to be, rather than something that you are.

⇨ You're in charge of your own education. As an ally, it's inevitable that you'll want to learn, but it's important to remember that bisexual people are not here to teach you. That may sound a little harsh, and certainly some bisexual people will be happy to share their knowledge with you, but you shouldn't expect that. Instead, seek out other resources by going online or heading to the library. You'll encounter a much wider range of perspectives that way, too.

⮕ You have privileges that other people don't have. You cannot ally yourself with bisexual people without examining your own privileges and recognising that, as a monosexual person (straight or gay), you are a member of a group that has historically sidelined, devalued, ignored and abused bisexuals. That doesn't mean that you personally are responsible for the marginalisation of the bisexual people, but it does mean that you have benefited from their marginalisation *even if you don't realise it*.

Quick and Dirty Tips for New Allies

Don't do it for the glory

If you're in it for praise, you're in it for the wrong reason. If you only condemn offensive jokes when a bisexual person is with you, or you're happy to let bi-erasure slide when no one's listening, you're not an ally.

> 'Oh, God, straight people at Pride. Where are they the rest of the year? They want to party but they don't want to get their hands dirty.'
> Lewis

Allies are active in their support for and advocacy of the bisexual community. They take responsibility for the biphobia perpetrated in monosexual culture and work to stop it, even when it's difficult, and even when it's inconvenient, and even when they won't be praised for it.

Choose to believe

When someone tells you they're bisexual, believe them. Don't ask for proof. Don't use a different word to describe their sexuality, especially if you're doing it because it makes it more comfortable for you. Don't ask if they're confused, or tell them they're 'bi now, gay later'.

We know ourselves better than you, and if we do change our minds later down the road, so what?

Learn when to speak…

As an ally, it is critical that you engage with people who are like you. Bisexuals do not need you to tell them, for example, that they're more likely to experience sexual assault than any other group—they already know. They need you to tell other people. Engaging with the people who respect and love you is one of the easiest ways to be an ally to bisexual people, and members of your peer group who might dismiss the words of bisexual people may well listen to you.

…and when to keep schtum

Being an ally is about speaking up, challenging the status quo in order to change it. Sometimes, though, it's better to stay quiet.

It's great to be vocal in your support of bisexual people, but it's important to be mindful of the space you're taking up. As much as you might have learned about bisexual experiences, you have not lived them, so sometimes the best thing you can do as allies is cede the floor and let bisexual people speak for themselves.

Think about the words you choose

The way we use language betrays a lot about us. When you use offensive language, even in jest, you imply that that language is acceptable. Your friends might know you're only joking, really, but does everyone else listening? Similarly, words that some people think are completely acceptable are offensive to others. Words that have been ostensibly 'reclaimed', like 'queer', still have the power to wound, especially for the older people in our community.

'My dad thinks it's hilarious to call me "confused.com". He thinks that because I know he doesn't mean it as a slur that it's not hurtful. But it

is. Firstly, it means he sees the core of my identity as something trivial, and secondly, it's an insultingly unoriginal joke. Totally Alan Partridge.
Have I ever mentioned it to him? No. I'd just be told I was "too sensitive".'
Lizzie

It's not just potentially offensive language that we need to be wary of, though. When you're speaking to bi people about their negative experiences, minimising language should also be avoided. Phrases like 'Some people have it worse than you' or 'It can't be that bad' may appear benign, but when we use them we trivialise hurt and discourage people from speaking up.

If someone is sharing their negative experiences with you, they are placing trust in you; do not abuse it. Even phrases like 'I know how you feel' can trivialise negative experiences. Can you really put yourself in our shoes?

Don't play 'oppression Olympics'

Sometimes it's tempting to compare the ways in which people are marginalised, or try to work out who is worse off. It is always a bad idea. Very rarely do we have enough information to make a truly informed comparison, and the value in making such judgements is tenuous at best. The truth is, most of us experience oppression or exploitation of one sort or another, and most of us also experience a number of privileges. Ranking them gets us nowhere.

Consider intersecting identities

However many things we might have in common, there is no such thing as a single bisexual experience, and other facets of a person's identity, such as their gender, race, class or religion, can affect both how they feel about themselves and how other people treat them. For more on the intersection of sexuality and other identities, see chapters 8 and 10.

Give yourself permission to make mistakes (and say sorry)

We all make mistakes. Making mistakes is part of being human and part of learning about something new. It's impossible to go through life without upsetting someone, saying or doing the wrong thing, or messing up.

If someone tells you that you've upset or insulted them, say sorry and listen to what they say, but don't beat yourself up about it. Instead, try and see it as an opportunity to make yourself an even better ally than you already are.

Know how to say sorry

An apology is worth nothing if you don't mean it, so before your apologise, take a moment to consider how your words or behaviour have hurt someone. To make your apology effective, you should take responsibility for your actions and express genuine regret. Statements like 'I'm sorry you feel that way' shift the blame to the hurt party. Instead, acknowledge the situation and your role in it by unequivocally accepting responsibility and asking for forgiveness.

Look after yourself

Take a bath. Play sports. Read a favourite book or watch a favourite show. Spend time with your favourite people. When you're feeling your best, it's much easier to do your best, and self-care is not an indulgence, it is a necessity.

Read this book

There are a million and one ways to be a great ally to bisexual people, from challenging biphobia when you see it, to letting your bi friend cry on your shoulder, to encouraging your friends to become allies themselves.

But the absolute best thing you can do is educate yourself. The best allies are those who really try to understand our experiences and the challenges we face. Reading this book will give you a good grounding in the current state of bisexuality in the UK, and when you're done, there are plenty of other resources you can seek out, from books, academic journals and studies, and information leaflets to websites, blogs and online magazines. Check the end of this book for a list of resources.

Okay, I Get It! Tell Me What I Can *Do!*

As an ally, you should take pointers on actions you can take from the people you're allying yourself with, but that doesn't mean there aren't things you can do alone. No matter how much time you have to spare, there's sure to be something you can do to further the cause.

One *minute*

Even in sixty seconds, you can support bisexual people. Sign a petition or post a bisexual-content website to social media. Text a bi friend a nice message. Challenge a biphobic joke or stereotype. Defend against biphobic bullying in your school, college or workplace.

Ten minutes

Go online. Read an article on a bi website or blog, donate to your favourite LGBT charity or go shopping for bi merchandise on Etsy.

Half an hour

Give a friend a call. Ask your local library, sexual health clinic, gay bar or community centre to stock more bisexual information leaflets and tell them where they can find more literature. Join a lobbying campaign. Encourage your friends to become allies.

One hour

Write a letter to your MP. Seek out a bi community project that could use your help. Listen to a queer podcast.

A few hours

Get creative! Make bisexual pin badges or stickers, write an article to submit to a bi website or magazine, or make a zine. Catch up on bi websites and blogs, and learn more about bisexual experiences. Go along with a friend to their first time at a bi group or event.

A day

Help out your friends attending or running a bisexual group or event. Visit a place of queer historical interest and brush up on your knowledge.

15

LET'S DO SOMETHING ABOUT THIS: GETTING STARTED IN BISEXUAL ACTIVISM

Editor: Marcus Morgan

If you've been reading the chapters of this book in sequential order, then by now you have a better understanding of bisexuality, the bisexual community in the UK, what biphobia is, and how bisexual erasure (or invisibility) hurts people.

If you've been paying attention, you might even be starting to get cross. What right do people have to oppress us, who decided that bisexuality would be erased, and what's the deal with the lack of services, information and support?

But, also, you might be thinking, what can be done about it? What can we do to fight against it? How can we raise bisexual people's voices so we are heard above the deafening background hiss of our heteronormative society?

There are a lot of big LGBTQIA+ organisations fighting homophobia and transphobia, working to support LGBT people, trying to teach people the message that it's not okay to be prejudiced. In recent years some of them have started to say 'and biphobia' in these contexts.

But not all of them really understand biphobia all that well. Not all of them notice that they don't, don't notice that their message is being shaped only by homosexual and trans people, don't notice (or don't care) that they're not representing bisexuals. People use 'gay' as an umbrella without irony, not realising that abbreviating a list down to the first item is like describing a group of apples, potatoes, mangoes and limes as 'apples'.

This is why we need activists, because thanks to institutional bisexual erasure, no one's going to suddenly clap a hand to their fore-heads and say, 'Silly me, guess who I've missed out!' without an awful lot of prodding. The most common thing I hear people say, gay or straight, when I'm talking about bisexuality is 'Oh, yeah. That makes sense. I guess I hadn't really thought about it.'

They really don't think about it. We're all trained by society not to. It can be like owning magical glasses that no one else has.

While a lot of bisexual people notice their own erasure, many re-main seething balls of rage and don't feel they're allowed to do any-thing about it. We read articles online that refer to LGBT people as 'gays' or talk about the homophobia that 'LGBT people' face. We roll our eyes when the bisexual TV character is a murderer, or weird. We sigh when the panellists at an LGBT event are feted for being inclu-sive of lesbian and trans people, because we've noticed they haven't included any bisexual speakers.

The barrier to doing something about it puts a lot of people off when they think about activism, but the truth is that the barrier to getting something done is so low that many a time it's possible to clear the hurdle without noticing you've done it.

There are no Secret Powers That Bi to oversee bisexual activism. We don't need anyone's permission to start. If what we're doing isn't pulling in the exact same direction as other people, that's okay — we're all working to make bisexuality either less erased or more vis-ible.

The erasure versus invisibility question is a prime example of an area where it's actually useful that people are taking different sides. For some people the invisibility idea is the perfect metaphor, while for others the erasure metaphor works better. The net result of people working on either is to wear down people's assumptions about sexuality in society, about who is straight and who is gay and which people could possibly be bisexual, expressed in questions like 'What, him? But he's married...' The more differences in the language and outlooks we use in our activism, the wider the audience we address. You might think you're a lone voice in your community, but you won't have the only ears. The first step for many people is realising there are other people, just like them, who are also bi.

Still, some people reading this will think that they can't make a difference. Surely activism takes certain skills, commitment, dedication and, especially, time? Not necessarily...

One First Step

I asked a number of existing bisexual activists what they would suggest that someone could do if they wanted to raise the profile of bisexuality in fifteen minutes. The common theme I could immediately see among their answers was something that I agree is the most immediate way and useful way to raise the profile of bisexuality in a community. It doesn't matter if the community is colleagues in a workplace, a friends list on Twitter or Facebook, family, church, a social group or a geographical setting. It's an immediate flare that says, 'There are bisexual people here!', and it startles some people, sure, but others see it and feel immense relief because it means they're not alone.

It's this: *come out*. Robyn Ochs, a bi activist for more than thirty years (and editor of *Bi Women Quarterly*) phrased it best.

'Come out to someone in a proud, affirming and unapologetic tone. Come out to a friend, a family member, on social media, in a comment or letter to the editor, et cetera. Remember: people will not be aware of our existence unless we let them know we're here.'

Robyn

A few years ago I was having second thoughts about coming out in a social group I'd joined; it was a very traditional masculine space and featured a lot of laddish banter that was typical of the sort of chauvinism that festers in all-male environments. On the night in question the topic had gotten around to the names of our first partners, and as I was feeling underinvested in the group (and was considering bailing out), I said abruptly that my first partner had been named David. This was in fact untrue; my first partner had been called Lai, but that wasn't a name that they would have recognised as male and so would not have pulled the conversation up short. After a bit of 'Oh, you're one of them are you?' from the oldest guy present (and my coming out as bisexual following the obligatory 'But I thought you were married'), the conversation moved awkwardly on, and I was at the time pleased to see the people of my age and younger steer it away from becoming actually homophobic. A bit of more 'You can't say that these days' rather than 'You're wrong about the gays' for my liking, but gratifying nonetheless.

A few months passed and that older guy rang me, to ask if I knew any resources for older bisexual men, as he'd been thinking a lot about what I'd said and how he realised it applied to him. He was in his seventies, and hadn't thought about it before. Could I, being Internet savvy, find him details of groups for older people thinking of coming out? Of course I could.

Bisexual awareness has no greater weapon than our coming out, becoming the signposts we would have wanted to see.

What Else Can We Do?

The other suggestions included posting bisexual links on social media without necessarily coming out each time (maybe your circle already knows?) and donating money to bisexual organisations. Sam Rankin (a South African bi activist who now works at the Equality Network based in Edinburgh) especially recommends Bi's of Colour, as the smaller organisations are the ones where the donations can make the most difference.

With more time to spare, there's more you can do. Helping other bisexual people know they're not alone is great activism to do, and aside from coming out (though as bisexuals it is sometimes necessary to do this more than once to the same people), it's really useful to be able to point people towards the bisexual community. In five minutes a day you can use Twitter to propagate the messages of a local or national bisexual group (the Bisexual Index tweet several times every day, so they're a good choice).

When I asked him what he suggested people do, I got a really good suggestion from Ian Watters (a long-time BiCon organiser who says he 'got into this by sticking his hand up to do a little and quickly ended up doing a bit more than that'): give feedback. Maybe you could review this book on your preferred online book store (which might not be Amazon)? Or ask your local LGBT organisation if it's doing anything about bisexuality for LGBT History Month, or IDAHOBIT (the International Day Against Homophobia, Transphobia and Biphobia), or Bisexual Visibility Day. Also, he suggests, you can give feedback to other bisexual activists by thanking them for their efforts.

Wait, did I say 'other bisexual activists'? Perhaps you were thinking that we were working up to that and these were going to be some sort of training steps, but the hurdle is so small it's possible you've already cleared it. An activist is simply one who is active—and even coming out makes you an activist when bisexuality is as erased as it is in our society. Being out as a bisexual person is itself an act of activism—it takes effort.

When I asked my pool of bisexual activists (don't picture that) what could be done with one evening a month, the replies were nearly unanimous: create a community, found a space, start a group. Margaret Robinson, former co-chair of the Toronto Dyke March, told me: 'With one evening a month free you can create bi community. You could attend, or organise and facilitate, a discussion, support or social group for bisexual people. This doesn't just have to be a bunch of people talking about bisexuality. You can have a games night. You could play a sport. One woman I know started a bisexual cabaret evening. You could do peer support around an issue that disproportionately impacts bisexual people, such as anxiety. It can even be a bi group that focuses on a different issue, such as bisexuals against animal cruelty.'

Almost all bisexual groups in the UK run on a monthly basis. Sure, there's almost always maintenance tasks that need doing outside of that one evening, but the nature of a group means it's often possible to spread the load. And the group doesn't have to be especially onerous. When I was at a bisexual conference in the US once, someone asked me for suggestions on what to do, as they wanted to revive their local bi group but didn't want to have to rent a room or find a bar that would put them up in the nearest suitable town. I asked a simple question: what else did they do in that town? The answer was 'go shopping on a Saturday'. My suggestion was then obvious: have the bisexual group less as an evening in a bar and more as a meetup. Tell people to look out for the purple soft toy on the table in the food court on Saturday lunchtime once a month, and see who turns up. If no one comes (which could happen at first), then you've still got somewhere to sit and eat lunch.

Another suggestion, which came from Meg-John Barker, was to volunteer at the local LGBT organisation and be the out and proud bisexual who volunteers there. I like this suggestion but would offer two notes: First, be prepared to be a lightning rod for everyone's curiosity and possibly a little initial biphobia. Second, make sure it's an organisation you'd support and volunteer at regardless; don't be doing it just to raise the profile of bisexuality, otherwise once you've set them on the right track, what do you do?

How we deal with organisations that aren't living up to their professed opposition to biphobia is an interesting issue. It can get us very angry, but oftentimes the attitudes of an organisation are just a conglomeration of the attitudes of the people who work or volunteer there. A lot of LGBT organisations seem to have an attitude of 'If you work here, you understand LGBT stuff', which is unfortunate when plenty of gay people have a poor understanding of bisexuality or the ways in which they themselves are unwitting perpetrators of biphobia.

When I asked Ian Watters what could be done with one evening a month, he gave me a different answer: write something. Now, this initially seems like a scary idea to a lot of people, as we're not all journalists or authors. But when you combine this with the most effective tool for visibility—coming out—then it becomes a really accessible weapon in the fight. Our stories, told by us and in our own words, can really resonate, and resonate most with the people who hear their own voices in our wording. The website bisexual.org collects bisexual stories as an awareness-raising project. And if you want to tell the story of how you're still bisexual despite society's expectations that bisexuality is a phase, then have a look at the video-blogging campaign site stillbisexual.com run by Nicole Kristal (who co-authored *The Bisexual's Guide to the Universe*).

One of the things you will have noticed in the suggestions and ideas so far is a certain squad size. It's you, or me, or that other person—and we're all going it alone. This does have some advantages. There's no committee to argue over the placement of commas, no waiting for everyone to reply to an email and certainly a lot less difficulty finding a time when everyone can go sit in the coffee shop to hash out ideas. It's also immensely rewarding to see a change implemented, whether that's an 'and bisexuals' in a mission statement or an ally arguing for our validity, when you know that you were the person that made it happen.

However, for some projects, we need a team. Whether that's someone to share work with, underlings to delegate to, specialists to fill our skill gaps, or a friend to meet us for coffee and pointedly say, 'So, what did you do this week to push Bisexual Project X forward?', there are advantages to teamwork. It's through activist teams that events like BiFests and BiCons happen, LGBT Prides are run, and bisexual charities or community-interest companies are set up.

And when we work together, we can bounce ideas around. Grant Denkinson, also appearing in this book, made a good point to me: we have very little funds for any of this, but everyone has resources or skills. If you want to have food at an event, maybe someone you're working with can also cook. 'Talk to other activists who work with no resources; they are incredibly resourceful,' he said. 'If it can't happen now, consider describing it to others and maybe it will happen another time—ooh, I remember someone who had an idea of a travelling bi bus...I now happen to have a bus.'

Dealing with Imperfection

It's also vital, every now and then, to have someone say those three important words that we need to hear to be effective activists. The three magical words we won't want to hear unless it's from another activist. Those words are 'You are wrong'.

Get good at hearing those words. I don't mean become accustomed to them on a regular basis. Instead, I mean become skilled at dealing with the words, separating them from knee-jerk emotional responses and defensiveness.

No one is the Super Activist who is always right, who fits into every (conflicting) minority and knows all the language. Any image, and any wording, could be better. Mike Szymanski, whose long-running column about bisexual issues started at Planet Out and now is published by the National Bisexuality Examiner, makes a good point: 'Don't feel guilty about not doing enough. Everyone can do more. No one can do everything. I always felt bad about not doing more; then I found out that people who have done far more than me also feel guilty the same way.' And he's right. Activism can be a calling, a cause, a fight, a struggle, but it's also important to remember that as it's unpaid, it has to have limits.

Sam Rankin agrees: 'Too many activists burn out really quickly. We cannot fight discrimination if we are constantly breaking ourselves. It's a marathon, not a sprint. Do not take on more than you can comfortably manage.'

Good enough to use isn't perfect, and perhaps perfection doesn't exist. You don't have to know everything if you can get good at receiving feedback. I don't mean praise. It's good to be able to take praise at face value and not get all awkward about it, but praise is easier to take most times than criticism. And constructive criticism is easier to take than someone screaming in your face.

Why do people shout at activists? I think it's because they've got tired of seeing people repeat the same myth or make the same mistake, and just when they were about to finally give in and let that issue become 'another one of those things that people with no clue keep doing' they see someone they expect (or hope) to be better at it making the same error. The *Sun* newspaper saying that is one thing, but someone you can see fighting for that one minority? Couldn't they be better?

I'm not perfect at handling criticism, but I'm trying to be better. My current steps when someone emails me with an angry correction to something on the Bisexual Index website runs like this:

1.   From their email, set aside the swearing, tone and shouting. That's for step 8.
2.   Look at what they're saying is wrong. Assume they're right.
3.   Go out and find further evidence they're right.
4.   Having invariably found other people who agree, change the wording.
5.   Email them as if they'd sent the politest typo-spotting email in the world. Thank them for the feedback. Tell them the page is changed and thank them for reading it in the first place.
6.   A week or so later, if they've not replied telling me it's still wrong, go back and look. Can it be improved any further?
7.   Go back to their tone, their insults, their anger. Now is the time to deal with those. Make a cup of tea, get ready and:
8.   Get over it.

If you're spotting things another bisexual activist is doing and you're thinking, 'Uh, wait—they're saying x means y, I'm saying y means y, noooo!', then please do remember to be gentle yourself when you give feedback. At the end of the day even the most established seeming hardened bisexual community leaders are just like you: unpaid individuals soldiering along because they can't stand to see no one else doing it.

The message we want to spread can be simple or it can be complicated. The change we want to make in the world can be stark or subtle. Some bisexual activists are trying to alter complex organisations, others just want to fill their local LGBTQIA+ scene with people in cool bi T-shirts. There's space for everyone. Here are some examples.

Emily Wright, a bi activist from Manchester, says her activism is about providing an alternative voice on bisexuality. She said, 'I want people to know that most fears and insecurities about being bisexual are not personal failings; they are the whisperings of biphobia, which tells us all we are "doing it wrong",' and she wants to reach out especially to isolated bisexuals in mixed-sex relationships because she thinks they are particularly isolated and most LG(BT) outreach fails them. I think she's right.

Margaret Robinson found a side effect: 'I got into activism because I wanted to change people's biphobic attitudes. I heard a lot about how bisexuals didn't contribute to the LGBTQ community. So I wanted to be visible as an activist and a bisexual person. I changed policy, making events officially inclusive of bisexual and trans people, which meant a lot to me. Ultimately what changed most was my attitude about my own bisexuality. I became confident. I became happy. And that, more than anything, changed how other people treated me.'

Meg-John Barker said, 'Tell potential bi activists this: It'll change you in ways that are unanticipated and incredibly challenging at times, but definitely for the better for you and everyone around you if you're up for embracing the vulnerability of the challenge.'

Why do I do it, or what do I hope to achieve? Through the training I've delivered, I've had the privilege of being the person to make the light bulbs go on over people's heads. It's very rewarding to watch a group of people arrive with uncertainty and questions, and then as the session progresses see them start to nod, see the ideas make sense. For me the simplicity and validity of bisexuality seem so obvious that maybe all many people need is someone to provide them with a clear definition and pull away the stereotypes and myths.

When I'm on the phone to someone looking to do 'something about bisexuality, because we've done trans last year' and I start to explain some common topics I cover, it's quite usual for them to start interrupting me excitedly with correlations and things they'd spotted too. 'I've never had anyone give me an answer to this, but...' comes up a lot too, and invariably it's a question that they've not knowingly asked a bisexual person. There's a great value in being the signpost, in being the person with their head above the parapet.

Sure, there's some rocks to dodge. But if we stare long enough at the horizon, we can see the future we want. All we have to do is pull everyone else there with us.

ACKNOWLEDGEMENTS

Purple Prose would like to thank:

BiCon Continuity for donation matching during the crowdfunding campaign.

DIVA magazine, the *Examiner*, the *BiCast*, *Biscuit*, the *Bisexual Index* and *Gay Star News* for publishing articles, interviews and book extracts during the crowdfunding campaign.

BiCon for donating day passes to the crowdfunding campaign.

Stonewall for donating 'Some People Are Bi' T-shirts to the crowdfunding campaign.

Everyone who pledged to the crowdfunding campaign.

Eve and Franklin at Thorntree Press for taking us on.

GLOSSARY

Notes

⇨ These are not intended to be exhaustive or one-true-way definitions, but guidelines. The language of LGBTQIA+ issues can be
complex and full of nuances.

⇨ When describing someone, it's generally best to use their identity as an adjective, not a noun: for example, 'a trans person'
rather than 'a transsexual' and 'a gay man' not 'a gay', although
'lesbian' is usually a noun. 'Bisexual' is probably best used as an
adjective ('a bisexual woman'), although it depends on context
('a group of bisexuals' is usually okay, particularly if you're one
of them).

⇨ Some of these definitions have been taken, with permission,
from rainbowteaching.co.uk.

⇨ The glossary is a group effort, but all responsibility for it rests
with the editor.

asexual (ace): does not experience sexual attraction.
aromantic (aro): does not experience romantic attraction.
bi: short for bisexual, also sometimes used by asexual people who
are attracted to more than one gender in order to avoid the 'sexual'
aspect of the word.
Bi Community News: Britain's bimonthly bi magazine. See
bicommunitynews.co.uk

BiCon: an annual weekend gathering of bisexuals and their friends/ allies in various locations around the UK, usually a university campus. See bicon.org.uk. Some years include BiReCon, an academic conference on bisexuality.

BiFest/BiFete: typically a one-day bi event with workshops, social space and often evening entertainments. See wikipedia.org/wiki/ BiFest.

bi-curious: thinking you might be bisexual, not being completely sure and wanting to explore it.

biphobia: similar to homophobia, the dislike of or prejudice against bisexual people.

bisexual: see chapter 1 for a discussion of definitions. In summary: having the potential to be attracted to more than one gender.

biromantic: having the potential to be romantically attracted to more than one gender, while not necessarily being sexually attracted to multiple genders.

cisgender: having a gender identity that matches one's gender assigned at birth (i.e. not transgender).

cishet: a shorthand term for cisgender and heterosexual.

demisexual: not experiencing sexual attraction unless one forms a strong emotional connection with someone.

disablism (can also be called ableism): discrimination or prejudice against disabled people; the ways in which society is set up to disadvantage disabled people.

frubbly: also known as 'compersion'; in polyamorous relationships, the sensation of being happy to see your partner with someone else (so the opposite of jealousy).

gay: another term for homosexual. Tends to be mainly used by men but can also be used by women.

genderqueer: a non-binary gender identity; outside societal gender norms; sometimes used to express existing anywhere in a broad spectrum of gender non-conformity.

genderfluid: a non-binary gender identity; shifting between different gender identities and/or expressions.

greysexual (or grey-a): an identity on the asexuality spectrum; experiencing sexual attraction infrequently or experiencing low sexual desire.

heterosexual: attracted only to a different gender than one's own. Note that the LGBTQIA+ umbrella can include heterosexual people, since many trans people and many people on the ace or aro spectrum are heterosexual.

heterosexism: discrimination or prejudice against non-heterosexual people; the ways in which society is set up to disadvantage non-heterosexual people.

homosexual: attracted only to people of one's own sex.

intersex: having a mix of physical characteristics (including hormones and chromosomes) which don't fit the typical definitions of male and female. These characteristics may be evident at birth or become so later in life, at puberty or when trying to conceive. For some, the characteristics may not be evident at all.

Kinsey scale: Invented by Dr. Alfred Kinsey in the 1940s, the Kinsey scale plots individuals on a range of sexual dispositions from exclusively heterosexual at 0 through to exclusively homosexual at 6. For a more 3D model of sexual orientation, see the Klein grid, designed by Dr. Fritz Klein, which plots attraction, behaviour, preference, etc. against past, present and ideal orientation.

lesbian: a woman attracted only to other women.

LGBT: an umbrella term for minority sexualities/genders; stands for lesbian, gay, bisexual, trans.

LGBTQIA+: an umbrella term for minority sexualities/genders; stands for lesbian, gay, bisexual, trans, queer/questioning, intersex, asexual, plus. Other terms used could include **QUILTBAG** (queer/questioning, undecided, intersex, lesbian, trans, bisexual, asexual, gay) or just **queer**.

metamour: in polyamorous relationships, your partner's partner.

microaggressions: 'The everyday verbal, nonverbal and environmental slights, snubs or insults, whether intentional or unintentional, that communicate hostile, derogatory or negative messages to target

persons based solely upon their marginalized group membership'
(definition from *Diversity in the Classroom*).

misgendering: being perceived or treated as an incorrect gender (e.g.
a woman being called 'sir', a man being directed to the ladies' toilets,
a non-binary person being assumed to be a man or a woman).

monosexual: attracted only to one gender.

monosexism: discrimination or prejudice against non-monosexual
people (bisexual, pansexual, etc.); the ways in which society is set up
to disadvantage non-monosexual people.

non-binary: Having a gender identity that is neither exclusively
male/man nor exclusively female/woman. Used as an identity label
in itself or as an umbrella term.

non-monogamy/non-monogamous: used here to mean ethical
non-monogamy, that is, open relationships, polyamory, swinging,
etc., with the knowledge and consent of all involved.

omnisexual: attracted to many or all genders.

pansexual: attracted to all genders or attracted to people regardless
of gender.

polyamory/polyamorous: capable of, or actively practising, ethical
non-monogamy, probably with multiple relationships.

Polyday: a one-day event similar to BiFest but for poly/non-
monogamous people. See polyday.org.uk.

queer: in general, falling under the LGBTQIA+ umbrella. Some people
don't like the use of the word 'queer' because it was historically a
slur; others have reclaimed its use. It can also represent a stance of
resisting boundaries and categories of sexuality and gender.

questioning (as part of the LGBTQIA+ acronym): someone who is
exploring their sexuality.

QUILTBAG: see LGBTQIA+.

secret non-monogamy: sometimes used as a less judgemental term
for cheating, that is, having sex (or something comparable) outside a
relationship without the consent of all involved.

straight: see heterosexual.

trans/trans*: an umbrella term for transgender and related identities. It is currently considered that trans without the asterisk is the

better usage, since trans* has been used to invalidate non-binary people and mark them as distinct from 'real' trans; it also has a history of transmisogynistic use.

transgender: an umbrella term for people whose gender identity differs from what is expected based on their sex characteristics at birth; includes non-binary people.

transsexual: sometimes used for people who are changing their sex characteristics to be more congruent with their gender identity; usually considered outdated and should be avoided.

FURTHER READING

Publications

Sue George. 1993. *Women and Bisexuality*. London: Scarlet Press.

Meg Barker, Christina Richards, Rebecca Jones, Helen Bowes-Catton, Tracey Plowman, Jen Yockney and Marcus Morgan. 2012. *The Bisexuality Report: Bisexual Inclusion in LGBT Equality and Diversity*. Milton Keynes: Centre for Citizenship, Identities and Governance and Faculty of Health and Social Care, The Open University.

Loraine Hutchins and Lani Kaahumanu. 1995. *Bi Any Other Name: Bisexual People Speak Out*. Boston: Alyson Publications.

Shiri Eisner. 2013. *Bi: Notes for a Bisexual Revolution*. Berkeley: Seal Press.

Surya Monro. 2015. *Bisexuality: Identities, Politics, and Theories*. Basingstoke: Palgrave MacMillan.

Ron Jackson Suresha and Pete Chvany, eds. 2005. *Bi Men: Coming Out Every Which Way*. New York: Routledge.

Robyn Ochs and Sarah Rowley, eds. 2009. *Getting Bi: Voices of Bisexuals Around the World*. Boston: Bisexual Resource Center.

Sam Rankin, James Morton and Matthew Bell. 2015. *Complicated? Bisexual People's Experiences of and Ideas for Improving Services*. Edingurgh: Equality Network.

Jacq Applebee. 2015. *The Bi's of Colour History Survey Report.* https://bisexualresearch.files.wordpress.com/2015/06/bis-of-colour-survey-report.pdf

Nancy Chater, Dionne Falconer, Sharon Lewis, Leanna McLennan and Susan Nosov, eds. 1996. *Plural Desires: Writing Bisexual Women's Realities* by Bisexual Anthology Collective. Sistervision Press.

Bi-focused or bi-friendly websites

bicommunitynews.co.uk
thisisbiscuit.co.uk
bisexualindex.org.uk
bisexualblogs.wordpress.com
bisofcolour.tumblr.com
bisexuallondon.tumblr.com
biuk.org
bicast.wordpress.com
bishuk.com
uncharted-worlds.org
purple-prose.co.uk
rainbowteaching.co.uk
rewriting-the-rules.com
scarleteen.com
captainawkward.com
thefword.org.uk
the-toast.net
themarysue.com

NOTES

Chapter 3

Page 39 Christopher Biggins quote

Scott Roberts. 2014. 'Christopher Biggins: "Bisexuals are not real people and they ruin women's lives."' *Pink News*. 28 April. http://www.pinknews.co.uk/2014/04/28/christopher-biggins-bisexuals-are-not-real-people-and-they-ruin-womens-lives/

Page 40 'Three Levels of Bi Erasure'

Jennifer Moore. 2014. 'Three Levels of Bi Erasure.' *Uncharted Worlds* [Blog]. 7 October. http://www.uncharted-worlds.org/blog/2014/10/three-levels-of-bi-erasure/

Page 41 'My "Superpower": Bisexual Invisbility'

Maxine Green. 2015. 'My "Superpower": Bisexual Invisibility.' *Jim & Tonic* [Blog]. 28 September. http://www.chaosbunny.com/archivetoon.php?toonid=766

Page 42 'Truly Bi' image

Jennifer Moore. 2006. 'Bi Identity: Obstacles and Paths.' *Uncharted Worlds* [Blog]. http://uncharted-worlds.org/bi/biidentity.htm

Page 44 *The Bisexuality Report*

Meg Barker, Christina Richards, Rebecca Jones, Helen Bowes-Catton, Tracey Plowman, Jen Yockney and Marcus Morgan. 2012. *The Bisexuality Report: Bisexual Inclusion in LGBT Equality and Diversity*. Milton Keynes: Centre for Citizenship, Identities and Governance and Faculty of Health and Social Care, The Open University.

Page 49 'Hypersexualised Objectified Bisexual'

Hannah Bee. 2015. 'Hypersexualised Objectified Bisexual.' *Hannah Bee's Bisexual Blog* [Blog]. 24 August. https://bisexualblogs.wordpress.com/2015/08/24/hypersexualised-objectified-bisexual/

Page 51 'Bisexuality: Integrated, Stable, Peaceful'

Jennifer Moore. 2011. 'Bisexuality: Integrated, Stable, Peaceful.' *Uncharted Worlds* [Blog]. 23 September. http://www.uncharted-worlds.org/blog/2011/09/bisexuality-integrated-stable-peaceful/

Chapter 4

Page 57 Research on experiences of bisexual men and women

Sue George. 1993. *Women and Bisexuality*. London: Scarlet Press.
Robin Ochs and H. Sharif Williams, eds. 2014. *Recognize: The Voices of Bisexual Men*. Boston: Bisexual Resource Center.
Kata Orndorff, ed. 1999. *Bi Lives: Bisexual Women Tell Their Stories*. Tucson: Sharp Press.

Page 58 Research on non-binary identities

Meg-John Barker and Christina Richards. 2015. 'Further Genders.' In *Handbook of the Psychology of Sexuality and Gender*, edited by Christina Richards and Meg-John Barker, 166–182. Basingstoke: Palgrave Macmillan.

METRO Youth Chances. 2014. *Youth Chances Summary of First Findings: The Experiences of LGBTQ Young People in England.* London: METRO.

Nat Titman. 2014. 'How Many People in the United Kingdom Are Nonbinary?' *Practical Androgyny* [Blog]. 16 December. www. practicalandrogyny.com/2014/12/16/how-many-people-in-the-uk-are-nonbinary

Chapter 5

Page 87 'Disadvantages of Polyamory'

Maxine Green. 2010. 'Disadvantages of Polyamory.' *Jim & Tonic* [Blog]. 12 February. http://www.chaosbunny.com/archivetoon. php?toonid=388

Page 101 Humorous take on polyamory advice

Elise Matthesen. 2000. 'How to Fuck Up.' *Heartless Bitches International* [Blog]. http://www.heartless-bitches.com/rants/ elise.shtml

Rebecca. 2010. 'Things to Do to Fuck Up Polyamory.' *Only More So* [Blog]. 29 May. http://only-more-so.blogspot.co.uk/2010/05/ things-to-do-to-fuck-up-polyamory.html?m=1

Page 106 Non-monogamy resources

Dossie Easton and Janet W. Hardy. 2009. *The Ethical Slut: A Practical Guide to Polyamory, Open Relationships, and Other Adventures.* Berkeley: Celestial Arts.

Franklin Veaux and Eve Rickert. 2014. *More Than Two: A Practical Guide to Ethical Polyamory.* Portland, OR: Thorntree Press.

Chapter 6

Page 119 'Geek-Sexual'

Maxine Green. 2015. 'Geek-Sexual.' *Jim & Tonic* [Blog]. 2 October. http://www.chaosbunny.com/archivetoon.php?toonid=773

Chapter 7

Page 122 Interview with Charlie

Patrick Strudwick. 2015. 'This Is What Dating Is Like When You're LGBT and Disabled.' *BuzzFeed News,* 15 October. http://www. buzzfeed.com/patrickstrudwick/this-is-what-its-like-coming-out-when-youre-disabled#.lkMBrl92WB

Page 128 Mental health

Meg Barker, Christina Richards, Rebecca Jones, Helen Bowes-Catton, Tracey Plowman, Jen Yockney and Marcus Morgan. 2012. *The Bisexuality Report: Bisexual Inclusion in LGBT Equality and Diversity.* Milton Keynes: Centre for Citizenship, Identities and Governance and Faculty of Health and Social Care, The Open University.

Hay Group. 2015. 'Removing Barriers to Success in the Civil Service: Survey Findings' [PowerPoint Presentation]. https://www.gov.uk/government/publications/removing-the-barriers-to-success-in-the-civil-service-survey-findings.

Page 140 Intersection of bisexuality and disability

Kath Browne and Jason Lim. 2008. *Count Me In Too: LGBT Lives in Brighton & Hove.* Brighton: Count Me In Too. www.realadmin.co.uk/microdir/3700/File/CMIT_Bi_Report_Dec08.pdf

Lisa Colledge, Ford Hickson, David Reid and Peter Weatherburn. 2015. 'Poorer Mental Health in UK Bisexual Women than Lesbians: Evidence from the UK 2007 Stonewall Women's Health Survey.' *Journal of Public Health,* 37 (3): 427–437. doi:10.1093/pubmed/fdu105.

Sam Rankin, James Morton and Matthew Bell. 2015. *Complicated? Bisexual People's Experiences of and Ideas for Improving Services.* Edingurgh: Equality Network.

Chapter 8

Page 157 'My Invisible Skin'

Omar Sakr. 2014. 'My Invisible Skin.' *Human Parts* [Blog]. 8 April.
    https://human.parts/my-invisible-skin-7ca44cdbaa28#.
    c41wpypqa

Chapter 9

Page 184 'You Trans-sexy Thing'

Charlie Hale. 2014. 'You Trans-sexy Thing.' *Feminist Halestorm*
    [Blog]. 25 January. http://charliehale.net/?p=5

Chapter 11

Page 207 Statistics on biphobia in schools

Meg Barker, Christina Richards, Rebecca Jones, Helen Bowes-
    Catton, Tracey Plowman, Jen Yockney and Marcus Morgan.
    2012. *The Bisexuality Report: Bisexual Inclusion in* LGBT *Equality
    and Diversity*. Milton Keynes: Centre for Citizenship, Identities
    and Governance and Faculty of Health and Social Care, The
    Open University.

Page 208 'My Harmful Heteronormative Education'

Hannah Bee. 2015. 'My Harmful Heteronormative Education.'
    Hannah Bee's Bisexual Blog [Blog]. 10 June.
    https://bisexualblogs.wordpress.com/2015/06/10/
    my-harmful-heteronormative-sex-negative-education/

Pages 211–213 Articles on women's transitioning sexualities

Eleanor Tucker. 2014. 'Living Secretly as Lesbians: Meet the
    Women Who Left Their Male Partners for Another Woman.'
    The Telegraph, 17 July. http://www.telegraph.co.uk/women/
    womens-life/10971051/Lesbian-affairs-Meet-the-women-who-
    left-their-male-partners-for-another-woman.html

Kira Cochrane. 2010. 'Why It's Never Too Late to Be a Lesbian.' *The Guardian*, 22 July. http://www.theguardian.com/lifeandstyle/2010/jul/22/late-blooming-lesbians-women-sexuality

Chapter 12

General resources

Acas (Advisory, Conciliation and Arbitration Service). *Equality and Discrimination*. www.acas.org.uk/index.aspx?articleid=1363

Citizens' Advice Bureau. *Discrimination because of Sexual Orientation*. www.adviceguide.org.uk/england/discrimination_e/discrimination_discrimination_because_of_sex_or_sexual_orientation_e/discrimination_because_of_sexual_orientation.htm

Equality and Human Rights Commission. *Equal Rights*. www.equalityhumanrights.com/your-rights/equal-rights/sexual-orientation

Stonewall. *Discrimination at Work*. http://www.stonewall.org.uk/help-advice/discrimination/discrimination-work

Glossary Notes

Page 299 Definition of 'microaggression'

UCLA Diversity and Faculty Development. 2014. *Diversity in the Classroom*. https://faculty.diversity.ucla.edu/resources-for/teaching/diversity-in-the-classroom-booklet

THE EDITORS

Jacq Applebee

Jacq Applebee is a black bisexual writer and activist. They co-founded and facilitate Bisexuals of Colour (bisofcolour.tumblr.com and @bisofcolour). Jacq would love to win the lottery so they could live in a lighthouse by the sea with a few dozen adoring fans.

Meg-John Barker

Meg-John Barker is a sex, gender and relationships geek who spends pretty much all of their time talking, thinking and writing about these topics. They write self help–style books which focus more on changing social norms than on changing individuals, and they work at the Open University and London Friend as a lecturer and therapist. They're chair of BiUK (www.biuk.org) and have been involved with bi activism for over a decade. Meg-John blogs on www.rewriting-the-rules.com and tweets as @megjohnbarker.

Elizabeth Baxter-Williams

Elizabeth is a thirty-something bisexual activist and writer living in South London. She edits thisisbiscuit.com, keeps getting involved in running bisexual events and bakes a really mean lemon drizzle cake.

Jamie Q Collins

Jamie Q Collins is a teacher and activist and as such is entirely too fond of acronyms. They have an inability to walk away from a project, and a fondness for tattoos, cats and glitter that renders them the living embodiment of a queer stereotype. They tweet as @theteatteacat.

Grant Denkinson

Grant Denkinson came out with surprise rather than shock just over twenty years ago, found bisexual community quickly and has felt at home there since. He tends to accrete and spawn new projects: editing *Bi Community News*, creating BDSM-bisexuals weekends, starting Polyday, running Leicester Pride, being a trustee of the Leicester LGBT Centre and BiCon Continuity Ltd. as they became charities, steering the Sexual Freedom Coalition, and organising Night of the Senses, SM Pride and other sex, sexuality and relationships events. He is interdisciplinary in his work life, supporting research in higher education and being a psychotherapist. He should probably try relaxing.

Kate Harrad

Kate Harrad is a fiction and non-fiction writer, bi activist, event organiser, and parent. You can find her novel *All Lies and Jest* at gwdbooks.com/kate-harrad.html, and her blog at fausterella.co.uk. She tweets as @katyha.

Symon Hill

Symon Hill is a bisexual, a Christian, an activist, an author and an ex-biphobe. He teaches courses on religion and history for the Workers' Educational Association. His latest book is *The Upside-Down Bible: What Jesus Really Said about Money, Sex and Violence* (published by Darton, Longman & Todd). Symon walked from Birmingham to London in 2011 as a pilgrimage of repentance for his former homophobia. He blogs at www.symonhill.wordpress.com. He wishes the Church was more like BiCon.

Juliet Kemp

[Photo credit Charlotte Barnes]
Juliet Kemp is a writer, activist and parent. She spends a lot of time staring at the river and drinking tea, which seems to be how the writing happens. She blogs (very) intermittently at julietkemp.com.

Fred Langridge

Fred Langridge is a bit of an administrator at heart, and applies this to activism and voluntary positions in the bi community and among Quakers when they're not at their day job. They also enjoy chairing meetings, reading, writing and…sums…and are far more interesting than this sounds, honest. They tweet as @SFLangridge.

Marcus Morgan

Since the early 1990s Marcus Morgan has been one of the UK's leading bisexual activists, delivering training about bisexuality and fighting for better bisexual inclusion. He is the only member of the Institute of Diversity and Equality Practitioners who is also a member of the Magic Circle. Find his various incarnations at magicmarcus.co.uk, @MarcusTeaches and www.facebook.com/MischiefMental.

Kaye McLelland

Kaye is a bi activist and event organiser. She has been on two BiCon teams and has helped run BiFests and other events, including BiReCon, the academic conference for bi research. She is also an associate researcher for BiUK, the UK national organisation for bisexual research and activism. In her day job she lectures in Shakespeare and is currently researching representations of disability in Renaissance writing. She uses her knowledge of Shakespeare to run 'Queering Shakespeare' drama workshops at BiCon and other LGBT events. Kaye is also a keen singer and the parent of five children. Occasionally she sleeps.

Milena Popova

Milena Popova is a PhD researcher interested in the politics of culture. In a past life, she also ran the LGBT network group of a large multinational corporation. She has far too many interests and is an activist on a range of issues, including violence against women, LGBTQIA+ issues and digital rights. She blogs about some of these things at milenapopova.eu and pornresearcher.eu and tweets as @elmyra.

INDEX

Barker, Meg-John
  activist, 290, 294, 308n, 313
  coming out, 35
  and gender, 69, 77, 78–79, 81
  identity, 62, 66, 186
  mental health, 128–29
  non-monogamy, 91–92
  and visibility, 59
Basic Instinct (film), 261–62
batting for both teams, 44
Baxter-Williams, Elizabeth, 11, 18, 22, 314
BDSM (bondage/discipline, domination/
    submission, sadism/masochism), 79,
    101, 181, 192
BDSM/kink, 181–83
Bee, Hannah, 48–50, 208–11, 308n, 311n
bi, bis. Abbreviations of bisexuality
Bi Community News, 118, 299
bi-curious, 1, 10, 300
Bi-friendly spaces (life story), 219–23
bi-gendered, 67, 71
bi + grey-a, 177, 187
bi now, gay later, 39, 158–59, 278
bi visibility. *See* visibility/invisibility
Bi Women Quarterly, 287
BiCon, 80, 81–82, 118, 135, 137–38, 148–49,
    219, 300
BiFest/BiFete, 118, 148, 300
Biggins, Christopher, 39, 307n
biphobia
  and activism, 285–87
  admitting bi exists, 44–51
  among lesbians and gays, 275–76
  against the BME community, 146, 152–53
  dealing with organisations, 290–91
  defined, 300
  internalised, 51–55
  in the NUS LG(B) community, 78
  organised, 43
  religious, 195–97
  in schools, 311n

on TV, 264
in the workplace, 251, 252
Biphoria, 135
bi (queer/pan), 76
BiReCon, 128, 300
biromantic/biromanticism, 167, 300
bisexual/bisexuality
  the actionable, 237–38
  being a proper, 14–17
  confused/indecisive, 44–45
  defined, 4–7, 300
  denial of, 38–39
  dress codes, 142–44
  everyone's bi, 45–46
  first realisation, 10–14
  and gender, 58–72
  in heterosexual relationships, 48
  how can you tell if you're, 5, 8–10
  identifying as, 61, 62–63
  issues, 54
  it's a phase, 45
  it's all about sex, 48–50
  it's real, but it's wrong, 44–45
  legal definition, 241
  meaning of, to you, 17–18
  older, 223–36
  proving it, 42–43
  and sex with both genders, 48
  as trendy or appealing, 39–40
  the unfaithful, 46–47
Bisexual Index, 6, 8–9, 16, 43, 289, 293
Bisexual Visibility Day, 132, 144, 197, 245,
    252, 289
'Bisexuality: Integrated, Stable, Peaceful'
    (Moore), 51, 308n
bisexuality/biromanticism, 167
Bisexuality Report, 44, 51, 145–46, 150–51,
    207–8, 308n
bisexuality, describing
  Bisexual Index, 6
  DH Kelly, 3

Also from Thorntree Press

More Than Two: A Practical Guide to
Ethical Polyamory
Franklin Veaux and Eve Rickert, 2014
"More Than Two may well be the best book on polyamory
I've ever read. No joke, it's really that fantastic."
— Andrea Zanin, blogger at *Sex Geek*

Stories from the Polycule: Real Life in
Polyamorous Families
Dr. Elisabeth Sheff, 2015
"Readers engaged in or curious about polyamorous
families will find plenty to ponder in this eclectic and
enlightening collection."
—*Publishers Weekly*

Ask Me About Polyamory: The Best of Kimchi Cuddles
Tikva Wolf, 2016
"Kimchi Cuddles is a snapshot of our changing culture.
A warm-hearted, wise, and brave comic: an invaluable
resource in the global polyamory movement."
—Dr. Anya, author of *Opening Love*

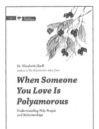

When Someone You Love Is Polyamorous: A Guide to
Understanding Poly People and Relationships
Dr. Elisabeth Sheff, 2016
An essential guidebook for family and friends of
polyamorous people.